NAVIGATING NEUTRALITY

THE REVOLUTIONARY AGE

Francis D. Cogliano and Patrick Griffin, Editors

Navigating Neutrality

Early American Governance in the Turbulent Atlantic

Sandra Moats

UNIVERSITY OF VIRGINIA PRESS
Charlottesville and London

University of Virginia Press
© 2021 by the Rector and Visitors of the University of Virginia
All rights reserved

First published 2021

ISBN 978-0-8139-4644-3 (hardcover)
ISBN 978-0-8139-4645-0 (ebook)

1 3 5 7 9 8 6 4 2

Library of Congress Cataloging-in-Publication Data is available for this title.

Cover image: USS *Constellation* firing upon *L'Insurgente*,
by Rear Admiral John William Schmidt. (Wikimedia / Naval History
and Heritage Command, National Archive ID# 428-KN-2882)

S|H   **The Sustainable History Monograph Pilot**
M|P   Opening Up the Past, Publishing for the Future

This book is published as part of the Sustainable History Monograph Pilot. With the generous support of the Andrew W. Mellon Foundation, the Pilot uses cutting-edge publishing technology to produce open access digital editions of high-quality, peer-reviewed monographs from leading university presses. Free digital editions can be downloaded from: Books at JSTOR, EBSCO, Internet Archive, OAPEN, Project MUSE, and many other open repositories.

While the digital edition is free to download, read, and share, the book is under copyright and covered by the following Creative Commons License: BY-NC-ND. Please consult www.creativecommons.org if you have questions about your rights to reuse the material in this book.

When you cite the book, please include the following URL for its Digital Object Identifier (DOI): https://doi.org/10.52156/m.5645

> We are eager to learn more about how you discovered this title and how you are using it. We hope you will spend a few minutes answering a couple of questions at this URL:
> **https://www.longleafservices.org/shmp-survey/**

More information about the Sustainable History Monograph Pilot can be found at https://www.longleafservices.org.

For Anna Stadick and in memory of Joyce Appleby

CONTENTS

List of Illustrations xi

Acknowledgments xiii

INTRODUCTION
"The Mischiefs of Foreign Intrigue" 1

CHAPTER 1
"Highway Robbery under the Protection of the Law":
American Privateers in the Eighteenth-Century Atlantic 9

CHAPTER 2
"Free Ships Make Free Goods":
Revolutionary Experiments in Neutrality 24

CHAPTER 3
"The Contests of European Nations":
George Washington and Neutrality 41

CHAPTER 4
"Americans in Politics":
Crafting a Neutral Proclamation 59

CHAPTER 5
"To Keep This Country in Peace":
French Violations and Executive Actions 78

CHAPTER 6
"A Rank Due to the United States":
Enforcing Neutrality across the Federal Government 103

CHAPTER 7
"My Objects Are, to Prevent a War":
Enforcing Neutrality across the Globe 127

CONCLUSION
"First in Peace":
George Washington, Statesman 141

Notes 147

Bibliography 187

Index 199

ILLUSTRATIONS

Figure 1. Continental Congress directive on privateering 21

Figure 2. Empress Catherine the Great of Russia 31

Figure 3. Society of Cincinnati medal 47

Figure 4. George Washington 63

Figure 5. Citizen Genet 83

Figure 6. USS *Constellation* 119

Figure 7. Captain Joshua Barney of Maryland 129

ACKNOWLEDGMENTS

This project had its origins in the *Papers of George Washington*. As I leafed through these volumes, I came across a slew of letters between Washington and the French officers who had served alongside him in the Continental Army. It took me several years and a few unsuccessful article submissions to realize that these letters explained Washington's steadfast commitment to American neutrality. From that kernel, this book was born.

I had the good fortune to be working on this project when the Fred W. Smith Library for the Study of George Washington opened at Mount Vernon in 2013. I was one of seven inaugural fellows, and during my five-month tenure, I made significant progress researching and framing this project. Living and working at Washington's beloved estate was a wonderful bonus. I am grateful to Doug Bradburn for his conversation and insights. The always efficient and pleasant Mary Jongema helped me with all manner of challenges, including mastering DeVos House. DeDe Petri, Wisconsin's representative on the Mount Vernon Ladies Association, has been a generous supporter. She hosted me at her home for a research presentation; she also invited me to speak at a gathering in Madison, Wisconsin. I am also grateful to Gwen White and Jon Taylor for their friendship during the fellowship period.

During the 2017–18 academic year, I enjoyed a second fellowship, this time at the Institute for the Research in the Humanities at the University of Wisconsin, Madison. (Thank you Lesley Walker for making me aware of this opportunity.) This nine-month respite from teaching and administrative duties allowed me to write for this book full time. I am grateful to Ann Harris for her cheerful assistance during my time in Madison and to Ullrich Langer, the program's director, who always called on me during the weekly research presentations. I also appreciate the comments and insights of the institute's other fellows. A special shout out to Melissa Vise for her friendship while in Madison and her willingness to share her office with me. This book would not have been completed without these two long-term fellowships. Both gave me time to research, write, and, most importantly, think.

The availability of online historical sources has exploded since I finished graduate school. The National Archives' Founders Online epitomizes the quality and accessibility the Internet can offer to anyone interested in the nation's founding generation. Nonetheless, print resources and in-person research remain indispensable for historians. This book offers its existence to the first-rate (and multivolume) *Papers of George Washington*. In addition to the library at Mount Vernon, my research led me to the excellent holdings at the Massachusetts Historical Society, the Library Company of Philadelphia, and the Pennsylvania Historical Society. Lastly, I benefited from the generous borrowing privileges that exist across the thirteen University of Wisconsin libraries. At Parkside's library, Heather Spencer and Liz Antaramiam deserve special recognition for their heroic efforts in tracking down sources from the other University of Wisconsin campuses.

I want to thank my departmental colleagues at Parkside, Ed Schmitt, Beth Brownson, and David Bruce, for their continued support as I took breaks from teaching to work on this book. Dean Peggy James has been supportive of my research, ensuring a sabbatical, course releases, and research time and money. I am also proud to call her a friend.

As I have worked on this project, I have gained from the insights of many scholars, including Ben Irvin and Rachel Hope Cleves. Lige Gould deserves special recognition for his generosity as a colleague. I discussed American neutrality with him *once* at Mount Vernon, and he became an enthusiastic supporter of me and this project. He good-naturedly wrote countless letter of recommendations on my behalf, and his help ensured the successful completion of this book.

Deep appreciation goes to my friends who have supported me, including Lesley Walker, Anna Stadick, Dana Oswald, Kenny French, Catherine Stephens, Peter O'Keefe, Lisa Kornetsky, and Sahar Bahmani. Henry Moats and Liam Moats have been supportive in their unique ways, with both ensuring that I got exercise. As I contemplated sailors and privateering, I was able to see Lake Michigan from my study, a vast body of water that is both inspiring and comforting. New York City boasts a first-rate classical public-radio station, WQXR. It has proved to be an essential companion as I researched, wrote, revised, and resubmitted.

Of course, this book would not be seeing the light of day without a publisher. Thanks to Cathy Kelly of the Omohundro Institute for steering me to Nadine Zimmerli at the University of Virginia Press. Nadine has been a strong supporter of this project, and her editorial insights and substantive comments have greatly improved the quality of the final manuscript. I am also grateful to the press's two anonymous reviewers, who offered generous comments and constructive suggestions, and to Frank Cogliano and Patrick Griffin for including me in The Revolutionary Age series.

The book's dedication honors two people who have proved indispensable to my scholarly career. Anna Stadick has been a steady and reliable friend throughout this long process, including enabling me to be away from home for long stretches. Sadly, my mentor, Joyce Appleby, passed away while I was working on this book. I want to thank her for the excellent training she gave me as an historian. I hope the final results are worthy of her efforts.

NAVIGATING NEUTRALITY

Introduction

"The Mischiefs of Foreign Intrigue"

FRANCE'S REVOLUTIONARY WAR against Britain could not have occurred at a worse time for President George Washington. In late March 1793, when the news reached Philadelphia, Washington had begun his second term in a job he was not sure he wanted anymore.[1] The growing partisanship among voters and within his cabinet, along with the increasingly personal attacks appearing in the nation's newspapers, had soured Washington on his presidential duties.[2] Nonetheless, he recognized the dangers a European war posed for the young nation, particularly one involving America's principal allies. Amid these international and partisan challenges, Washington achieved the near impossible when he forged a consensus neutrality policy in his deeply divided cabinet and then utilized the authorities contained in the Constitution to implement American neutrality at home and abroad to keep the nation at peace.

The United States' commitment to neutrality began on April 22, 1793, when Washington and his cabinet issued the Neutrality Proclamation to shield the young nation from the latest round of warfare between France and Great Britain. Recognizing the significant risks that this conflict posed for the recently independent United States, the proclamation announced America's desire to pursue friendly commercial and diplomatic relations with all nations, including its two principal trading partners, while avoiding hostilities. Amid a century of fighting on the high seas in which ship seizures and privateering were the norm, this proclamation boldly declared America's right of free trade even during wartime. Proclaiming neutrality, however, proved easier than maintaining it, and enforcing neutrality contributed to America's transformation from a paper republic into an autonomous nation fully embracing its constitutional responsibilities.

Neutrality stands as a familiar theme in American foreign policy, influencing diplomatic decisions well into the nineteenth century.[3] The term "neutrality" also enjoyed a revival in the twentieth century during the debates over American involvement in the two world wars, although this had more to do with isolationism than free trade.[4] Historical treatments of the 1793 proclamation have either focused on the diplomatic crises associated with this policy or have exaggerated the partisan disagreements surrounding it.[5] While diplomatic challenges did arise in the 1790s, these studies would be stronger if they situated the resulting agreements, such as Jay's Treaty and Pinckney's Treaty (both 1795), within the nation's overriding ambition to remain neutral.[6] Two older works dealing with the policy's formulation in Washington's cabinet emphasize the partisan fireworks and policy disagreements between Treasury Secretary Alexander Hamilton and Secretary of State Thomas Jefferson while overlooking the compromises they and others reached that resulted in a successful proclamation.[7] Despite the concept's ubiquity in American politics and diplomacy, in other words, no book has looked at the systematic implementation of neutrality across the government or overseas. Through a comprehensive examination of its origins, formulation, and implementation, *Navigating Neutrality* demonstrates this policy's far-reaching effects in building an economically independent, institutionally strong, and politically sovereign nation.

The concept of neutrality did not originate on American shores, nor was the United States the first nation to adopt this policy, of course.[8] This idea emerged from Enlightenment philosophers, who saw neutral trade as a rational practice that could foster harmony among nations.[9] Additionally, many smaller European nations pursued neutrality to protect their maritime economies from the incessant continental warfare of the seventeenth and eighteenth centuries. Denmark, Sweden, and the Netherlands had declared themselves neutral in treaties and alliances in the hope of pursuing free trade without interference from warring powers.[10] Even the American Revolution provoked a neutrality agreement, with Russia organizing its European neighbors into the League of Armed Neutrality in 1780 to avoid taking sides in this increasingly global conflict.[11] Most of these neutrality agreements inevitably fell victim to wartime realities. With the Atlantic Ocean serving as a watery battleground during European hostilities, most nations relied on state-sponsored "privateers" to harass enemy merchant ships and to capture their cargoes. Privateering provided a cost-effective way for nations to undercut their opponents while enriching themselves and the authorized ship captains. Merchantmen claiming to be neutral frequently fell victim to wartime privateering since nations at war viewed all vessels as potential carriers of supplies for their enemies.[12]

For America to achieve its goal of wartime neutrality, the federal government needed to develop the capacity to enforce this policy among its citizens and across diplomatic channels or risk sinking into irrelevance at home and abroad.[13]

Proclaiming and enforcing neutrality forced the U.S. government to leave its safe constitutional moorings and exercise its responsibilities in the Atlantic's tumultuous waters. *Navigating Neutrality* tells this story through an examination of the historical circumstances and precedents, the political decisions, and the governing authorities that defined and ultimately led to the enforcement of American neutrality.

The 1793 proclamation announced the international and economic role the United States sought in its founding decades. Yet violations of this policy quickly washed up on U.S. shores as France's new minister, Citizen Genet, commissioned American ships and sailors as privateers, with many eagerly accepting these lucrative opportunities. Remaining neutral during the 1790s required the constant vigilance of all three federal branches as the national government crafted policies and exercised its authorities to prevent these infringements. In its quest to avoid entanglements in European warfare, the enforcement of this bold and far-reaching statement helped build the national government.

Neutrality's international and commercial components, as well as its enforcement requirements, explain its outsized role in the federal government's development. Since diplomacy is the exclusive responsibility of the national government, the neutrality policy energized federal institutions, authorities, and constitutional responsibilities.[14] Additionally, its implementation required the expansion of the government's diplomatic and commercial presence across all three federal branches.[15] The executive branch, possessing authority over foreign affairs, formulated this policy and then implemented it in U.S. ports and among foreign diplomats.[16] The other two branches also assumed their institutional responsibilities, with Congress regulating commerce and the courts adjudicating violations.

Other policies of the 1790s also built the federal government's authority, of course. The national government in its founding decade tackled such challenges as the Revolutionary War debt, Indian warfare, westward expansion, the Whiskey Rebellion (1794), and the codification of chattel slavery. Yet none of these issues built the government as extensively as neutrality did. The latter cut an unusually wide swath across all three branches and also required a permanent institutional presence to be successful: diplomatic envoys, custom officers, district attorneys, federal judges, naval officers and sailors, and state militias. In contrast, the Indian wars of the 1790s, for example, required a military presence in the West but did not lead to a permanent standing army.[17]

The one program that equaled the scale and reach of the neutrality proclamation was Hamilton's landmark "Report on the Public Credit." Issued in 1790, this ambitious economic proposal included a sweeping plan to pay off the war debt, including those of the states; establish a Bank of the United States; and institute tariffs to protect nascent American manufacturing. In building federal institutions and establishing the scope of the government's role and authority, Hamilton's report (and resulting initiatives) matched the influence of the neutrality proclamation, but in the domestic realm.[18]

With its emphasis on the United States' international role, *Navigating Neutrality* joins a growing collection of histories that recognize the importance of state building in implementing the Constitution and in establishing the new government in the 1790s and beyond.[19] As the popular biographies of John Adams and Hamilton (and a resulting television show and Broadway musical, respectively) have demonstrated, the reading public is fascinated by the lives and careers of the founding generation.[20] But personalities alone did not build the U.S. government or energize the Constitution. With the renewed focus on political, diplomatic, and even military histories, scholars have turned their attention to the national institutions that supported these endeavors in the late eighteenth and early nineteenth centuries, including the relationship of war and money, the work of the custom houses in regulating American commerce, and the president's cabinet as a governing entity.[21] *Navigating Neutrality* expands this field by focusing on the practical ramifications of enforcing a key policy across the entire government, not just in one agency or department. This interdisciplinary study also engages the fields of politics, diplomacy, law, philosophy, and the Atlantic world and beyond as well as the role of American citizens in negotiating commerce and warfare.

Washington's leadership in guiding the formulation and implementation of this proclamation demonstrates his underappreciated skills as a savvy political negotiator and his enduring presidential legacy as a statesman. This book joins others that have increasingly recognized Washington as more than a symbol of republican government but as an active and engaged champion of its successful launching. Additionally, his presidential accomplishments have emerged from the long ideological and partisan shadows cast by his sparring cabinet members Hamilton and Jefferson.[22]

As Washington and his cabinet discussed neutrality, no one, including Hamilton and Jefferson, wanted to become involved in a European war. Where they disagreed was how to translate this stance into a viable policy.[23] The president held the strong belief that the United States needed to explicitly distance itself from a European conflict that would only harm the young nation. Unlike Hamilton and Jefferson, who viewed Britain and France through ideological and philosophical prisms, Washington understood the activities of these two nations more pragmatically. As a military officer in the Seven Years' War (1756–63) and later the American Revolution, Washington had encountered the British and the French as both enemies and allies. For him, the Anglo-French war of 1793 was just another chapter in a longstanding imperial rivalry that had nothing to do with the United States. This battlefield perspective explains Washington's steadfast commitment to American neutrality throughout his presidency, concluding with the advice contained in his Farewell Address to avoid "the mischiefs of foreign intrigue" and "to steer clear of permanent alliances."[24]

To produce a successful statement on neutrality, Washington recognized the need to gain the support of Jefferson and Hamilton as well as their cabinet allies, Attorney General Edmund Randolph and Secretary of War Henry Knox, respectively. The president did not bully or cajole his cabinet, nor did he force his views on them. Instead, he solicited the opinions of all four cabinet members, sought common ground among their ideas, and then crafted their suggestions into a final proclamation that epitomized compromise and consensus. Each cabinet member could point to crucial provisions that reflected their concerns and suggestions, even if the statement contained elements they did not favor. (For example, Jefferson successfully pushed for the omission of the word "neutrality," preferring "impartial" instead.)[25] In the 1793 proclamation, Washington and his cabinet spoke in a single voice to announce America's intention to remain at peace and to prohibit its citizens from becoming involved in European warfare.

Threats to U.S. neutrality were not limited to the Atlantic. In 1794, Washington's administration issued a second neutrality proclamation to ban the nation's citizens from participating in a French-led invasion of Spanish Louisiana. This western proclamation underscored the volatility of the nation's trans-Mississippi boundary as Indigenous peoples, Americans, and other Europeans fought for land and navigation rights.[26] Rather than seeing the porous boundaries of the Atlantic, the South, and the West as mutually exclusive, this book acknowledges that some neutrality violations also occurred along the nation's territorial border with Spanish Louisiana. Just as the original proclamation and the cotton gin came into existence the same year, the cotton crops this machine processed required unfettered passage in transatlantic ships headed to textile mills in Liverpool and Manchester.[27] Many studies have emphasized the turmoil along the nation's western and southern boundaries in explaining early American history. This book argues for the continued relevance of America's disputed Atlantic coastline as well.[28]

If the formulation of neutrality demonstrated Washington's skills as a political leader, its implementation, both at home and abroad, revealed his equally underappreciated role as a statesman. With violations of this policy occurring with impunity, Washington led his administration, including Hamilton and Jefferson, through a series of enforcement decisions intended to prevent Americans from privateering or otherwise aiding the European war.[29] The president and his cabinet directed the Treasury Department's collectors of the customs, located in port cities, to serve as the first line of defense in reporting neutrality violations. The U.S. attorneys, under the secretary of state's supervision, were instructed to prosecute these transgressions in the newly established federal court system.

While the neutrality proclamation established the executive branch as the leading voice of foreign policy, rampant privateering made Washington realize he needed the assistance of the entire government to enforce this policy.[30] The district courts and the Supreme Court struggled the most to define their legal and constitutional duties but eventually embraced their responsibilities.[31] Congress, which possessed the constitutional mandate for regulating commerce, codified the two neutrality proclamations into law and sought ways to protect American trade and port cities. Without a standing army or navy, state militias, under the command of the governors, policed U.S. waters for illegal privateering activities. During a long summer of privateering violations in 1793, Washington came to realize a *bold* proclamation did not necessarily mean an *effective* one. In response, he employed his considerable political skills to encourage all three branches of government to embrace their constitutional duties in order to successfully enforce federal policy.

On the diplomatic front, Washington and his cabinet dealt with a litany of violations caused by Genet and a growing list of complaints from the British minister about assaults on his nation's vessels. With these transgressions occurring on an almost daily basis, Secretary of State Jefferson assumed primary responsibility for diplomatic communications and negotiations with foreign nations, particularly France and Britain. At the same time, Washington sought a more permanent solution to resolve these assaults on U.S. sovereignty. With America's transatlantic commerce increasingly under siege, the president posted envoys (in addition to U.S. ministers) to Britain, Spain, the West Indies, and the Barbary Coast to secure free-trade agreements and to recover captured American ships from foreign ports. In keeping the nation at peace during the international turmoil of the 1790s, Washington achieved his most enduring legacy as president as a pragmatic diplomat and prescient statesman.

In recognizing Washington's substantial achievements as president in attaining peace over war, this book also engages the new diplomatic history. This previously moribund field has enjoyed a revival thanks to the globalization of U.S. history and the expansion of "diplomacy" to include not just the official government functions of treaties and ambassadors, but also the activities of ordinary citizens living and working throughout the world. This revival has also sought to broaden the chronological reach of this field beyond the twentieth century and into the neglected foreign affairs of the early republic, a period dating from 1789 to 1861.[32] The ship captains and seamen discussed in this book found themselves immersed in international politics and commerce in the Caribbean Sea, the Mediterranean Sea, and, of course, the Atlantic Ocean, sometimes at their own peril.[33] But they were not the only ones. Along with official diplomats, unofficial American consuls, and the maritime community, Americans permeated global affairs as merchants, missionaries, and even scientists.[34] Mixing the old with the new, this book shows that during the 1790s, the Washington administration's official stance of neutrality not only benefited the new nation internationally but also aided U.S. citizens who ran into difficulties overseas.

As Washington led his cabinet through the issues surrounding the formulation and implementation of neutrality, all five men brought a professionalism to these discussions as well as a strong awareness of their institutional and constitutional duties, despite their personal and partisan differences. While the president employed meetings to resolve the major issues surrounding neutrality, he also encouraged the cabinet to submit their ideas in writing in order to elicit their insights and forge a consensus.[35] Thanks to Washington's desire to build a common ground on neutrality, written documents, particularly letters, emerged as an essential tool of early American governance.[36] Additionally, with an eye to posterity, Hamilton, Jefferson, Randolph, and even Knox eagerly provided detailed responses to the president's queries about the best ways to formulate and implement U.S. neutrality. Jefferson, who increasingly found himself in the minority, kept detailed notes on the debates and decisions from the numerous cabinet meetings. These summaries provided a venue for him to record what was said in order to highlight his own disagreements for future partisan purposes. As the enforcement of neutrality spread across the government, each cabinet member contributed drafts for Washington's annual addresses to Congress announcing this policy and also submitted suggestions for the letter to France that would lead to Citizen Genet's recall. Early in his presidency, Washington famously said that he "walked on untrodden ground."[37] As he and his cabinet formulated and enacted the nation's first major statement on foreign policy, with its domestic and institutional ramifications, they followed in his footsteps and established precedents for the new government on an almost daily basis.

America's declaration of neutrality in 1793 represented a desire to avoid European warfare; it also served as a manifesto of the young nation's quest to abandon its colonial status and to be recognized as an independent country. Neither Britain nor France respected U.S. neutrality, with Britain still regarding American ports and ships as colonial holdings and France possessing unrealistic expectations about America's support for its own revolutionary war against monarchy. As both an Enlightenment idea and a policy goal, neutrality defined America's stance in the transatlantic disputes that roiled the 1790s. Through an exploration of this concept's legal origins, its political formulation, and its domestic and international enforcement, this book explains neutrality's profound and enduring consequences in the 1790s and beyond. Beginning in 1789, the government found multiple arenas in which to assert its authority: in fiscal matters, in the West, among Indigenous peoples, and with U.S. citizens. Neutrality provided an additional area for the government to exercise its constitutional responsibilities. This policy also stands as a testament to Washington's skills as a political leader in forging and implementing this policy and his enduring presidential legacy as a visionary statesman who kept the United States at peace. Because of the far-reaching scope of this policy domestically and internationally, its longevity into the nineteenth century, and its engagement with all three branches, neutrality played an unexpectedly large and underappreciated role in launching the U.S. government. Becoming neutral represented one of America's earliest domestic and international aspirations. Creating a government capable of supporting these ambitions resulted in neutrality contributing to the building of the American nation.

CHAPTER 1

"Highway Robbery under the Protection of the Law"

American Privateers in the Eighteenth-Century Atlantic

THE ESTABLISHMENT OF THE British North American colonies along the Atlantic coastline in the seventeenth century ensured the central role this dynamic and turbulent ocean would play in America's economic development. While the colonies derived tremendous commercial benefits from the transatlantic trade, these advantages could quickly evaporate depending on the controversies and conflicts occurring 3,000 miles away in Europe. Britain's involvement in a series of continental wars during the eighteenth century disrupted maritime commerce, forcing American ship captains, merchants, and seamen to consider alternative ways of remaining at sea. With the British government encouraging its colonial subjects to serve as privateers to supplement the Royal Navy's strength, war provided additional economic opportunities for America's seafaring community. During the American Revolution, the maritime community employed its privateering skills to assist the tiny Continental Navy. Once the United States became an independent nation, reconciling the longstanding practices of America's seafaring citizens with the government's desire to remain neutral in international affairs and to pursue free trade challenged both groups. Until then, the turbulent Atlantic offered the promise of jobs and adventure, along with an ironclad guarantee of dangers, for anyone seeking a livelihood there.

WITH THEIR PRIME LOCATION along the Atlantic, the British North American colonies entered the world economy as seafaring communities. Small port cities sprung up along the coast to negotiate the transfer of raw materials from forests and fields into ships headed to Europe and the Caribbean. The exports emerging from these towns reflected what was grown and harvested in the surrounding area. Northern cities like Boston, with a more limited growing season, tended to ship items harvested from its natural environment: fish and whale oil. Colonies to Boston's south, with more extensive agricultural production, exported their leading commodities such as wheat, pork, and beef from New York City and Philadelphia; tobacco from the Chesapeake region of Maryland and Virginia; and rice and indigo from Charleston, South Carolina. (Cotton would not become a significant southern export until the nineteenth century, following the cotton gin's invention in 1793.)[1]

In exchange for these items, finished goods arrived from Europe, raw materials came from the West Indies, and enslaved men, women, and children involuntarily emigrated from Africa through a horrific journey known as the "middle passage."[2] While all thirteen colonies participated in transatlantic commerce to ensure their economic livelihood, northern port cities such as Boston, New York, and Philadelphia provided the shipbuilding and seamen that permitted the American side of this trade to flourish.[3]

As hubs of America's maritime trade, Boston, New York, and Philadelphia evolved from tightly knit villages into centers of commercial exchange. Functioning as seafaring "company towns," these port cities offered inhabitants a wide range of employment options related to the transatlantic trade, most of which did not require leaving the harbor. Before ships and crews could transport goods across the Atlantic, vessels had to be constructed, loaded, and staffed with experienced seamen. Each waterfront city possessed a range of artisans engaged in shipbuilding and repair, including riggers, sailmakers, shipwrights, and coopers. Merchants and ship captains, many of whom co-owned the vessels, regularly and closely worked together to arrange the transport of goods. For those men too young, too old, or too inexperienced to serve on vessels, jobs were available loading and unloading cargo, with very few ships leaving American harbors with empty holds.[4] Residents of New England port cities also utilized the shipbuilding services to engage in commercial fishing or whaling operations in northern Atlantic waters.[5]

The artisans, seamen, and ship captains who made a port city's maritime economy hum came together in waterfront neighborhoods nicknamed "sailor towns." Coffeehouses, taverns, boardinghouses, stores, and private homes and tenements fed, housed, and supplied the mariners who entered, departed, and inhabited the port. Taverns played a particularly important role as centers of entertainment, information, and business transactions for ship captains, sailors, and artisans in need of food, drink, lodging, socializing, lines of credit, and job opportunities. New York City and its taverns emerged as the hub of transatlantic information for the North American colonists because it was the port that received the English packet boats carrying news, mail, and gossip.[6] In general, these colonial port cities functioned as single-industry maritime communities that thrived during times of peaceful transoceanic trade but struggled to adapt to the disruptive warfare increasingly permeating North Atlantic trade routes.

A vibrant shipping industry could not exist on land alone, and the experienced seamen and ship captains who staffed these vessels provided the essential element to keep America's transatlantic trade afloat. Most sailors came from port cities (or the surrounding towns), the Atlantic Ocean having been in their sights since boyhood. While some sought adventure, riches, and freedom, many went to sea simply because "it was there," following family and community traditions.[7] Added enticements included wage payments in cash, a rarity at the time, and short stints on the water (ranging from three weeks to three months) combined with long respites onshore.[8] Alongside these perks were the physical demands of sailing that made it a young man's profession, with apprenticeships beginning at the age of twelve or thirteen and retirements occurring in a sailor's early thirties. John Paul Jones, a naval hero of the American Revolution, embarked on his first transatlantic voyage when he was thirteen, a seemingly youthful age that reflected the maritime norm.[9] With ships at the mercy of wind power to travel, too much weather in the form of storms could damage vessels, while too little wind could render a ship vulnerable to attack or incapacitate it and risk spoiling its fragile cargo of raw materials.[10] The risks accompanying sailing, including drowning or sinking, as well as the long apprenticeship meant that experienced sailors remained a small but desirable group in America's transatlantic economy.[11] Indeed, their abilities as "able seamen" made them vulnerable to impressment by a British navy in need of skilled men to support its imperial ambitions.[12] For those seamen who avoided death or capture at sea, their post-Atlantic retirement brought them home to port cities where they might open a maritime-related business or even return to the sea as ship captains.[13]

Ship captains occupied a seminal space in North America's transatlantic economy, serving as the conduits between the coastal merchants, who hired them to ship goods, and as commanders of the seamen who made these journeys possible. Before embarking on a new voyage, experienced sailors enjoyed a certain amount of onshore autonomy due to their cash wages and their skills. Once men signed the "articles of a ship"—a contract establishing wages and rules for the voyage—they relinquished their freedoms to the ship captain. He then became the sailor's legal guardian and fully controlled the sailor's work and his physical body, including punishments.[14] Commercial ships maintained small crews, typically four to five men, in addition to the captain and the first mate, and the work required to keep a schooner or sloop afloat was hard and constant.[15] A ship's cargo determined its final destination, another decision that resided with the captain rather than the crew. As European warfare increasingly encroached on transatlantic shipping, the ship's captains and its owners might choose to profit from these tensions through the legal practice of privateering.

As Britain's economic influence and political power increased in the late seventeenth and early eighteenth centuries, rivals sought to challenge its emerging hegemony on the European continent, in the Atlantic and the Caribbean, and in North America. Further intensifying these conflicts was the concept of mercantilism, which provided the accelerant needed to fuel a succession of fiercely competitive European trade wars at this time. Mercantilism posited that the world contained a limited amount of wealth, with warfare offering the pathway to controlling more of it.[16] With the expansion of empires beyond Europe, the raw materials transported in the Atlantic trade provided a convenient target to increase a nation's riches and its political standing. In the seventeenth century, Britain engaged in a series of "blue water" (or oceanic) trading wars with the Dutch Republic, and by the eighteenth century, France's growing commercial presence in the Atlantic and Caribbean made that nation Britain's chief maritime rival and antagonist.[17] These imperial and economic wars, disrupting the Atlantic trade, transformed the relationship between seafaring North American colonists and their mother country, Britain.

Originating in twelfth-century Europe, "privateering" referred to the legally sanctioned practice of seizing enemy ships, including their crews and cargoes, during times of war. Unlike its illegitimate sibling "piracy," privateering possessed the legal backing of the state. (In fact, privateersmen resented being associated with the unsavory world of piracy, a practice that had largely ended by the 1730s.)[18] Nations issued "letters of marque" or "commissions" to ship captains authorizing them to engage in this practice. In Britain, where the High Court of the Admiralty enforced and regulated privateering, ship captains were also required to post surety bonds as a guarantee that they would obey British maritime laws and regulations once they left port. When an authorized privateer captured an enemy vessel, that "prize" would be transported to the nearest British admiralty court to be "condemned," that is, redeemed for money. If the court determined that the prize had been legally obtained, including belonging to Britain's enemy, the privateer would receive a portion of the ship's value and would return to the Atlantic to attempt additional captures.[19] Other European nations that engaged in privateering followed a process similar to Britain's. In

France, consuls, stationed in busy ports, issued letters of marque and adjudicated the prize claims of their nation's privateers, known as "corsairs."[20]

Privateering proved to be a "win-win" situation for warring states and their maritime subjects, although less so for neutral nations. Prior to the eighteenth century, most nations had small or nonexistent navies.[21] Privateering, essentially "privatized warfare," gave European countries greater coverage over Atlantic shipping lanes without the cost and logistical challenges of launching a state-supported navy. Also engaging in privateering were the English and Dutch East India Companies, which preemptively attacked hostile ships to prevent the seizure of their own valuable shipments.[22] With warring nation's embracing the mercantilist concept of limited wealth, seizing an enemy's cargo deprived it of valuable supplies while enriching the privateer and the state, which split the proceeds of the condemned prize.[23] Many ship captains invested these windfalls into profitable trading companies of their own.[24] The financial benefits associated with privateering helped balance its dangers, including the capture of one's ship, the impressment of sailors, or even death.[25] Privateering remained popular into the nineteenth century, when signatories to the Congress of Paris (which did not include the United States) finally agreed to ban this practice in 1856 in the aftermath of the Crimean War (1853–56).[26]

Adding to the intensity and aggressiveness of privateering was a collection of maritime rules and laws emanating from medieval Europe known as the Consolato del mare ("the code of sea laws").[27] Originating in thirteenth-century Spain and first practiced on the Mediterranean, this compendium contained the provision that a ship's cargo, not its flag or its registry, determined its wartime affiliation.[28] Under these guidelines, for example, France's enemies could seize a neutral Portuguese ship carrying French cargo because these items could be used to support France's war effort. While neutral cargo on either warring or peaceful ships was not subject to seizure, privateers considered neutral vessels fair game as potential carriers of enemy goods. The Consolato del mare became expressed in diplomatic agreements as "enemy goods make enemy ships"; its converse was the phrase "free ships make free goods," with the exception of contraband used for war, such as gunpowder and weapons. Beginning in the mid-seventeenth century, Britain and France increasingly embraced the notion of freedom of shipping, at least diplomatically, although what happened to neutral vessels in open waters remained another matter.[29]

Enlightenment ideas on free trade brought temporary relief to those European nations hoping to pursue maritime commerce without combat. The recognition of neutral rights made its first diplomatic appearance in 1650, with the insertion of the phrase "free ships make free goods" in a treaty between Holland and Spain.[30] Longtime combatants France and Britain abandoned the Consolato del mare in several seventeenth-century treaties and then reaffirmed this stance in the influential Treaty of Utrecht of 1713, declaring "that free ships shall also give a freedom to goods," except for specifically defined contraband.[31] This change in policy offered relief to Portugal, the Netherlands, and other smaller nations, who hoped to maintain friendly commercial relations with all nations but whose ships had been vulnerable to wartime seizure. This free-trade détente would come to an abrupt end in the 1750s, when the global Seven Years' War triggered the resumption of Anglo-French fighting. Due to wartime exigencies, Britain and France returned to the aggressive practice of attacking any ship and seizing any cargo it perceived as aiding its enemy, regardless of a vessel's nationality or its captain's desire for neutrality.[32] While a diplomatic precedent for honoring neutrality had been established, powerful nations such as Britain and France still controlled maritime rules through treaties and warfare.

Privateering originally spread to the North American side of the Atlantic in the aftermath of Columbus's successful journey in 1492 and emerged as a legitimate and enduring way to negotiate economic and imperial power in this vast, lucrative, and contested ocean. Although England staked its territorial claim in the Americas later than Spain or Portugal, its ship captains and explorers such as Walter Raleigh and Francis Drake wasted no time in embracing transatlantic privateering during the sixteenth century.[33] English privateers attacked Spanish ships carrying valuable cargoes of gold and silver, enriching themselves and their patron, Queen Elizabeth I.[34] As England became a wealthier and more powerful nation in the seventeenth and eighteenth centuries, it found itself increasingly fighting wars to defend its position and to expand into new markets.[35] In need of naval reinforcements to harass its Spanish, Dutch, and (most importantly) French enemies, the British government looked to the maritime inhabitants of its North American colonies.[36]

Prior to 1689, most North American warfare occurred largely on land and involved territorial disputes between English colonists and Native American nations. While some colonists had engaged in wartime privateering in the seventeenth century, this practice had occurred on a small scale, with the British government and some colonies occasionally issuing commissions to ship captains.[37] During the early rounds of European warfare—the Nine Years' War (1688–97) and the War of Spanish Succession (1702–13)—the North American maritime economy experienced more disruptions than benefits.[38] Following the Treaty of Utrecht in 1713, the seafaring colonists enjoyed a twenty-six-year hiatus from

Anglo-French hostilities. During this period, North American port cities grew into vibrant maritime communities without the disturbances and damages associated with warfare. In 1739, when hostilities resumed, the British government discovered an untapped pool of ship captains and sailors who could support its imperial ambitions as privateers.[39]

The War of Jenkins's Ear, beginning in 1739, marked the North American colonists' full-scale immersion into British privateering.[40] This conflict concerned Britain's desire to access the Spanish-controlled Caribbean trade, and North America's vibrant maritime communities proved ideally situated to support these ambitions.[41] Aspiring American privateers followed the same procedures established in England, with colonial governors deputized as vice admirals and placed in charge of their own admiralty courts. These vice-admiralty courts, operating in eleven colonies since 1689, had the authority to issue letters of marque to American ship captains, collect surety bonds, and condemn any prizes that American privateers might bring to port.[42] Not surprisingly, the cities with the most active maritime communities also hosted the busiest vice-admiralty courts: Boston, Newport, New York City, Philadelphia, and Charleston.[43] Privateering's influence on these ports could also be seen in the growing importance of taverns as informal spaces for these transactions to occur. British officials and naval officers relaxed in these establishments, where some of the work involved in enlisting privateers—recruiting ships, raising crews, inspecting ship articles, and auctioning prize ships and cargoes—also took place.[44] During the transatlantic warfare of the eighteenth century, privateering provided a way for Britain's seafaring subjects to stay in business, and to even profit, from these conflicts.[45]

The colonial privateering boom that began in the 1740s lifted the economic fortunes of North American port cities, at least as long as the wars lasted.[46] Unlike peaceful merchant ships, privateers required larger crews to function and also needed to be faster and armed. Both of these changes resulted in increased employment for artisans, who built new ships and transformed existing ones, and for seamen, who served on them. Port-city artisans such as shipwrights, blacksmiths, sailmakers, mast makers, and caulkers added gunsmiths to their ranks in order to retrofit and construct larger and faster warships capable of outrunning and capturing enemy vessels.[47] The privateering boom resulted in 164 ships being constructed in Boston in 1741 alone, compared with an annual peacetime total of about 40–50 ships in the late 1730s.[48] A well-armed privateer required 100 seamen to function, in contrast to the 5–10 sailors needed on a merchant ship. With more ships needing larger crews to perform its military functions, demand increased for seamen in the 1740s.[49] Between 1750 and 1850, wartime demand raised pay as high as fifty dollars a month, with peacetime reducing this amount to four dollars.⁵⁰ While seamen might also receive a share of the prize money for a captured ship, the amount would be small or nonexistent. Instead, steady employment and higher wages provided the real reward for sailors who served on privateers.⁵¹ The overall rise in wages and demand for workers benefited port-city businesses, particularly taverns, because artisans, ship captains, and sailors would have more money to spend on "drinking, gambling, whoring, and carousing."⁵²

Ship captains enjoyed the most immediate rewards of privateering by splitting a larger share of the captured goods with the British government. This practice encouraged risky behavior—the more ships they seized, the wealthier these captains became. Merchants also benefited from privateering as war contractors. Thomas Hancock, uncle of John Hancock (whose prominent signature adorns the Declaration of Independence), reconfigured a vigorous trading business into an even more successful privateering enterprise by sending ships out to claim prizes and by supplying military expeditions. These wartime activities yielded the elder Hancock wartime profits of 12,000 pounds sterling, making him one of the wealthiest men in Boston.⁵³

The symbiotic relationship between Britain's imperial ambitions and colonial Americans' willingness to serve as privateers reached its pinnacle in size, scope, and autonomy during the global Seven Years' War, which began in the North American frontier in 1754 and expanded to the Atlantic, Europe, India, and the Caribbean.⁵⁴ Soon after the war's North American start, colonial governors issued letters of marque to American ship captains to encourage privateering against French (and later Spanish) ships in the lucrative West Indian trade.⁵⁵ Recognizing the important role neutral countries played in transporting French colonial commerce out of the West Indies, Britain established the "Rule of 1756" to deny free-trade status to noncombatants such as the Netherlands.⁵⁶

With Britain and France now abandoning their earlier understanding that "free ships make free goods," the number of potential prizes multiplied.⁵⁷ As a result, the legal privateering and illegal trading that accompanied this war produced another economic boom in American port cities, particularly in New York and Philadelphia, with seamen and shipbuilding in high demand.⁵⁸ Young men flocked to the coastal cities to work in the maritime trades, and the increased need for sailors resulted in wage increases. As many as 10,000 men served on privateers from Newport, Rhode Island, with another 3,000 men coming from New York City.⁵⁹ American ship captains proved so effective at seizing French naval ships that by 1759 none remained to be captured.⁶⁰

Despite the economic lift privateering offered, dangers still persisted, such as capture by enemy ships, economic downturns, and the risks of a crew's impressment. In response, American colonists employed a variety of strategies onshore and at sea to cope with these challenges. Although privateers possessed the legal backing of the state, these vessels entered legally murky waters once they began attacking and capturing enemy ships. Even the most law-abiding captain quickly adapted to the realities of life on the sea to ensure a vessel's survival and its success, regardless of the legal promises he had made in port.[61] The experiences of Captain George Walker, a British privateer during King George's War (1744–48) and its European counterpart, the War of Austrian Succession (1740–48), demonstrated the excitement and uncertainty involved in raiding enemy ships. Initially assigned to transport cargo from South Carolina, Walker spent four months in 1740 pursuing two Spanish privateers that had docked on the Carolina coast. His efforts resulted in the successful retrieval of a captured British vessel, the *Neptune*. His next mission took him to Barbados, where his ship sprung a leak and sunk. He waited over a year in the Caribbean before British officials entrusted him with a new vessel to command. Even during a string of successful privateering campaigns that resulted in prize money amounting to 220,000 pounds sterling, Walker had to contend with a mutiny among his crew.[62]

Aside from the personal risks and physical challenges involved in privateering, episodic European wars resulted in "boom and bust" cycles in maritime cities, teaching savvy ship captains to place profit before patriotism to stay in business.[63] Many embraced trading opportunities with Britain's Spanish and French opponents in neutral Caribbean waters.[64] At sea, ship captains disguised themselves as "neutrals" through fabricated paperwork and the hoisting of "unthreatening" flags in the hopes of escaping capture.[65] In port they might bribe or threaten British customhouse officials to avoid punishment or seek to exploit the inconsistent enforcement of laws in the various colonial vice-admiralty courts.[66] And when all else failed, American ship captains sought to outrun other privateers to avoid the long and expensive ordeal of being captured and held in port.[67] The willingness of these captains to defy British laws in favor of maritime profits made disregarding government authority an acceptable business practice in the eighteenth-century Atlantic.[68]

No group was more susceptible to the lawlessness of the open water than the "able seamen," whose highly demanded skills made them vulnerable to impressment by British naval ships. American sailors, desirous of controlling their labor and their wages, employed numerous strategies to avoid capture, including "hiding, running (or swimming), wearing disguises, pretending to be employed in another occupation, deserting to another ship, or jumping overboard."[69] Amid these small and individual acts of resistance, colonial waterfront communities, which depended on skilled sailors and unencumbered shipping for their survival, responded en masse to particularly aggressive or egregious examples of impressment. Such was the case in Boston's Knowles Riot of 1747. British commodore Charles Knowles and his crew brazenly impressed forty-seven men from the city's harbor, including an outbound ship's entire crew, as well as several waterfront apprentices. In response, Bostonians rioted for three days, burnt a barge, and took several of Knowles's crewmembers hostage until the commodore agreed to release most of the impressed men.[70] Additional press riots occurred in Portsmouth, New Hampshire, in 1757 and in New York City, where three occurred in 1760 alone.[71] The vibrant Atlantic trade offered both opportunities and risks, and American maritime communities embraced acts both small and large, legal and illegal, to protect their livelihood in these turbulent waters.

In the aftermath of the Seven Years' War, tightly knit port cities rallied together to protest the onerous taxes and duties the British government attempted to impose. Even before the 1760s, American colonists had taken a lax approach to complying with British trade laws and regarded those royal custom officials who attempted to enforce them with disdain.[72] With the introduction of a series of postwar revenue measures intended to offset the cost of the recent fighting, colonists devised new strategies to elude British officials. Waterfront residents in Boston and elsewhere took to loading and unloading their ships at night to avoid paying duties, while smuggling became widespread throughout the colonies.[73] Regarding these revenue measures as a threat to their economic survival, maritime communities publicly punished those who too eagerly complied with these British laws by tarring and feathering captains and burning their boats.[74] While the Boston Tea Party of 1773 stands as the most famous example of these waterfront protests, it represented just one of many throughout the colonies, each of which showed the interdependence and coordination among port-city residents who relied on the Atlantic trade for their survival.

These waterfront protests, of course, contributed to the outbreak of the American Revolution, which itself provided an opportunity for interested ship captains and able seamen to apply their maritime talents to the cause of American independence. Decades of privateering had prepared ship captains for this latest round of warfare, and northern states quickly authorized this practice to protect maritime commerce. The trade-dependent state of Massachusetts led the way on November 1, 1775, when its legislature passed "An Act for Encouraging the Fixing out of Armed Vessels to defend the Sea Coast of America, and for erecting a court to try and condemn all vessels that shall be found infesting the same."[75] The Continental Congress (the national government during the Revolutionary War) followed suit in December 1775 when it established the Continental Navy by purchasing and converting frigates into warships. When Britain issued the Prohibitory Act in December 1775, which banned all trade with the rebellious American colonies, Congress was forced to take more aggressive actions to protect American shipping. On March 23, 1776, delegates approved authorizing privateers but envisioned them as a water-based militia, delegating the implementation of this program to the participating states. During the war, Congress authorized an estimated 2,000 letters of marque, but the individual states assumed the responsibility for issuing commissions and collecting the $5,000 (in continental dollars) for surety bonds from ship captains.[76] States also established their own admiralty courts to deal with captured prizes, including "condemning" the vessel and its cargo.[77] Eventually joining Massachusetts in sanctioning privateers were other states with strong maritime economies: New Hampshire, Connecticut, Rhode Island, New York, Pennsylvania, New Jersey, Maryland, and Virginia.[78]

The resulting American naval presence consisted of the Continental Navy, with 57 vessels, supplemented by 2,000–3,000 state-sponsored privateers employing approximately 200,000 sailors.[79] Just as an earlier generation of colonial ship captains had harassed Britain's enemies to undercut their ability to fight, revolutionary privateers now employed these tactics against British commercial ships. Most of the seizures occurred in the Atlantic's open waters near the busy (and British-occupied) port cities of New York and Philadelphia.[80] The success of American privateers in capturing enemy commercial ships demonstrated that financial rewards continued to be an essential motivation, even amid revolutionary sentiment. For example, the British insurer Lloyd's of London estimated that American privateers seized about 2,200 British vessels during the war, with Massachusetts alone claiming 1,200 ships.[81] Privateering, already a longstanding colonial practice, became embedded in America's struggle for independence, sanctioned by the newly established state and national governments.

While numerous American seamen supported revolutionary politics through the Sons of Neptune, the water-based counterpart to the Sons of Liberty, many served on privateers, motivated as much by self-interest as patriotism.[82] Despite the risk of impressment or capture, privateering offered many advantages over enlisting in the Continental Army, including a shorter term of service and the possibility of enrichment. A broadside from the port city of Beverly, Massachusetts, declared: "Any seamen or landmen that have an inclination to make their fortunes in a few months, may have an opportunity" by applying to serve on the brigantine *Washington*.⁸³ Many Continental soldiers finished their military service and joined British and American privateers, lured by pay advances of up to $100.⁸⁴ In addition, sailors from the French and British navies deserted during the war in hopes of serving on more lucrative and less authoritarian American merchant ships.⁸⁵ Even as many Americans fought to become an independent nation, the lure of riches often trumped patriotism for those who made their living on the Atlantic.⁸⁶

Despite the relative advantages associated with privateering, ships continued to encounter significant risks once they reached the open waters of the Atlantic. The wartime experiences of Captain Christopher Prince of New London, Connecticut, best illustrate the opportunities and perils associated with privateering. From 1777 to 1783, Prince captained at least seven American privateers, sailed repeatedly into lucrative Caribbean waters, and successfully acquired several enemy prizes. The British captured him in 1779 and again in 1782, holding the captain for several months in a London prison until his eventual release.⁸⁷ Less fortunate than Prince was American seaman Nathaniel Fanning, who embarked on the American privateer *Angelica*, "a new vessel, mounting sixteen carriage guns, and carrying 98 men and boys, on a six month cruise." Within weeks of his departure, a British ship seized Fanning and his fellow crewmembers, installing them on a British privateer. Subsequently captured by the French, Fanning became a lieutenant in their navy before eventually returning home to New York.⁸⁸ Another American, Thomas Painter, briefly served on a privateer, but the British caught him and placed him on a prison ship. He escaped by jumping overboard and swimming to safety in New York harbor. This experience soured Painter on a career as a privateersman: "I came to the conclusion, that privateering, was nothing better than Highway Robbery under the protection of law."⁸⁹

Reflecting the ubiquity of eighteenth-century American privateering, even George Washington participated in a practice he would eventually attempt to curtail. Upon his arrival in Cambridge, Massachusetts, to assume command of the Continental Army, Washington realized British ships could sail into Boston's harbor with little resistance. Tapping into the experienced maritime communities of Gloucester, Marblehead, and Plymouth, he organized a flotilla of six privateering vessels to patrol the entire Massachusetts coastline, from Cape Ann to Cape Cod, in order to intercept enemy supply ships coming from Canada and across the Atlantic. From 1775 to 1777, Washington's so-called "navy" captured fifty-five British vessels.⁹⁰ Privately, he also owned a share of one privateer, aptly

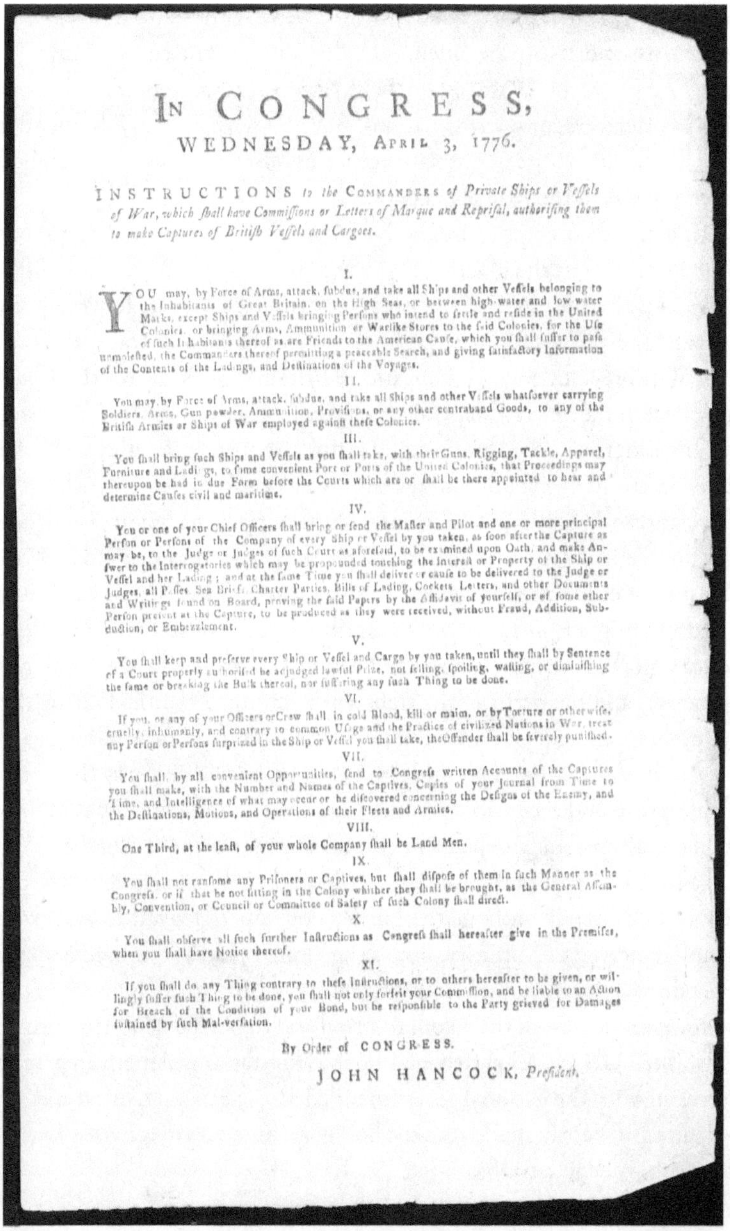

IN CONGRESS,

WEDNESDAY, APRIL 3, 1776.

INSTRUCTIONS *to the* COMMANDERS *of Private Ships or Veſſels of War, which ſhall have Commiſſions or Letters of Marque and Repriſal, authoriſing them to make Captures of Britiſh Veſſels and Cargoes.*

I.

YOU may, by Force of Arms, attack, ſubdue, and take all Ships and other Veſſels belonging to the Inhabitants of Great Britain, on the High Seas, or between high-water and low-water Marks, except Ships and Veſſels bringing Perſons who intend to ſettle and reſide in the United Colonies, or bringing Arms, Ammunition or Warlike Stores to the ſaid Colonies, for the Uſe of ſuch Inhabitants thereof as are Friends to the American Cauſe, which you ſhall ſuffer to paſs unmoleſted, the Commanders thereof permitting a peaceable Search, and giving ſatisfactory Information of the Contents of the Ladings, and Deſtinations of the Voyages.

II.

You may, by Force of Arms, attack, ſubdue, and take all Ships and other Veſſels whatſoever carrying Soldiers, Arms, Gun powder, Ammunition, Proviſions, or any other contraband Goods, to any of the Britiſh Armies or Ships of War employed againſt theſe Colonies.

III.

You ſhall bring ſuch Ships and Veſſels as you ſhall take, with their Guns, Rigging, Tackle, Apparel, Furniture and Ladings, to ſome convenient Port or Ports of the United Colonies, that Proceedings may thereupon be had in due Form before the Courts which are or ſhall be there appointed to hear and determine Cauſes civil and maritime.

IV.

You or one of your Chief Officers ſhall bring or ſend the Maſter and Pilot and one or more principal Perſon or Perſons of the Company of every Ship or Veſſel by you taken, as ſoon after the Capture as may be, to the Judge or Judges of ſuch Court as aforeſaid, to be examined upon Oath, and make Anſwer to the Interrogatories which may be propounded touching the Intereſt or Property of the Ship or Veſſel and her Lading; and at the ſame Time you ſhall deliver or cauſe to be delivered to the Judge or Judges, all Paſſes, Sea Briefs, Charter Parties, Bills of Lading, Cockets, Letters, and other Documents and Writings found on Board, proving the ſaid Papers by the Affidavit of yourſelf, or of ſome other Perſon preſent at the Capture, to be produced as they were received, without Fraud, Addition, Subduction, or Embezzlement.

V.

You ſhall keep and preſerve every Ship or Veſſel and Cargo by you taken, until they ſhall by Sentence of a Court properly authoriſed be adjudged lawful Prize, not ſelling, ſpoiling, waſting, or diminiſhing the ſame or breaking the Bulk thereof, nor ſuffering any ſuch Thing to be done.

VI.

If you, or any of your Officers or Crew ſhall in cold Blood, kill or maim, or by Torture or otherwiſe, cruelly, inhumanly, and contrary to common Uſage and the Practice of civilized Nations in War, treat any Perſon or Perſons ſurprized in the Ship or Veſſel you ſhall take, the Offender ſhall be ſeverely puniſhed.

VII.

You ſhall, by all convenient Opportunities, ſend to Congreſs written Accounts of the Captures you ſhall make, with the Number and Names of the Captives, Copies of your Journal from Time to Time, and Intelligence of what may occur or be diſcovered concerning the Deſigns of the Enemy, and the Deſtinations, Motions, and Operations of their Fleets and Armies.

VIII.

One Third, at the leaſt, of your whole Company ſhall be Land Men.

IX.

You ſhall not ranſome any Priſoners or Captives, but ſhall diſpoſe of them in ſuch Manner as the Congreſs, or if that be not ſitting in the Colony whither they ſhall be brought, as the General Aſſembly, Convention, or Council or Committee of Safety of ſuch Colony ſhall direct.

X.

You ſhall obſerve all ſuch further Inſtructions as Congreſs ſhall hereafter give in the Premiſes, when you ſhall have Notice thereof.

XI.

If you ſhall do any Thing contrary to theſe Inſtructions, or to others hereafter to be given, or willingly ſuffer ſuch Thing to be done, you ſhall not only forfeit your Commiſſion, and be liable to an Action for Breach of the Condition of your Bond, but be reſponſible to the Party grieved for Damages ſuſtained by ſuch Mal-verſation.

By Order of CONGRESS.

JOHN HANCOCK, *Preſident.*

FIGURE 1. A 1776 directive from the Continental Congress authorizing the use of privateers against the British during the American Revolution. (Library of Congress, Rare Book and Special Collections Division, Continental Congress & Constitutional Convention Broadsides Collection) named the *General Washington*, with his twenty-two-year-old stepson, John Parke Custis, and two other men, including his distant cousin Lund Washington.[91] As president, Washington would attempt to prevent Americans from serving as privateers for warring nations. But his own earlier involvement, however small that enterprise might have been, demonstrated how deeply embedded privateering was in the Atlantic economy.

During the eighteenth century, North America's maritime communities became immersed in the practice of privateering, both as British colonists and as American revolutionaries. The prospect of independence, however, offered Americans the possibility of engaging in the transatlantic trade without the burden of its previous colonial obligations. Britain's imperial rivalries would no longer concern the newly independent American nation (or at least that was the hope). Instead, the United States could assume an international role that better reflected its status as a young and relatively weak country.

For eighteenth-century Americans, the Atlantic provided an essential economic lifeline in a watery environment teeming with personal risks. Working on the sea not only could bring a sailor adventure and wealth but also could result in drowning, sinking, disease, or capture. Nearly constant warfare between America's mother country, Great Britain, and its European enemies magnified the promises and the perils of the eighteenth-century Atlantic. During the colonial period, residents of American port cities embraced privateering as a way to survive in a maritime economy often defined by war. Privateering emerged as a widespread and acceptable practice ingrained not only in ship captains and seamen but also in trade-dependent coastal communities. As America contemplated a future free from British laws, obligations, and expectations, the opportunity to trade freely without the burdens of imperial rivalries and wartime exigencies emerged as a priority. But as the United States embraced its political independence, would its maritime citizens be willing to abandon the familiar economic practices from the colonial period and to pursue neutral commerce as newly minted U.S. citizens? Reconciling the longstanding American practice of privateering with the national government's desire to remain neutral and pursue free trade significantly challenged the new government as it exercised its authority over its sovereign citizens.

WHILE THE CONTINENTAL CONGRESS endorsed privateering as a wartime necessity, this governing body also envisioned a postrevolutionary world of peaceful Atlantic commerce when it proposed the Plan of Treaties (or Model Treaty) in 1776. John Adams, a congressional delegate from the maritime-dependent state of Massachusetts, drafted this document for the committee charged with establishing diplomatic relations and military alliances with Europe.[92] Inspired by Enlightenment ideas, he incorporated the concept that "free ships make free goods" into the Model Treaty. Adams envisioned the newly independent United States enjoying peaceful relations and free trade with other nations. As a neutral nation uninvolved in warfare, the United States would not need to engage in privateering or worry about warring states seizing its ships or blockading its ports. Congress's two-handed approach of authorizing privateering and endorsing the Model Treaty illustrated America's idealistic vision of its future clashing with the commercial and military realities of not only winning the American Revolution but also doing business on the Atlantic.

CHAPTER 2

"Free Ships Make Free Goods"

Revolutionary Experiments in Neutrality

THE ENLIGHTENMENT IDEAS THAT inspired the American Revolution encouraged many Americans to think boldly and broadly about the transformations they hoped to institute in the newly established nation. Having engaged in wartime privateering as colonists and revolutionaries, they now sought less combative ways to participate in maritime commerce. Free trade emerged as a top priority of the Continental Congress, with John Adams spearheading the effort to translate these Enlightenment concepts into practical diplomacy. His draft Plan of Treaties of 1776, more commonly known as the Model Treaty, represented America's blueprint for interacting with other nations: commercial agreements would replace burdensome military alliances. Yet winning a war with free trade alone proved to be a losing proposition. Most European nations had no interest in alienating Britain by recognizing its rebellious colonies, preferring to pursue their own neutrality instead. Even Britain's archenemy, France, required more than the promise of American commerce to enter the conflict. The realities of winning the war forced the Continental Congress to secure the entangling alliances they had hoped to avoid. With American diplomats scattered across Europe, Congress first pursed an international path to independence, with the prospect of free trade on the horizon.

THE ORIGINS OF the 1793 Neutrality Proclamation can be found within the ideas of Enlightenment philosophers and the resulting treaties that embraced these concepts. Most European nations subscribed to the reigning economic concept of the sixteenth and seventeenth centuries—mercantilism. As a result, warfare and trade became closely intertwined as these countries sought to gain a greater share of finite commerce. The Atlantic became a dangerous place to do business, particularly for neutral nations. To gain advantage over their maritime enemies, warring adversaries employed privateers encouraged to operate under the concept that "enemy goods make enemy vessels."[1]

Relief from this cutthroat approach came from Enlightenment philosophers, who viewed trade through the more benign prism of reason and balance. In contrast to European monarchs who regarded trade as a combative enterprise, writers such as Montesquieu and Adam Smith saw free trade as a positive good that could elevate people and societies. Montesquieu argued that "the spirit of republics is peace and moderation," in contrast with warring monarchies. Smith believed "free and open trade between nations" would offer the "greatest good for all mankind."[2] A seventeenth-century Dutch legal scholar, Hugo Grotius, had inspired these philosophical conceptions by declaring in his book *Mare Liberum* (The free sea) that the oceans should be open to all, not just a few powerful nations such as Spain and Portugal.[3] If trade had previously functioned as a tool of war, free trade imagined a world of neutral commerce in which ships traded without regard to nationality and without risk of entangling warfare.

As European nations experimented with free trade in the seventeenth and eighteenth centuries, the resulting diplomatic agreements and the Enlightenment ideas that inspired them traversed the Atlantic and entered the homes, minds, and colleges of Americans living in the thirteen English colonies.[4] As the political situation in America heated up after the Seven Years' War, revolutionary leaders looked to a wide range of historical and philosophical sources from ancient Greece and Rome and from Europe, specifically Renaissance and Enlightenment scholars, for inspiration.[5] Amid this vast collection of writings, one emerged as an indispensable guidebook for revolutionary Americans contemplating the nascent country's diplomatic future: Emer de Vattel's *The Law of Nations*. Vattel, a Swiss philosopher, published this four-volume work in 1758, offering a comprehensive understanding of the role a nation should take in state building and international relations.[6] For an eighteenth-century audience already steeped in natural rights and free trade, Vattel's chapter on neutrality (contained in the third book, *Of War*), served as the definitive handbook for nations wishing to purse a neutral diplomatic path.

Following in the tradition of other Enlightenment philosophers, Vattel proclaimed that the laws of nature applied to nations, making them "free, independent and equal."[7] He then demonstrated the specific ways a nation's freedom, independence, and equality found expression in trade and diplomacy. Like Grotius, Vattel believed in the freedom of the seas: "No nation, therefore, has a right to take possession of the open sea, or claim the sole use of it, to the exclusion of other nations."[8] Freedom of the seas also meant free trade. Vattel affirmed, "Every nation, in virtue of her natural liberty, has a right to trade with those who are willing to correspond with such intentions," chiding those who might "injure" this right.[9] While advocating treaties and diplomacy among nations, he also recognized that wars might occur. In his chapter "Of Neutrality," Vattel affirmed the right of a nation to remain neutral during wartime as long as unbound by treaty to participate. He also offered other rules of neutrality, including the need to adhere strictly to this status and to treat all combatants equally. He encouraged nations to make their neutral status explicit through formal treaties with the warring parties so there were no misunderstandings. Most importantly, Vattel reiterated the importance of neutral nations being able to trade without interference, writing, "An attempt to interrupt or put a stop to this trade would be a violation of the rights of neutral nations, a flagrant injury to them." In other words, neutrality was a meaningless concept if ships could not trade freely without risk of capture. Vattel made an exception for specifically defined contraband needed for war, such as "arms, ammunition, timber for ship-building, every kind of naval stores, [and] horses," recognizing too that searching neutral vessels would be inevitable. Nonetheless, he urged respect for a ship's bill of lading to avoid unnecessary seizures and captures.[10]

With the convening of the First Continental Congress in 1774, *Law of Nations* served as an indispensable guidebook for America's early diplomats and political leaders as they contemplated an independent nation. The delegates made use of Philadelphia's public library to obtain works by Vattel and Montesquieu.[11] Later, when Congress established its own library, Vattel's four-volume work appeared among the collection's 300 books. Benjamin Franklin, who relied on a donated copy, wrote to the book's donor to describe its popularity among the delegates: "It came to us in good season, when the circumstances of a rising state make it necessary frequently to consult the law of nations."[12] Even after the revolution, Vattel's ideas continued to permeate political discussions. During the lively debates on the draft Neutrality Proclamation in 1793, Washington's cabinet members—Jefferson, Hamilton, Randolph, and Knox—resembled sparring graduate students as they vied to demonstrate their superior mastery of Vattel's ideas.[13] One historian succinctly summarized *Law of Nations* as providing the "textbook for the State Department and the federal courts" in the 1790s.[14]

Illustrating the book's importance in the education of a future generation of political leaders, Vattel's writings (along with those of Grotius, John Locke, Montesquieu, and other Enlightenment scholars) infused the curriculums and libraries of the colonies' colleges.[15] Having earlier benefited from a loaned copy of Vattel, Franklin returned the favor by donating copies of *Law of Nations* to Harvard College, the Boston Public Library, and the Library Company of Philadelphia.[16] Washington ordered this book, along with many others, for his stepson John Parke Custis, who was a student at King's College (present-day Columbia University).[17] Hamilton, then also at King's College, studied Vattel, as did future secretary of state and president John Quincy Adams, who read his father's copy while at Harvard.[18] Jefferson, who trained law students while also serving in public office, included Vattel (as well as law books, historical studies, and the writings of other Enlightenment philosophers) on the extensive reading list he prepared for his students.[19]

The most immediate and direct effect of Vattel's and other Enlightenment writers' ideas on free trade appeared in the Plan of Treaties, adopted by the Continental Congress in September 1776. American diplomacy formally began in 1775, when Congress established the "Secret Committee" to initiate negotiations with potential European allies, particularly France, which eagerly sought ways to undercut Britain's economic and political hegemony.[20] A year later Richard Henry Lee's resolution on independence made America's diplomatic needs explicit when it stated "that measures should be immediately taken for procuring the assistance of foreign powers."[21] The fledging nation's Declaration of Independence would be meaningless unless foreign countries recognized the United States as a sovereign nation. In the busy summer of 1776, Congress appointed a committee "to prepare a plan of treaties to be proposed to foreign powers" to attain international recognition, to cultivate wartime alliances, and to develop transatlantic trading relations.[22]

As newcomers to international diplomacy, many in Congress naively believed that unrestricted commercial treaties would offer European nations so many benefits that they would happily support American independence and even contribute resources to the war effort.[23] John Adams emerged as the leading advocate of this approach.[24] As he sat down to draft what would become the Model Treaty in 1776, Adams's diplomatic experiences were more academic than practical. In keeping with the college curriculums of the eighteenth century, he had studied Enlightenment philosophers while at Harvard. As an attorney in Boston during the revenue crises, he had participated in the debates on the Stamp, Townshend, and Tea Acts. These practical experiences, combined with his thoughtful writings on republican government, made him an influential figure in both the First and Second Continental Congresses. Despite his leading role in writing America's first diplomatic statement, the Model Treaty, his posting to France in 1778 marked his first journey outside the American colonies.

This idealistic approach to international relations might explain Adams's overconfidence in the power of free trade to attract European allies.

During the intellectually fertile summer of 1776, Adams sketched out his thoughts on "a model of a treaty" in his diary. In an initial entry, he outlined the very specific provisions he sought in a treaty with France: "1st. No Political Connection. 2nd. No military connection. Receive no Troops from her. 3rd. Only a commercial connection, i.e. make a Treaty, to receive her ships in our Ports. Let her engage to receive our Ships into her Ports—furnish us with Arms, Cannon, Salt Petre [sic], Powder, Duck, Steel."[25] In subsequent writings, he expanded on the importance of American autonomy: "That we should avoid all alliance, which might embarrass us in after times and involve us in future European Wars." Instead, Adams saw a nonbinding commercial treaty as the pathway to American independence because it would liberate the colonies from existing trading restrictions with Britain while opening up additional commercial markets across Europe.[26] As the following list suggests, he believed the benefits to France of a Franco-American alliance would be substantial and endless: it would "encourage her manufactures, increase her exports of the produce of her soil and agriculture, extend her navigation and trade, augment her resources of naval power, raise her from her present deep humiliation, distress and decay, and place her on a more equal footing with England, for the protection of her foreign possessions, and maintaining her independence at sea." At the same, these significant political and economic advantages "would be an ample compensation to France for acknowledging our independence, and for furnishing us for our money or upon credit for a time, with such supplies of necessaries as we should want, even if this conduct should involve her in a war."[27] As a major proponent of commercial diplomacy, Adams emerged as the obvious choice to write the draft treaty.[28]

With the right of free trade being increasingly affirmed in European diplomacy, Adams had numerous examples to choose from as he composed the Model Treaty. His challenge was finding the versions that best suited American needs and aspirations. Relying on several books on European diplomacy that Franklin, a one-man lending library, had shared with him, Adams focused on Anglo-French treaties from the late seventeenth and early eighteenth centuries. He liberally copied the free-trade provisions from these agreements, including navigation rights, the definition of contraband, and limits on privateering, into Articles XIV–XXX of his draft agreement.[29] Adams's decision to model his treaty on these Anglo-French efforts made sense. He wanted to create a successful document that would include language and provisions familiar to European diplomats. While several Anglo-Dutch and Anglo-Spanish agreements also provided potential templates, Adams wanted to incorporate language on free trade from treaties that France had already endorsed.[30] By substituting "America" for "Britain" in his version, he also placed the revolutionary nation on equal sovereign footing with France and Britain.[31]

When completed several weeks later, the Model Treaty consisted of thirty articles and envisioned a friendly commercial relationship with Louis XVI, "the most Christian king," in the hope that France would return the favor by declaring war on Britain.[32] The treaty's economic provisions promised commercial reciprocity between the United States and France, with French ships enjoying the same privileges as American ones, including the same rate of duties and freedom of navigation in U.S. waters. The nascent country also requested French protection from the Algerian pirates in the Mediterranean. Most importantly, the agreement affirmed the concept "that free ships shall also give a freedom to goods, and that everything shall be deemed to be free and exempt . . . , contraband goods being always excepted." At the same time, the Model Treaty implied the possibility of war between Great Britain and France, even a wartime alliance between America and France. In the event of an Anglo-French conflict, the treaty offered several self-serving provisions for the American cause. First, the United States agreed to remain neutral but requested that France not privateer against America or invade Canada. Second, France should not expect to acquire Canada or Florida as a prerequisite for an American alliance. In its definition of contraband, the treaty listed sixty-eight items, primarily weapons and ammunition but also tobacco, salted fish, cheese, butter, beer, wine, sugar, and salt while excluding cloth, shipbuilding materials, and most other food items.[33] Adams nonetheless had crafted a treaty that demonstrated a strong adherence to Enlightenment ideas on free trade. While some critics in Congress wanted it to acknowledge the political situation, Adams and Franklin, his diplomatic colleague, believed its commercial provisions provided enough incentives to attract France's military assistance without sacrificing American sovereignty.[34]

Free trade as a wartime strategy proved to be a short-lived policy, despite Congress's adoption of the Model Treaty in September 1776. (Congress had also authorized the competing policy of wartime privateering.)[35] France would not enter the conflict without an explicit military alliance, and the struggling American war effort needed more than free trade to be successful. America would need to win its independence on the battlefield before it could attain its dream of political and commercial neutrality. In December 1776, Congress abandoned the Model Treaty and instructed its commissioners in Paris—Franklin, Silas

Deane, and Arthur Lee—to make more tangible concessions to France in the hopes of securing military help. After more than a year of slow and delicate negotiations, Franklin and Deane secured two treaties with France: the Treaty of Alliance and the Treaty of Amity and Commerce. (Adams had replaced Lee as the third envoy, but by the time he arrived in Paris, most of the work on the two treaties had been completed.)[36] The thirty-one-article Treaty of Amity and Commerce borrowed liberally from the thirty-article Model Treaty's vision of commercial agreements, including its affirmation of the right of free trade in Article XXIII: "And it is hereby stipulated that free Ships shall also give a freedom to Goods."[37] A month after Congress accepted these treaties, Great Britain declared war on France on June 14, 1778. The American Revolution had become a global conflict.[38]

The Franco-American alliance (which would also include Spain) had the ironic effect of encouraging less powerful nations such as Russia and Sweden to form the League of Armed Neutrality to attain the political neutrality and freedom of trade that the fledgling United States had sought in its Model Treaty.[39] Spearheading this effort was Empress Catherine II of Russia (Catherine the Great), who had grown frustrated with Britain's previous neutrality violations and wanted to signal Russia's unwillingness to ally with that kingdom to fight France, Spain, and the Americans. As an added bonus, an alliance of neutral nations could bolster Russia's naval power and its influence over European affairs.[40]

The roots of Armed Neutrality can be found in the delicate maritime relationship that made Russia dependent on Britain. Possessing only 17 merchant ships compared with Britain's 414, the transport of Russian goods relied on the kindness of foreign captains. Further complicating this relationship was Britain's continued reliance on the Consolato del mare as a wartime strategy against enemy shipping during its eighteenth-century wars. British (and Spanish) warships captured and seized Russian cargoes and vessels (and those of other nations) despite the desire of these smaller countries to avoid involvement in these conflicts.[41] Amid these offenses, Britain arrogantly assumed that Russia would join forces with them to counter the Americans' alliance with the Bourbon powers of France and Spain. Aside from political considerations, Britain desired this alliance because Russian forests produced valuable raw materials useful in building and repairing ships.[42] Catherine the Great, however, had other plans. Steeped in the Enlightenment ideas of free trade and understanding the realities of her weak navy, the empress sought to unite the other neutral nations that had fallen victim to the aggressive practices of Britain and the other great powers. Spain's seizure of a Russian ship (rather than a

FIGURE 2. Catherine the Great, who organized the League of Armed Neutrality in 1780 to shield Russia and other smaller nations from belligerent actions during the American Revolution. (Wikipedia.com; painted by J. B. Lampi, ca. 1780)

British transgression) provided the violation Catherine needed to launch her diplomatic offensive on neutrality.[43]

On March 11, 1780, Russia issued the Declaration of Armed Neutrality to the warring nations of Britain, France, and Spain to announce its intention to remain neutral. Demonstrating the continued influence of Enlightenment ideas on free trade, the statement's preamble declared Russia's high regard "for the rights of neutrality and the liberty of universal commerce." The statement added that Catherine's "subjects would peaceably enjoy the fruits of their industry and the advantages belonging to a neutral nation." The declaration then announced to these belligerents the five principles of neutrality Russia intended to follow during the current war. The first item declared the right of neutral vessels "to navigate freely from port to port and along the coasts of nations at war." The second provision affirmed the principle that "free ships make free goods." The third article made exceptions for contraband amid a list of "free goods" but permitted each nation to define what specifically qualified. The fourth item defined a blockaded port and the potential dangers in entering a heavily fortified harbor. The last provision established the rules for dealing with the disposition of prizes.[44]

The Declaration of Armed Neutrality prompted swift diplomatic reactions across Europe, with most nations responding favorably to its provisions.[45] The Bourbon powers of France and Spain eagerly embraced this statement because it enabled them to trade freely with participating nations. On April 18, Spain, by way of its foreign minister, affirmed its support for Russia's declaration: "To show to all the neutral powers how much Spain is desirous of observing the same rules in time of war as she was directed by whilst neuter, His Majesty conforms to the other points contained in the declaration of Russia." A week later France also offered its backing for the rights of neutral nations during wartime: "The King has been desirous, not only to procure a freedom of navigation to the subjects of the Empress of Russia, but to those of all the States who hold their neutrality, and that upon the same conditions as are announced in the treaty to which His Majesty this day answers."[46]

The strength of these responses encouraged other neutrals to join Russia. By the summer of 1780, Denmark and Norway had signed the Armed Neutrality Conventions, with Sweden and the Netherlands coming aboard by the end of the year. To enforce the provisions of the declaration, Russia, Sweden, Denmark, and Norway increased funding for their navies to defend their commercial ships, while Russia's tiny merchant navy sought to decrease its reliance on British ships by expanding its fleet to 141 vessels by 1787.[47] The emerging league also owed its success to "strength in numbers": as additional nations embraced neutral trade, the agreement grew in symbolic and strategic significance.[48] By the end of 1782, the Holy Roman Empire, Prussia, Austria, and Portugal had become members of the League of Armed Neutrality as well. When the Two Sicilies joined in 1783, this agreement consisted of ten member nations.[49]

The outlier amid this diplomatic enthusiasm for neutrality was, not surprisingly, the chief practitioner of aggressive trading practices: Great Britain. Increasingly isolated, it bristled at this agreement, regarding assertions of neutrality as a blow to its economic reputation and its commercial influence. In its April

23 response to Russia's declaration, Britain complained that it had become the victim of "the unprovoked aggression of France and Spain." Instead of offering a sweeping affirmation of neutral rights, as its two European antagonists had, it reiterated that "the king, from the commencement of these troubles, gave the most precise orders respecting the flag of Her Imperial Majesty, and the commerce of her subjects, agreeable to the law of nations." Taking a "business as usual" approach to maritime violations, Britain reiterated, "in case any infringements, contrary to these repeated orders, take place, the courts of admiralty . . . are established to take cognizance of such matters."[50] Despite the league's desire to trade freely during the current conflict, Britain intended to employ the full range of wartime tactics available to it, including seizing the cargoes of neutral vessels.

Britain demonstrated further disregard for Russia's neutral status when it made a second attempt to secure a military alliance with Empress Catherine, despite her stated desire to avoid involvement in the American conflict. In retaliation for Russia spurning its proposal and to weaken the league's enforcement powers, Britain declared war on the Netherlands in December 1780, the strongest maritime member of the Armed Neutrality Convention.[51] Many Americans, including Washington, Adams, and members of Congress, believed Russia and its neutral allies would offer military support to the Dutch since its membership in the league had triggered the declaration of war.[52] But Catherine remained steadfast in her commitment to Russian neutrality and declined to aid her erstwhile Dutch ally, then demonstrated her expanding influence in European affairs by offering to broker an Anglo-Dutch peace treaty instead.[53]

For the Americans in Paris, Franklin and Adams, the Declaration of Armed Neutrality exposed the revolutionary nation's precarious diplomatic standing across Europe. Despite America's role as a leading participant in the current war (and also as a supporter of privateers against Russian ships), most European nations perceived the United States, not as a sovereign entity, but as thirteen British colonies in rebellion against their powerful mother country. Because of its dependent political status, America did not warrant official acknowledgement in Russia's plans.[54] Stuck in an international "no man's land," Adams and Franklin offered Congress competing advice on the best way to respond to the Armed Neutrality Convention.

Adams, who maintained a sanguine view of European diplomacy, interpreted the declaration as a favorable philosophical and strategic development for the American cause.[55] He saw the obvious intellectual connections between his Model Treaty and the emerging League of Armed Neutrality, believing that its members' shared commitment to free trade made these nations natural allies for the American cause. Adams also regarded the league as a powerful bulwark against the British war effort, equivalent to a declaration of war by these nations. He wrote to the Continental Congress, "The Improvement in the Law of Nations which the Empress aims at, and will undoubtedly establish, is hurtful to England, it is true, to a very great degree: but it is beneficial to all other Nations, and to none more than the United States of America, who will be Carriers, and I hope forever Neuters."[56] With Russia and other nations rejecting British hegemony, Adams believed the time was ripe for expanded European recognition of American independence as well as additional military alliances.[57] Once again, his idealism blinded him to international realities. Russia had formed the league in order to avoid participating in the Anglo-American war. If a powerful country like Britain could not cajole it into an alliance, thirteen American colonies stood little chance of being more successful.

Nonetheless, in subsequent letters to Congress, Adams advocated a return to the "militia diplomacy"—the American practice of sending ministers to European capitals even if they had not been invited—to capitalize on the common cause with Europe that Armed Neutrality revealed.[58] He wrote, "I could wish that the United States had a Minister at each of the Maritime Courts, I mean Holland, Russia, Sweden and Denmark," a reference to the participants in the convention.[59] A month later Adams lamented the lack of information about America's revolutionary efforts in European capitals: "Neither the Cause, nor the Country of America are understood in any Part of Europe, which gives Opportunity to the English to represent Things as they choose."[60] With American diplomats promoting the fledgling nation's interests in these neutral capitals, he hoped that the United States would be invited to join the League of Armed Neutrality and also receive acknowledgment of its independence.[61]

Franklin, more experienced in the rules and mores of European diplomacy, offered a more tempered response to Armed Neutrality.[62] In Franklin's capacity as America's only recognized minister in Europe, his dispatches officially notified Congress of the dramatic change to international law: "For whatever may formerly have been the Law of Nations, all the Neutral Powers at the Instance of Russia, seem at present disposed to change it."[63] Underscoring America's ambiguous status as an unrecognized combatant, he nonetheless recommended that Congress acknowledge the changing maritime law and alert American privateers to its implications: "As it is likely to become the Law of Nations that free Ships should make free Goods, I wish the Congress to consider whether it may not be proper to give Orders to their Cruizers [sic] not to molest Foreign Ships, but conform to the Spirit of that Treaty of Neutrality."[64] Franklin, a stickler for diplomatic protocol, stopped short of endorsing Adams's enthusiasm for militia diplomacy, having long dismissed this approach as "suitoring for Alliances." Instead, he advocated what he considered the more effective approach of waiting for nations to choose to ally with the Americans.[65]

From the battlefield, General Washington also offered his assessment of the new policy of the Armed Neutrality Convention. Writing to the president of the Continental Congress, he agreed with Franklin and Adams's views that "the accession of Holland and Portugal to the Northern League of Neutrality will be undoubtedly very embarrassing to Great Britain." While Adams saw diplomatic opportunity in Britain's difficulties, Washington offered a more realistic interpretation of the situation. He concluded, "But this, I think, may be relied upon, that the more she is insulted and oppressed by the European Powers, the more she will endeavor to revenge herself upon us."[66] Later Washington praised the military benefits of the league's agreement because its enforcement greatly weakened "the naval pride and power of Great Britain."[67] A career officer who had fought alongside and now against the British, Washington viewed the complexities of European rivalries from a battlefield perspective.

In its official response to the Declaration of Armed Neutrality, the Continental Congress embraced pragmatism over protocol by adopting the competing recommendations of its two diplomats. Advancing the stalled American war effort proved more important than resolving a philosophical debate occurring 3,000 miles away. In deference to Franklin, Congress officially responded to Russia's statement on October 5, 1780. Acknowledging that "their most Christian and Catholic Majesties and most of the neutral maritime powers of Europe have declared their approbation" of the Russian declaration, the delegates also affirmed their "regard to the rights of commerce, and their respect for the sovereign." Additionally, they instructed the Board of Admiralty to "prepare and report instructions for the commander of armed vessels commissioned by the United States" to respect "the principles contained in the Declaration of the Empress of all Russia, on the rights of neutral vessels." In that same statement, Congress also entertained hopes that Russia might include the United States in the League of Armed Neutrality when delegates "empowered" the American ministers in Europe "to accede to such regulations ... of the said declaration" if invited to do so by "Her Imperial Majesty."[68] Although this statement stressed Russia's role in offering America an "invitation" to the agreement, Congress also embraced Adams's recommendation that its diplomats preemptively pursue European alliances.

Despite Franklin's misgivings, Congress revived the practice of militia diplomacy in October 1780 by authorizing unsolicited missions to Russia and the Netherlands. American leaders hoped that diplomatic recognition or even a commercial or military alliance would bolster America's sagging cause.[69] In a cost-saving move, Congress appointed diplomats who were already in Europe, with Adams posted to the Netherlands, and his secretary, Francis Dana, dispatched to Russia.[70] With Britain now at war with the Netherlands, Adams's instructions had been expanded to include securing a treaty of amity and commerce with the Dutch, modeled on the French agreement of 1778.[71] In addition to seeking inclusion in the League of Armed Neutrality, Congress authorized Dana to pursue a similar treaty with Russia that acknowledged American independence.[72] While the Declaration of Armed Neutrality offered the immediate incentive for these missions, the emissaries brought America's signature calling card to these negotiations: free trade and friendship with the United States in exchange for recognition and financial assistance.

Contrary to American hopes, militia diplomacy quickly ran afoul of the secretive rules and protocols of the royal courts and the complex entanglements that defined Europe's geopolitical arrangements. Adams complained to Congress, "It is very difficult to discover, with Certainty the secret springs which actuate the Courts of Europe, but whatever I can find with any degree of Probability, I Shall transmit to Congress, at one Time or another."[73] As Dana embarked for Russia, Franklin warned him of the pitfalls of militia diplomacy because it "lessens our reputation and makes other[s] less willing to form a connection with us." Instead, Franklin believed that America should focus its diplomatic energies on the country that had already chosen to be its ally: France.[74]

Despite their summertime arrival, Dana and his youthful secretary, John Quincy Adams, encountered an icy silence as they set foot in the Russian capital of Saint Petersburg.[75] Catherine II and her ministers refused to meet with the American, an unrecognized diplomat from rebellious British colonies. Instead, Dana and young Adams lived in virtual seclusion at the Hotel Paris, isolated from the other diplomats attending court at the Hermitage Palace. Further marginalizing his efforts was France's minister to Russia, the marquis de Verac, who believed that the Franco-American alliance authorized him to represent America's diplomatic interests in the empress's court. Dana also found the favoritism, blackmail, and bribery that regulated diplomacy in Catherine's court unseemly. During his two long years in Russia, he received an unsolicited tutorial on the limits of both militia diplomacy and the Armed Neutrality Convention.[76] Despite Catherine's boldness in challenging British aggressiveness, she nonetheless carefully avoided antagonizing Britain and becoming an unwilling participant in the American conflict. For starters, Russia had cited a Spanish transgression, rather than a British one, as the impetus for pursuing and declaring Armed Neutrality. Similarly, recognizing American independence remained out of the question as long as Britain still claimed the colonies as its own.[77] In the end, American victories on the battlefield, which led to progress at the negotiating table in Paris, ultimately obviated the need for Russian diplomatic recognition, permitting a disheartened Dana to finally leave Saint Petersburg in September 1783.[78]

Meanwhile in Amsterdam, John Adams's efforts at militia diplomacy also ran afoul of a nation's political priorities. While the outbreak of hostilities between Britain and the Netherlands had signaled an opening for the Americans, the Dutch preferred peace over war. Throughout 1781 and 1782, Adams, lacking proper diplomatic credentials, looked on helplessly as a series of negotiations ensued between these two nations, with a nonaligned Russia serving as mediator.[79] Adams's situation became even more precarious when his own government turned on him. On July 10, 1781, he received word that Congress was revoking his commission, then Franklin found a way to tangibly oppose militia diplomacy by eliminating funding for the mission.[80] Despite these monumental setbacks, Adams remained in Amsterdam. His diplomatic fortunes finally improved when news of the British surrender at Yorktown reached the Continent in November 1781. The Dutch had failed in their efforts to negotiate a peace treaty, and in the meantime Britain was preparing to recognize American independence. With these obstacles cleared away, Adams belatedly achieved the diplomatic successes he had sought from the Dutch, including recognition of the United States and a treaty of amity and commerce.[81] Yet these pyrrhic victories had more to do with America's decisive military triumph on the battlefield (aided by the French alliance) than with the colonies' ragtag efforts at militia diplomacy in European capitals.[82]

Neutrality assumed one other guise during the Revolution as Native American nations unsuccessfully attempted to avoid taking sides in this conflict. The Oneida Nation spoke for many Natives when they declared their friendship to "old and new England" as well as their neutrality toward a conflict between "two brothers of the same blood."[83] Despite these efforts, Indigenous tribes found themselves and their lands situated in the middle of a conflict that did not reflect their concerns, in contrast to European nations, which could declare their ports and ships as neutrals but did not have to worry about threats to their territory. With battles raging around them, Native Americans found it impossible to stay out of harm's way. Additionally, both American and British leaders sought their help on the battlefield. Unable to remain neutral, most Natives preferred to ally with the British, who offered vital trading relationships and did not encroach on their lands.[84] But a handful of nations joined forces with the Americans, including the Delaware and the Tuscarora and Oneida, who broke with the other four members of the Iroquois Confederacy.[85] The failure of Indian neutrality had disastrous consequences for these nations. The war weakened many of those who participated and resulted in the collapse of the once-powerful Iroquois Confederacy. Native American interests were not represented at the Treaty of Paris, and the American victory meant the additional loss of Indigenous lands to settlers without British officials to intervene.[86] Territorially and diplomatically vulnerable in a way that European nations were not, neutrality proved to be an attractive but ultimately elusive goal for Native Americans.

With the end of fighting, the United States could now turn its attention to the role it sought in international affairs as a newly independent nation. During the war, many Americans in Congress had optimistically viewed Russia's Armed Neutrality as an opportunity for an alliance because of its embrace of free trade.[87] Instead of that declaration establishing a common ground for neutral commerce, however, the experiences of Dana and John Adams exposed the frustrating complexities of European diplomacy, with its alliances, intrigues, and self-interests. With peace negotiations underway in Paris, the Continental Congress announced a dramatic shift in American policy when it advised its negotiators there, Franklin, Adams, and John Jay, to avoid joining the League of Armed Neutrality or any other European free-trade pact. Chastened by wartime diplomacy, Congress explained in its June 13, 1783, instructions, "the true interest of these states requires that they should be as little as possible entangled in the politics and controversies of European nations."[88] On October 29, Congress formally instructed its ministers in Europe "that no further measures be taken at present towards the admission of the United States into that [Armed Neutrality] Confederacy."[89] While free trade and commercial relationships remained a priority for Congress, alliances with European countries did not. Although America's national government institutionally evolved from 1776 to 1787, from the Continental Congress to the Confederation Congress and finally to the federal authority under the U.S. Constitution, the nation's commitment to avoiding international entanglements, including the Armed Neutrality Convention, remained a top diplomatic priority, even if these dealt with free trade.[90]

U.S. political leaders emerged from the revolution still committed to economic neutrality. But after a bruising exposure to the pitfalls of European diplomacy, they realized that their quest for free trade must also include political neutrality: foreign relationships without entanglements. While the Treaty of Paris of 1783 affirmed U.S. political independence from Britain and the new nation's territorial sovereignty, the agreement fell short in establishing the commercial relationship America sought with Britain, which remained its principal trading partner.[91] As an alternative, congressional officials launched an ambitious campaign to attain the economic and political relationships that had eluded them during the war.[92] Congress appointed Jefferson to join Adams and Franklin in Paris to pursue commercial agreements and diplomatic recognition from no fewer than sixteen European nations, including Great Britain, as well as the Barbary States. Jefferson crafted his own Model Treaty, based on Adams's 1776 template, which reaffirmed the concept that "free ships make free goods" and promised most-favored-nation status to other nations (rather than commercial reciprocity). Despite Congress's high hopes, Jefferson (and his deputies) achieved only two commercial treaties—with Prussia in 1785 and Morocco in 1786—both offering more-symbolic value than actual economic or strategic benefits.[93] Further complicating America's postwar aspirations were colonial and revolutionary entanglements: Britain continued to impress American sailors, and France sought American reciprocity during its revolutionary wars based on the 1778 alliance.[94] While America's political status had changed since the American Revolution, its political stature had not, at least in the eyes of most of Europe, further complicating efforts to gain recognition of its political sovereignty and economic autonomy.[95]

As the ineffectual Confederation Congress made way for a stronger national government under the Constitution of 1787, the nation's political leaders continued to stress the importance of politically unencumbered free trade. The detailed responsibilities given to Congress in Article I, Section 8 includes the power to "regulate commerce with foreign nations." In one *Federalist* essay (Number 11), Hamilton, its author, highlighted the economic influence a strong government would wield in international commerce.[96] Referring to America's lack of a trading agreement with Britain, Hamilton wrote of the pending Constitution, "Would it not enable us to negotiate, with the fairest prospect of success, for commercial privileges of the most valuable and extensive kind, in the dominions of that kingdom?" He also emphasized that free trade (or economic neutrality) was impossible without a strong government: "The rights of neutrality will only be respected when they are defended by all adequate power. A nation, despicable by its weakness, forfeits even the privilege of being neutral."[97] At the same time, the new national government prepared for the combative realities of transatlantic commerce, with Article I, Section 8 also giving Congress the power to declare war, to issue letters of marque and reprisal, and to make rules about seized ships and cargo, just as the Articles of Confederation had authorized. Challenging colonial precedent, however, the Constitution, in Article I, Section 9, also explicitly prohibits states from issuing letters of marque and reprisal, making clear that waging war was the national government's prerogative.[98]

REVOLUTIONARY AMERICA EMBRACED international diplomacy with high ideals and high aspirations for the role it intended to play in the world. Despite facing the monumental task of defeating the British Army on the battlefield, American politicians believed they could also pursue and promote free trade across Europe. Buffeted by the challenges involved in securing commercial and military alliances among reluctant European nations, neophyte American diplomats received an education in the self-interests that drove international affairs. Upon achieving their country's independence from Britain, American leadership did not abandon its quest for free trade or friendly relations with other states. Instead, the leaders of the young nation realized that the best way to achieve these goals was independently and unilaterally, without the encumbrances of other nations' concerns. While U.S. political leaders received insights on the pitfalls of European diplomacy, Washington gained his own battlefield education on imperial rivalries as he fought alongside the French to defeat the British.

CHAPTER 3

"The Contests of European Nations"

George Washington and Neutrality

GEORGE WASHINGTON, as the chief architect of the neutrality policy, brought a unique and longstanding perspective on foreign affairs to his administration that differed from the experiences of most early American politicians. While revolutionary leaders like Benjamin Franklin, John Adams, and Thomas Jefferson received their education on the pitfalls and complexities of European diplomacy during their overseas missions, Washington obtained his tutorial on North American battlefields. As a military officer, he had encountered the British and French as both allies and enemies in two different wars. Most recently, he had befriended the French officers who had served with him during the American Revolution. As president, he exchanged correspondence with these French generals, who described, to Washington's dismay, a hopeful revolution of their own now quickly descending into violence and chaos. These epistolary reports of France's volatile revolution, coupled with Washington's previous military experiences, inspired two landmark presidential decisions: not to pursue an alliance with France and instead to establish a position of American neutrality. Despite their desire for free trade, American leaders' revolutionary experiences had cooled their enthusiasm for international entanglements. With France and Britain engaged in their latest conflict in 1793, Washington took the decisive step of combining his own perspectives on European affairs with the lessons of revolutionary diplomacy to enshrine neutrality as an enduring American priority.

TWO INTERCONNECTED EVENTS—the death of Washington's father followed by the passing of his half-brother, Lawrence—occurring largely beyond his control, shaped Washington's early career and his developing view of international affairs. The premature death of Washington's father meant that the estate had insufficient funds to send him to college. Fortunately for the young man, Lawrence, fourteen years his senior, assumed the role of mentor and surrogate father. He encouraged Washington to pursue a career in the military, as he himself had done. Lawrence also provided Washington with his only opportunity for "international" (really intercolonial) travel when he accompanied his ailing half-brother to the British colony of Barbados. Lawrence's death from tuberculosis in 1752 (he was thirty-four) meant that the position of Virginia's adjutant general, which he had held, was now vacant. Washington applied and embarked on the second major turning point of his early life. In 1753, he began his career as a military officer with the colonial rank of major and, from this position, his serendipitous introduction to international affairs.[1]

That same year the Virginia colony sent its newly appointed adjutant general to the Ohio River valley to investigate reports of French encroachments on British-controlled lands. Washington's assignment seemed simple enough, but he was entering a complex and volatile situation in which the profound international and territorial stakes extended far beyond the Pennsylvania frontier. Since 1689, France and Great Britain had engaged in a series of dynastic wars, with a small portion of these conflicts spilling onto American soil.[2] In 1749, as part of its strategy during the War of Austrian Succession, France had built forts along the Ohio River to increase its territorial presence in North America. While Britain and its colonists possessed land claims along the Ohio, so too did France and the powerful Haudenosaunee Confederacy nations.[3] One historian described the Ohio Valley at this time as "one of the most sensitive boundary regions in the world."[4] In his first military assignment, the twenty-three-year-old officer walked into a delicate situation that would have challenged even the most seasoned diplomat.

During this mission, Washington endured physical hardships as he traversed dense forests and crossed frozen streams; he also faced diplomatic obstacles as he attempted to meet and negotiate with French, British, and Haudenosaunee representatives. The French officials he encountered refused to relinquish their forts and other territorial gains on the Ohio River. Under instructions from Virginia's governor to push them out, Washington returned to the area in May 1754 with 200 Virginia militiamen and a handful of Seneca Indians. An attack ensued, with Washington and his troops killing several French soldiers. Reflecting the confused and volatile environment of the Ohio frontier, this skirmish quickly escalated into the opening battle of the Seven Years' War. Unlike earlier conflicts over European succession, the governments of France and Britain justified this latest round of hostilities as a contest over their territorial holdings in North

America. Washington and his troops unwittingly provided the small spark needed to ignite this North American tinderbox that spread into a global war.[5]

Despite Washington's dubious distinction as the colonial officer who started the years-long fighting, his wartime experiences proved to be somewhat more positive. He served in the British Army from 1754 to 1758, although not quite in the rank he had hoped. The regular army did not recognize his status as a colonel in the colonial militia, nor did he receive a royal commission. Nonetheless, as a captain and aide-de-camp, Washington served directly under British general Edward Braddock, witnessing both the strengths and weaknesses of his commander's efforts. More importantly, Washington's service with the British Army expanded and regularized his training as a career military officer. He received valuable instruction during this period, "learning how to build forts, transport supplies, dispense justice, train and command soldiers, and give orders."[6] He also acquired the demeanor and authority of the British officers he met.[7]

Washington's wartime service also continued his education in the complexities of European diplomacy and the colonies' minor role in it. Despite his participation in a global war in which he fought with the British against the French, the Virginian viewed his achievements largely from a colonial perspective. He served alongside British regulars, not as one of them, and he always saw British war aims and accomplishments as separate from those of the colonies. When Washington resigned his commission in 1758, his service had been in the Virginia militia, not in the British Army. He also believed by that time that his work in securing the Pennsylvania frontier for his fellow colonists had been completed, although the Anglo-French war continued for several more years. Washington might not have grasped the full intricacies of European diplomacy during his time in the Ohio River valley. Yet the escalation of his fact-finding mission into a global war made a lasting impression concerning the complexity and volatility of European affairs.[8]

From 1758 to 1775, Washington enjoyed a domestic hiatus. During these seventeen years, he served in the Virginia House of Burgess, married Martha Custis, and began a lifetime of renovations on his beloved Mount Vernon estate. This break from military service came to end in June 1775, when the Second Continental Congress appointed Washington commander in Chief of the Continental Army. The man who assumed this post had matured into a thoughtful forty-three-year-old leader, with nearly two decades to reconcile his youthful military ambitions with a more realistic understanding of their deadly consequences.[9] With Great Britain now assuming the role of enemy and France eventually becoming an ally, this appointment continued Washington's education on the diplomatic chess game that defined European rivalries and alliances. From a position of experience and authority, he could influence international events rather than just being caught in their maelstrom.

The Treaty of Alliance between the United States and France and its commercial companion, the Treaty of Amity and Commerce, transformed the American Revolution into a global conflict in 1778, with France and Britain once again at war.[10] This alliance offered the American cause the additional troops and resources it desperately needed, while France saw an opportunity to undercut Britain as America's primary trading partner in order to alter the European balance of power.[11] As the commander of the Continental Army, Washington bore the responsibility for working with his former enemies in the French military. When negotiating with those officers, he emphasized pragmatism, respect, and most importantly, putting American needs first.[12]

The Franco-American alliance began on an optimistic note in July 1778 with the arrival of comte D'Estaing, a lieutenant general and vice admiral, and his naval fleet of sixteen warships and 4,000 soldiers. Many Americans, including Washington, believed that D'Estaing and his fleet would quickly break the British navy's stronghold on the American coastline, allowing the tide of war to shift dramatically. Instead, the French navy encountered a series of disappointments, first in its failure to challenge British hegemony in New York harbor, then in a poorly coordinated effort with American troops to capture Newport, Rhode Island. After two futile months D'Estaing and his fleet retreated to the West Indies, with no immediate plans of returning to the American conflict. Despite Washington's personal misgivings about the French as allies and his disappointment in their recent naval failures, he understood the diplomatic necessity of publicly supporting this essential international agreement, especially among his troops.[13] Writing to Major General John Sullivan after the French retreat, Washington recommended "the cultivation of harmony and good agreement, and [also] your endeavors to destroy that ill humor which may have got into the officers."[14] Despite these precautions, the future direction of the French alliance remained uncertain.

Prior to the 1778 alliance, several French citizens had joined the American cause on their own accord, and Washington's reaction to their involvement captured his ambivalent feelings about foreign officers. Of particular note were two men, the marquis de Lafayette and the marquis de La Rouerie, who both sought commissions in the Continental Army in 1777, commanded American troops, and eventually rose to the rank of general. Unlike a seasoned officer such as the fifty-one-year-old D'Estaing, the twenty-year-old Lafayette eagerly sought to learn the art of warfare from Washington, who was twenty-five years his senior. Furthermore, Lafayette's willingness to make the financial commitments required of an officer, such as purchasing horses, equipment, and uniforms, convinced Washington that he was not merely a glory-seeking "soldier of fortune." This deferential relationship resulted in a lifelong friendship between the two men, with Washington regarding Lafayette as an adopted son.[15] A letter written to Gouverneur Morris, an American businessman and later U.S. minister to France, succinctly captured the general's appreciation of Lafayette's talents and his exasperation with the other European officers: "I do most devoutly wish, that we had not a single foreign officer among us, except the Marquis de Lafayette, who acts upon very different principles from those which govern the rest."[16]

In 1780, two years after the unsuccessful deployment of its navy, France sought a quick and decisive return on its investment in the American theater and sent over approximately 5,500 men under the command of Lieutenant General comte de Rochambeau. Washington had not been consulted on these plans, and he now faced the prospect of welcoming formerly hostile French troops onto American soil. Despite the potential for awkwardness, both commanders treated each other with respect. In fact, the French government had specifically instructed Rochambeau, a fifty-five-year-old career military officer, to defer to Washington.[17] Some barriers remained, though. The Francophone Rochambeau and the Anglophone Washington required the use of a translator to discuss strategy, a role Lafayette performed on several occasions. More significantly, when they first met in September 1780, they could not agree on the best way to use their two armies. Eight months elapsed before their next meeting, and even the plans they agreed on at their May 1781 conference changed dramatically at the last minute. Washington advocated a joint invasion of New York, to which Rochambeau reluctantly concurred while secretly encouraging the French navy to enter the Chesapeake Bay. The fleet's attack in the Chesapeake demonstrated British vulnerability in the south. Washington, to his credit, responded quickly to these changing circumstances and endorsed Rochambeau's plan to attack in Virginia instead of New York.

Whatever differences had been present in planning the offensive had disappeared as the two armies traveled southward and smoothly executed their joint assault. The infusion of additional French and American troops overpowered the British army, forcing Lieutenant General Lord Cornwallis to surrender at Yorktown, Virginia, on October 17, 1781. France's crucial resources and its officers' strategic insights had brought the American Revolution to a successful conclusion.[18] Overnight, the victory transformed the French generals into American heroes and forged a bond between the two nations and its military leaders, even if those sentiments had not always been present to that time.[19]

In the aftermath of the British surrender, Washington offered praise for all those who had participated in the decisive victory, including the French officers and their army. In his orders of October 20, 1781, Washington wrote that "he requests the Count Rochambeau will be pleased to communicate to the Army under his immediate command the high sense he [Washington] entertains of the distinguished merits of the officers and soldiers of every corps."[20] As the Continental Army disbanded and the French generals and their troops assumed postings in the Caribbean and back in France, Washington's remarks might have signaled the end of these revolutionary friendships. But the formation of the Society of the Cincinnati in the United States and France gave the general and those French officers who assumed leadership roles in this new veterans organization reasons to stay in touch.[21]

In the aftermath of their near-mutiny at Newburgh, New York, over pay and pensions in 1783, American revolutionary officers formed the Society of the Cincinnati to advocate for their concerns. This fraternal and hereditary organization elevated the sacrifice and heroism of officers above that of the common soldiers and even the civilian population. The popularity of this organization spread to France, with officers there eagerly responding to the American Cincinnati's invitation to organize their own chapter. Members on both sides of the Atlantic wore a coveted blue-and-white ribbon, which symbolized the alliance between the two nations. Because the French chapter had more stringent membership requirements than the American one, many officers below the rank of colonel appealed to the leadership of the two societies for a dispensation. These epistolary requests were forwarded to Washington, president-general of the American society, from the French society's leaders: General Lafayette, its president; Admiral D'Estaing, its vice president for the navy; and General Rochambeau, its vice president for the army. General La Rouerie, although not one of its leaders, was an early member of the French society and a strong proponent of its high membership standards.[22]

These seemingly mundane exchanges over eligibility launched a new phase of transatlantic correspondence between Washington and his French generals. During the battles of the American Revolution, from roughly 1777 to 1781, the correspondence between these men had largely dealt with military instructions. In the postwar period of 1784–88, their letters acquired a more personal tone as Washington and these French officers reminisced about the war, built friendships, and established the Society of the Cincinnati. After 1789 these letters grew

FIGURE 3. The Diamond Eagle Ribbon, a gift from French officers to George Washington, symbolizing the role the Society of the Cincinnati played in fostering postwar friendships. (The Society of the Cincinnati; designed by Duval and Fancastel, 1784)

in significance as every man assumed a role in his country's politics. From 1777 until their respective deaths, Washington exchanged the most letters (167) with his "adopted son," the marquis de Lafayette. He and comte D'Estaing penned 58 letters, 48 of these dealing with naval instructions during the American Revolution. Washington exchanged 32 letters with comte de Rochambeau and 26 with the marquis de La Rouerie. Unlike his other European correspondents, such as Catherine Macaulay Graham and Edward Newenham, Washington had forged a trusted bond with these men on the battlefield while also sharing a commitment to the ideas of liberty and republican government that had inspired their service in or alongside the Continental Army. Besides a greater intimacy with Washington, Lafayette also outlived his French military colleagues.[23]

As Washington and his French generals engaged in the business of launching the society, their letters celebrated a shared republican ideology based in military sacrifice and honor as officers, masculine friendships, and an aristocratic liberalism premised on individual rights and constitutions.²⁴ These exchanges transformed them into an epistolary "band of brothers," with their correspondence laying the groundwork for future Franco-American relations. Rochambeau, writing to Washington about membership rosters and charitable contributions, concluded that the society would "perpetuate ... the tender sentiments of fraternity and friendship that we entertain for our brothers of your army, and for the celebrated chief whom we will respect and love till our last."²⁵ These men also discussed the possibilities of transatlantic visits. Washington, who had never traveled outside of the western hemisphere, wrote to Rochambeau, "Should fortune ever put it in my power to come to France, your being at Calais would be an irresistible inducement for me to make it a visit."²⁶ La Rouerie, who was still in America, promised "to take a journey to Virginia ... to see once more the man which [sic] I shall love, respect and admire all my days."²⁷ Lafayette, always willing to put in an extra effort for Washington and the American Revolution, visited the United States from August to December 1784.²⁸ Unable to arrive in time for the Society of the Cincinnati's first meeting, he nonetheless received a hero's welcome, which included traveling with Washington, visiting the retired general at Mount Vernon, and receiving honorary U.S. citizenship.²⁹

Beyond professions of friendship, these men shared the philosophical bonds, particularly a commitment to liberty, that had inspired their revolutionary service. General D'Estaing, who had rarely communicated with Washington during the Revolutionary War, became an effusive and prolific correspondent on matters relating to the society and to postwar remembrances.³⁰ Writing to him on December 25, 1783, D'Estaing emphasized the values that united American and French officers together, such as being "citizen-soldiers" and their "civil and military virtues" as well as their "gallant" conduct. He presented Washington with an American eagle sculpture that symbolized the freedom achieved during the American Revolution, writing, "Liberty (of which it is the happy and august symbol) has risen of itself, supported by wisdom, talents, and disinterestedness, by every virtue—by General Washington."³¹ Washington echoed this sentiment in a letter to Rochambeau, describing his "pleasure" that "we have been contemporaries and fellow-laborers in the cause of liberty, and that we have lived together as brothers should do—in harmony and friendship."³² These letters expressed their shared philosophical sensibilities on government—support for individual rights, particularly liberty; respect for constitutional authority and the rule of law; and the belief in the enlightened leadership of the elites. In short, the French generals' aristocratic liberalism matched Washington's republicanism, making these men trusted informants for one another.³³

By the time Washington became president in 1789, he had already participated in two global wars between France and Great Britain. The letters he received from his French generals, a happy byproduct of the latter of these, offered him a front-row seat to the rumblings that would eventually lead to a third war between the two European rivals. As president, Washington received international news from other correspondents and sources in Europe as well.[34] But the letters from his trusted brothers in arms, who had already served with him in one revolution and who now played leading roles in another, offered a firsthand perspective on European affairs that his other correspondents could not match. These reports played a crucial role in Washington's decisions to not aid France and, more importantly, to pursue a policy of neutrality toward warring Europe.

The year 1789 was a watershed one for America and for France. The United States entered a new phase of its revolution by launching a constitutionally based republican government, while France embarked on its own political makeover, with revolutionaries charging the Bastille prison, the members of the National Assembly pledging to write a new constitution, and these deputies proclaiming the people's natural rights in the Declaration of Rights of Man and the Citizen. As Americans celebrated the ratification of the Constitution and the establishment of their new national government, they also saluted the achievements of their French counterparts, who seemed to be wisely following the American path to political liberty and republican government.[35] The French achievements of 1789 enjoyed almost universal support among Americans, including Washington and other future Federalists. This enthusiasm spilled into the streets and led to widespread celebrations of revolutionary France, despite glaring differences between it and the American experience. Although this initial burst of optimism would devolve into partisan acrimony in the United States and political violence in France, both sides, at least for the time being, enjoyed the idea that their revolutions would inspire political change throughout the world.[36]

From the perspective of Washington and his generals, the French Revolution can be understood as actually two revolutions. The first one, occurring from 1789 to 1791, saw aristocratic liberalism and enlightened French officers and elites as ascendant, whereas the second one, taking place from 1791 to 1793, erased the accomplishments and ideas of the first with more democratic impulses.[37] During the initial stage of revolutionary hopefulness, beginning in 1789, these French officers assumed prominent positions in their country's army or in revolutionary politics and offered their insights to America's newly elected republican president. Comte D'Estaing, who had led the French navy in North America, was now the commanding general of the Versailles National Guard, a citizen-based militia group with jurisdiction over the king's palace. Comte de Rochambeau, the commander of French forces during the American Revolution, became the marshal of France in 1791, the last one Louis XVI would appoint. Now-comte La Rouerie, who had been a brigadier general in the Continental Army, found himself involved in political affairs when he served as a delegate from Brittany to the National Assembly in 1788. Among this group of generals, however, the marquis de Lafayette possessed the greatest ambitions for both himself and his nation's revolution, hoping to become the George Washington of France. In June 1789, after the fall of the Bastille, Louis XVI appointed Lafayette as the commander of the Paris unit of the National Guard, a newly established citizens' militia responsible for maintaining order throughout France.[38] This new position placed Lafayette at the center of revolutionary unrest, including protecting the controversial king who had selected him.

During the first year of the French Revolution, Washington and his former officers contrasted America's successful implementation of its new constitution against France's attempt to draft one. As promised in its Tennis Court oath of August 1789, the National Assembly set writing a new constitution as its sole priority. Members of the Third Estate and aristocratic liberals advocated a constitutional government, freedom of speech and press, and spreading the burden of taxation fairly and equally. In January 1789, Rochambeau summarized this leading, but not necessarily unanimous, approach to constitutional reform: "I am of the little number of the noble men that have voted in favor of the equal representation of the third order [the Third Estate]; your pupil Lafayette has voted for the same opinion, as you may believe it, but we have here a great number of aristocratical [*sic*] men that are very interested to perpetuate the abuses."[39] Despite the excitement of 1789, these noblemen wondered if France possessed the leadership and the ideological consensus to translate these ideas into political change.

La Rouerie's letter to Washington of June 18, 1789, captured the early ambivalence of an experienced military officer eager to make a political contribution but who found the French situation lacking in leadership and direction. After fulsomely praising Washington as a "mighty eminence . . . born every three or four hundred years," La Rouerie lamented France's failure to produce men with similarly selfless qualities: "Our affairs in this part of the world do not go as honest and impartial men could wish." He then chronicled his own relationship to the French Revolution: "I have been pretty active last year and in the beginning of this, when I thought the activity of an individual could be of service to his country." But La Rouerie's service was short lived due to a "long and hot skirmish" with members of the Assembly of Notables who opposed natural and civil rights. Contrasting his revolutionary service in America with that in France, La Rouerie concluded his letter with a prescient prediction: "I fear two great evils for my country, anarchy on one hand, despotism on the other."[40]

In his October 1789 response, Washington expressed his hopes when he juxtaposed America's positive experiment with republican government alongside his wish that France would enjoy a similar outcome. First, he concurrently announced America's successful launching of republican government to La Rouerie, Lafayette, Rochambeau, and D'Estaing: "I shall add to your satisfaction by informing you that the political affairs of the United States are in so pleasing a train as to promise respectability to our government and happiness to our citizens." Washington then linked the two revolutions together: "I am persuaded I express the sentiments of my fellow Citizens, when I offer an earnest prayer that it may terminate in the permanent honor and happiness of your government and people."[41] In other words, the United States had proceeded smoothly from revolution to republican government, and so could France.

The correspondence of 1790 continued to be hopeful about revolutionary progress on both sides of Atlantic, although the reports from the American side were increasingly optimistic, while those from France expressed growing anxiety about the future. Washington based his claims on the firsthand observations he had made during his presidential tours to the New England states in 1789 and to Rhode Island in 1790.[42] Meanwhile, his French generals increasingly fretted about a revolution that continued to be strong in ideas and passion but weak on leadership and constitutions.

A letter from Rochambeau dated April 11, 1790, contrasted the pace and volatility of the American and French Revolutions by recalling a moment during his service with the Continental Army. He wrote to Washington: "Do you remember, my dear general, of the first repast that we have made together at Rhode Island. I did you remark [sic] from the soup the difference of the character of our two nations, the French in burning their throat, and all the Americans waiting wisely of the time that it was cooled. I believe, my dear general, you have seen since a year that our nation has not change [sic] of character. We go very fast—God will that we come at our aims."[43] Washington attempted to reassure his friend and colleague by replying: "But if there shall be no worse consequence resulting from too great eagerness in swallowing something so delightful as liberty, than that of suffering a momentary pain or making a ridiculous figure with a scalded mouth; upon the whole it may be said that you Frenchmen have come off well, considering how immoderately you thirsted for the cup of liberty."[44]

With the differences between the two experiences becoming more apparent, many in France feared that their revolution would not end as happily as the American one had.

Lafayette sought to portray the upheavals in France as a type of constructive chaos that would produce positive political changes and stability.[45] Writing to Washington in January 1790, he explained, "We have come thus far in the revolution without breaking the ship either on the shoal of aristocracy, or that of faction," then concluded, "we are stirring towards a tolerable conclusion." Although he acknowledged that the "new building" might not be "perfect," it would be "sufficient to ensure freedom."[46] Several months later Lafayette cemented the connections between the American and French Revolutions, and between Washington and himself, when he sent the president the key to the Bastille prison.[47] He explained that the Bastille had represented a "fortress of despotism" and credited his former commander with inspiring in him the principles of liberty that resulted in his ordering the prison's destruction. Lafayette also reaffirmed his bond to Washington when he declared the key "a tribute which I owe as a son to my adoptive father, as an aide-de-camp to my general, as a missionary of liberty to its patriarch."[48] Yet comte de Chateaubriand, the future foreign minister of France, dismissed these keys "as rather silly toys which passed from hand to hand," offering at least one critique of the symbolic links Lafayette attempted to establish with his American role model.[49]

Despite Lafayette's confidence in his leadership abilities and France's long-term political prospects, Washington's other correspondents in 1790 blamed the National Assembly (now officially called the National Constituent Assembly) for its failure to fulfill its oath and write a constitution. The revolutionary excitement of 1789 had produced a leadership vacuum in Paris, with deputies to the National Assembly, which had displaced Louis XVI as the nation's sovereign authority, showing more interest in fighting among themselves than establishing a new government. La Rouerie described the self-centered politicians, whose intrigues merely exacerbated the chaotic French political situation: "I do not know indeed what to relate to you of the transactions which rascality, madness, avarice, and that super powerful love for disorder, which seems to be liberty to the eyes of insurrecting slavery." He then blamed the constitution writers as emblematic of the leadership problems plaguing France because these men "dispute, slander, fight and kick each other most unmercifully" without considering the common good of the nation.[50]

The turning point in Washington's views on the French Revolution came in late 1790, when he understood what his French officers had been describing—the unwillingness of the National Assembly to draft a new constitution—and he urged quick action. On June 20, 1790, the National Assembly presented a resolution to the president of the United States honoring the life of Benjamin Franklin, who had died on April 17. In this resolution, the deputies stressed the bonds that linked the two nations together, declaring: "At last the hour of the French has arrived—we love to think that the citizens of the United States have not regarded with indifference our first steps towards liberty."[51] In other words, America and France shared the common bonds of liberty and freedom. In his response, Washington celebrated "the blessings of liberty" that linked the two nations together, then he added "the sincere, cordial and earnest wish, I entertain, that their labors may speedily issue in the firm establishment of a Constitution, which, by wisely conciliating the indispensable principles of public order with the enjoyment and exercise of the essential rights of man, shall perpetuate the freedom and happiness of the People of France."[52] The president agreed that liberty and freedom were wonderful concepts, but until the French created a stable government to protect these rights and promote the public order, their revolution would be incomplete and might possibly even fail.

In the aftermath of this exchange with the National Assembly, Washington began to openly express his concerns about the instability of French politics to Congress, to his French generals, and to U.S. diplomats in Europe. In his annual address to Congress on December 8, 1790, Washington recommended that the United States shield itself from European conflicts, particularly in the area of transatlantic trade. He declared, "The disturbed situation of Europe, and particularly the critical posture of the great maritime powers," could have a disruptive effect on American commerce as these countries make "preparations for a War." He added that European turmoil "ought to make us more thankful for the general peace and security enjoyed by the United States." He additionally warned the nation and Congress to protect American economic interests from these external threats by relying on U.S. ships rather than foreign merchantmen: "Our fisheries and the transportation of our own produce offers us abundant means for guarding ourselves against this evil."[53] Reflecting the influence of his French generals on his diplomatic outlook, this address in December 1790 marked the first time Washington had mentioned European warfare and U.S. foreign policy to Congress, while also providing an early indication of his inclination toward neutrality.

Washington also employed this more assertive approach in his correspondence with his French generals, urging them to focus on governance rather than political rhetoric and excitement. Abandoning the bland reassurances contained in earlier letters, the president wrote to Lafayette on March 19, 1791, "My affection for the French nation, my sincere wish that their government may be respectable, and the people happy, will excuse the disclosure of this sentiment, the only one, I believe, that I have ventured to offer on the subject of the revolution."[54] Several months later Washington emphasized to him that the political disorder in France would not subside "until your Constitution is fixed—your government organized—and your representative body renovated—much tranquility cannot be expected—for, until these things are done, those who are unfriendly to the revolution, will not quit the hope of bringing matters back to their former state." He concluded, "But we do not wish to be the only people who taste the sweets of an equal and good government—we look with an anxious eye for the time when happiness and tranquility shall prevail in your country."[55] In the aftermath of the king's attempted flight that June, Washington offered Lafayette "his sincere regard for the French nation" and "his constant anxiety for [Lafayette's] personal safety," conceding, "it does not appear likely that the clouds which have long obscured your political horizon will be soon dispersed."[56] The president hoped France would fulfill its revolutionary mandate, but the National Assembly's failure to write a constitution made such an outcome unlikely.

Washington also wrote to U.S. diplomats in Europe to share his views on France's growing instability. In a March 16, 1791, letter to David Humphreys, the American minister to Portugal, the president explained the difficulty: "Of the state of things in France we can form no just idea, so various and contradictory are our accounts from thence."[57] In another letter, Washington made explicit his desire to remain aloof from European affairs, telling Gouverneur Morris on July 28, "But I trust we shall never so far lose sight of our own interest and happiness as to become, unnecessarily, a party in their political disputes."[58] In a subsequent letter to Morris, who was now minister to France, Washington observed, "gloomy indeed appears the situation of France at this juncture," adding, "who can say with any precision how these things will terminate."[59] He advocated distancing the young republic from such uncertainty, including any previous economic commitments, writing, "In the present state of things we cannot expect that any commercial treaty can now be formed with France."[60] Two years before issuing the Neutrality Proclamation, Washington was prepared to shield the United States from troublesome European alliances, a preemptive stance made possible by the intelligence he had received from his French generals.

Amid this gloominess, late 1791 brought a brief glimmer of hope when the National Constituent Assembly completed the new French constitution, and the king accepted it. On September 19, Louis XVI (who had signed the Treaties of Alliance and Amity and Commerce in 1778) shared the news with his ally, President Washington, in a brief letter: "Very dear, great friends and allies. We make it our duty to inform you that we have accepted the Constitution which has been presented to us in the name of the nation, and according to which France will be henceforth governed. . . . It is with real pleasure we take this occasion to renew to you assurances of the sincere friendship we bear you."[61] The president responded in an equally optimistic fashion, declaring: "Very great, good, and dear Friend and Ally. I receive as a new proof of friendship to the United States, the letter wherein you inform me that you have accepted the Constitution presented to you in the name of your nation, and according to which it is henceforth to be governed."[62] Writing to Lafayette, Washington reiterated his excitement and relief that the French people had translated their revolutionary ideas into a viable constitutional form: "I cannot conclude this letter without congratulating you most sincerely on the King's acceptance of the Constitution presented to him by the National Assembly. . . . [W]hen your affairs are completely settled under an energetic and equal government the hearts of good men will be gratified."[63] France's attainment of the constitutional stability Washington had long advocated offered hope that it would follow America's example and successfully fulfill its 1789 revolutionary mandate.

The only problem was that, for myriad reasons that soon became apparent, France was not the United States. The French constitution, rather than taming revolutionary impulses the way the U.S. Constitution had, instead unleashed that country's longstanding economic, social, and political tensions in violent and explosive ways. True to its Tennis Court oath, the relatively moderate National Constituent Assembly disbanded and gave way to the more egalitarian Legislative Assembly, where ideological orthodoxy, recrimination, and violence became the driving impulses. The aristocratic liberalism that had informed the first years of the French Revolution and the resulting constitution gave way to more provocative ideas designed to remake all of society.[64] Despite the brief burst of optimism in late 1791, France's entry into the democratic phase of its revolution affirmed the wisdom of Washington's earlier decision to distance the United States from its ally.

With the collapse of aristocratic liberalism and the violent assault on its supporting components, including the king, the nobles, and the constitution, Washington witnessed his military friends becoming victims of a revolution they had once supported. The marquis de Lafayette, who had such high aspirations for himself and his country's future, attempted to support the new government in late 1791, despite the Legislative Assembly's overt hostility to the new constitution and to the anemic king. In December, he became one of three commanders of the French army, along with Rochambeau and baron de Luckner.[65] Writing to Washington on January 22, 1792, Lafayette described his ambivalence in accepting this position: "I had refused every public employment that had been offered by the people, and still more had I denied my consent to my being appointed to any military command—But when I saw our liberties and Constitution were seriously threatened and my services could be usefully employed in fighting for our old cause, I could no more resist the wishes of my country men, and as soon as the King's express reached my farm, I set out for Paris."[66] In his response, Washington expressed concerns for France's political future: "We are however anxious that the horrors of war may be avoided, if possible.... [W]hile despotic oppression is avoided on the one hand, licentiousness may not be substituted for liberty or confusion take place of order, on the other."[67] Acknowledging the personal cost of France's revolutionary chaos, he also expressed concern for Lafayette's well-being: "I assure you, my dear Sir, I have not been a little anxious for your personal safety, and I have yet no grounds for removing that anxiety," a statement that demonstrated Washington's helplessness and his prescience.[68]

The year 1792 marked the full-scale debut of French radicalism, with the Legislative Assembly launching a war on monarchy, both internationally and domestically. By April, hostilities between revolutionary France and monarchical Austria resulted in an official declaration of war between the two countries, with Prussia joining Austria's side by June. Lafayette and Rochambeau led their troops into Austria, believing they were defending not only France but also the king and the country's new constitution. By August, though, the Bourbon monarchy had been overthrown, and a month later the French republic had been declared.[69] Radicals then turned their attention to violently purging the government and the military of anyone viewed as sympathetic to the monarchy, a policy that placed Washington's officers, and other aristocratic liberals, in a precarious position.

From 1792 onward, the violent excesses of the French Revolution hit Washington close to home as his former military comrades became victims of the political chaos he had warned against. Lafayette was the first of those officers to succumb to French radicals due to the prominent role he had played in protecting the king as head of the Parisian National Guard.[70] Although he attempted to escape from the Austrian front in 1792 and even make his way to America, Lafayette was instead captured and imprisoned in Prussia that same year.[71] His fate weighed heavily on Washington, who wrote to Lafayette's wife and to his own secretary of state to offer assistance.[72] The president, with his cabinet's approval, even took the unusual (and unsuccessful) step of contacting King Frederick William of Prussia in the hopes of gaining Lafayette's release.[73] Five years would pass before Washington would hear again from his beloved "adopted son," who was released from the Olmutz prison in 1797.[74]

Over the next few years, Washington watched as his other military friends succumbed to this once-promising revolution. La Rouerie, who had participated in revolutionary politics in 1788 and who had shared with Washington his growing disillusionment with its excesses, attempted to escape but died in hiding in 1793.[75] Even in death, La Rouerie's opponents hounded him. Accused of being a royalist, French radicals exhumed his body three weeks after his death, decapitated it, and displayed his head in the newly formed National Convention.[76] Rochambeau and D'Estaing, aristocratic liberals who had protected and supported the monarchy, albeit a constitutional one, became ensnared in the Great Terror of 1794. D'Estaing, who had guarded the king as head of the Versailles National Guard, was arrested in March 1794 and executed by guillotine in April.[77] Rochambeau, the last Bourbon marshal of France, proved more fortunate than his military colleagues, spending only six months in prison. He retired to his family estate upon his release and died in 1807.[78]

As Washington witnessed these personal examples of France's political turmoil, he received an unsettling letter from the National Convention, a popularly elected body charged with writing a republican constitution and determining the Louis XVI's fate, explaining the rationale behind its campaign against the king and his supporters. The letter calmly explained: "This revolution was necessary. Royalty was still existing, and in every constitution where it exists there is no true liberty. Kings and equality are incompatible with each other."[79] Washington did not offer a response to this campaign of regicide and political purges, particularly in the name of constitution writing and republican government. The mandate of the National Convention ushered in even more violence and turmoil in 1793, with the execution of Louis XVI in January and the expansion of France's antimonarchical European war to include Great Britain and the Dutch Republic in February, then Spain in March.[80]

France's declaration of war against Great Britain in 1793, America's primary trading partner, required the United States to formally reconsider its relationship with its revolutionary ally.[81] In a second round of letters to his foreign ministers in Lisbon and Paris, Washington offered a preview of how the U.S. government intended to respond. Writing to Humphreys on March 23, Washington articulated his desire to protect the young nation from European upheavals: "I ardently wish we may not be forced into it by the conduct of other nations" and instead be "permitted to improve, without interruption" to utilize "the great advantages which nature and circumstances have placed within our reach."[82] Having spent the past few years warily watching continental affairs, with the help of his French generals, Washington immediately understood how his administration needed to respond. Two months into his second term as president, he and his cabinet began to formulate a statement of American neutrality to shield the young republic from foreign turmoil, including distancing the nation from its erstwhile ally.[83]

WASHINGTON'S DIPLOMATIC EDUCATION occurred on the North American battlefields of two major wars, which he fought with increasing degrees of responsibility. These wartime experiences also yielded transatlantic friendships with trusted French generals who kept him abreast of European affairs once he became president. While Washington received many letters about the French Revolution, the ones from Lafayette, La Rouerie, Rochambeau, and D'Estaing occupied a special place because of the strong political and personal bonds these men shared with him. His participation in two global conflicts, with Great Britain and France trading places as America's ally and its enemy from one to the other, provided Washington with a unique perspective on the dangers and pitfalls of becoming involved in this longstanding European rivalry. Influenced by his battlefield experiences and the insights of his French generals, Washington pursued a policy of neutrality to protect the young nation from conflicts that did not concern the United States.

CHAPTER 4

"Americans in Politics"

Crafting a Neutral Proclamation

ON JULY 7, 1793, Secretary of State Jefferson urged Congressman James Madison "to take up his pen" and respond to Secretary of the Treasury Hamilton's published essays in support of the Neutrality Proclamation.¹ With Hamilton's opinions appearing in partisan newspapers, Jefferson hoped to continue the debates that had begun in Washington's cabinet.² A few months earlier, the president had solicited detailed opinions on neutrality from his cabinet members, fully aware of the strong philosophical and personal differences that divided them. In both the formulation and the implementation of the Neutrality Proclamation, Washington shrewdly encouraged the full expression of these diverse views in order to produce a program that had the support of the entire cabinet. While Hamilton and Jefferson submitted lengthy treatises in the hopes of gaining the partisan advantage, the president had a different goal in mind.³ During the busy spring of 1793, he labored to reconcile the divergent philosophical, ideological, and historical viewpoints within his cabinet to formulate a single, unified response to the nation's first international challenge. The resulting proclamation, issued on April 22, 1793, became the first step in Washington's consensus-based efforts to shield the United States from European warfare.

IN LATE MARCH 1793, word reached the United States that its principal trading partners, Britain and France, had been at war for two months. Washington realized that the country needed to quickly distance itself from this latest European conflict. On April 19, he convened his cabinet to begin work on a statement that announced America's intention to remain friendly with both France and Britain but to avoid taking sides in a war that did not concern the young nation.⁴ Over the next month, Washington's deeply divided advisors engaged in vigorous and detailed debates on the best way to announce U.S. intentions, including whether to issue a proclamation of neutrality. Although Washington and the cabinet ironed out their differences in order to produce a final document, Hamilton and Jefferson still continued to spar. During the summer of 1793, the debate over neutrality moved into the nation's highly partisan newspapers. Hamilton wrote what became known as the "Pacificus" essays in support of the proclamation, while Jefferson sought to undercut a policy he had once supported through Madison's "Helvidius" series. As the United States sought to be neutral, partisanship did not threaten the success of this policy. Instead, the greatest challenges to American neutrality came from French privateering, British cargo seizures, Americans eager to profit from this war, and a national government unable to keep pace with these violations.

American neutrality was not a new idea for Washington. Thanks to the correspondence with his former French generals and other reports from Europe, the president was well aware of the volatility of the political situation in Paris. He had long held the belief that America should be allowed to grow and prosper without outside interferences. As he had explained to Minister to France Morris: "And unwise should we be in the extreme to involve ourselves in the contests of European Nations, where our weight could be but small—though the loss to ourselves would be certain."[5] In April 1793, Washington masterfully guided his politically divided cabinet toward a united policy of promoting U.S. interests and protecting the nation from European warfare.

Prior to that spring, U.S. foreign policy focused on two major concerns: the institutional expansions needed to support the new Constitution and the outstanding issues from the Revolutionary War and the subsequent peace treaty. Under the Constitution, all three branches of government have some stake in foreign affairs, with the executive assuming the largest role because of its ability to negotiate treaties and appoint ambassadors. Congress as a whole possesses the power to declare war, while the Senate has the exclusive responsibility to offer its advice and consent on treaties and ministerial appointments. Lastly, the courts can weigh in on international disputes. Making clear that foreign policy belongs exclusively to the national government, Article I, Section 10 prohibits states from entering into treaties and alliances with foreign governments.[6] Congress further codified the executive branch's leadership in diplomatic matters when it passed the Foreign Affairs Act in 1789. This law established the Department of Foreign Affairs (later renamed the Department of State) and created a cabinet-level secretary to handle diplomatic affairs and appointments.[7] During its busy first session, Congress also created the Departments of War and the Treasury, while the attorney general was considered a legal advisor to the president and Congress (and so did not require a supporting department).[8]

On the policy front, the federal government continued to confront a laundry list of outstanding diplomatic issues from the Revolutionary War, particularly in the West, despite a peace treaty that had acknowledged U.S. sovereignty and independence. Britain refused to cede its military posts in the Old Northwest, and Spain blocked American commerce on the Mississippi River. In addition, both nations encouraged hostilities with Native American nations and with settlers in the Kentucky and Vermont territories.[9] The U.S. Army's war against Native Americans in the Ohio River valley in 1791 resulted in a disastrous defeat for Arthur St. Clair and his troops.[10] On the Atlantic, the U.S. government still hoped for trading agreements, particularly with Britain and Spain, but these remained elusive. While the Treaty of Amity and Commerce had established a commercial relationship with France, this agreement did not produce a surge in demand for American trade goods. Instead, a financially strapped France preferred that America repay its outstanding wartime loans.[11] As a young nation, America's diplomatic ambitions consistently exceeded its power and influence to achieve these goals.

Amid these unresolved issues, reports from Europe in 1793 helped train U.S. diplomatic attention on a single matter. On March 27, an American ship traveling from Portugal to Philadelphia carried word that France and Britain had been at war for almost two months. While George Washington learned of this dramatic development from Philadelphia's *General Advertiser*, his two sparring cabinet members also shared the news with the president.[12] On April 1, Secretary of State Jefferson wrote, "France had declared war against several nations, involved in that declaration almost every power of Europe," and on the fifth Secretary of the Treasury Hamilton announced that "war had been declared by France against England, Russia, and Holland."[13] Despite the importance of the two European powers to the United States, neither nation had bothered to communicate this development through diplomatic channels. Nonetheless, with its principal allies at war, it seemed to be only a matter of time before this conflict would wash up on American shores. Regardless of how the news arrived, the American government needed to issue a quick and preemptive response if the United States hoped to avoid participating in a European war.

The wars of 1793 coincided with the start of Washington's second term as president. He had reluctantly sought reelection in 1792, worn down by the partisan disagreements and infighting occurring within his cabinet, in Congress, and in the public realm through newspapers and nascent party organizations.

These differences had originated during the 1790 debate over Hamilton's "Report on the Credit," which envisioned a strong economic role for the federal government, including paying off the states' Revolutionary War debts. By 1793, these opposing viewpoints had coalesced into Hamilton's Federalists and Jefferson and Madison's Democratic-Republicans. In addition to offering competing understandings of what responsibilities the federal government should have and how strictly the Constitution should be interpreted, these coalitions also disagreed on the value of France's revolution and the importance of Britain as a principal trading partner.[14] Despite the Federalists' early enthusiasm for the French revolution, the transatlantic news of 1792–93 had soured them on its violent excesses.[15] In the spring of 1793, Washington's cabinet still consisted of its original members, with Hamilton serving as secretary of the Treasury; Knox as secretary of war; Jefferson as secretary of state; and Randolph as attorney general. Hamilton and Knox, both Revolutionary War veterans, tended to ally together, while the Virginia lawyers, Jefferson and Randolph, generally agreed on policy matters.[16]

As Washington contemplated America's response to the European conflict, he realized he would first need to calm the ideological and increasingly personal disputes that divided Hamilton and Jefferson. Soon after learning about the current Anglo-French hostilities, the president wrote similar letters to each man urging the development of a policy of "strict neutrality between the powers at war" that would discourage American citizens from entangling themselves (and the United States) in these conflicts. Washington was particularly concerned about reports "that many vessels in different parts of the Union are designated for privateers and are preparing accordingly."[17] In anticipation of the cabinet's first meeting to craft a policy, he urged them "to give the subject mature consideration" so that "measures ... deemed most likely to effect this desirable purpose may be adopted without delay."[18] As Washington steered the nation toward a neutral stance, he also needed to tame the partisan divisions within his cabinet in order to speak with a single voice on the world stage.

Even before receiving the April 12 letter, Hamilton had started to draft questions related to neutrality with the help of John Jay.[19] In an April 9 letter to Jay, he referred to a conversation the two men had had in which they had agreed "that the Minister expected from France should be received." Given the turmoil surrounding Louis XVI's execution, though, Hamilton asked Jay "whether he [the minister] should be received *absolutely* or with *qualifications*?" He further posited whether France's political changes drew into question the "applicability of the [1778] treaties."[20] In a second letter, also written on the ninth, Hamilton

FIGURE 4. George Washington as he appeared during his second term when the neutrality policy was formulated and implemented. (Mount Vernon Ladies' Association; painted by Charles Willson Peale, 1795)

solicited his opinion on the propriety of "a proclamation prohibiting our citizens from taking commissions on either side" and whether such a statement "should include a declaration of neutrality." Lastly, Hamilton asked Jay "if he could draft such a thing."[21] To Jefferson's great irritation, these questions formed the basis of the upcoming cabinet discussion on the war in Europe.

On April 18 Washington began the long process of forging a compromise on neutrality when he distributed a thirteen-point query to solicit his cabinet's opinions.[22] Although these questions borrowed heavily from Hamilton and Jay's discussions, the president penned the final document himself in an effort to camouflage its content's origins. But Jefferson remained suspicious, concluding "that the language was Hamilton's."[23] At other times in his administration, Washington had utilized questionnaires to reach a consensus on contested issues.[24] The war between Britain and France posed significant challenges to America's independence and autonomy, so producing a unified statement that protected and promoted U.S. interests possessed an urgency that surpassed earlier controversies.

In the introduction to his query, Washington defined the predicament the United States faced: "The posture of affairs in Europe, particularly between France and Great Britain, places the United States in a delicate situation; and requires much consideration of the measures which will be proper for them to observe in the war between those powers."[25] The first question addressed the fundamental issue: Should the United States issue a proclamation to discourage American citizens from interfering with this war, and should the United States proclaim its neutrality as well? Questions two, three, and twelve asked whether the United States should maintain diplomatic relations with France, including sending and receiving ministers, or should America wait until it establishes a new government? Questions four through nine tackled the complex issues of America's obligations to France under the 1778 treaties.[26] Pursuant to the Treaty of Alliance, what military support did the United States owe to France in its current war, particularly in its "guarantee" to protect French territories in the West Indies? As outlined in the Treaty of Amity and Commerce, would France be allowed to bring prizes into U.S. ports, while its British opponent would still be banned from outfitting privateers in these harbors?[27] The query concluded with question thirteen: was it necessary to call together the two houses of Congress to discuss the situation in Europe? Washington then directed his cabinet to meet at his house the following morning to discuss their "reflections" on these questions.[28]

At the April 19 meeting, then, the cabinet reached agreement on the first two issues: a proclamation to forbid citizens from participating in the European war, including carrying contraband, and unanimous support for welcoming the recently arrived minister from the newly constituted French republic (although disagreements remained whether any exceptions should apply, per question three).[29]

When Washington and his cabinet met again three days later, they recognized that the priority was announcing America's neutral stance at home and abroad rather than wasting valuable time attempting to reach a consensus on the remaining eleven issues. Although Hamilton took the initial role in composing the query and collaborated with Jay on a draft proclamation, the job of writing the final statement went to Jefferson's ally, Attorney General Randolph.[30] Despite their equal participation in cabinet deliberations and decisions, Randolph and Knox have not received the scholarly attention of their two colleagues.[31]

Amid the partisan posturing in Washington's cabinet, no one wanted to become involved in a European war, including Jefferson. Where he and Hamilton differed was how strongly to convey this message to the European powers: Hamilton preferred an explicit declaration that favored Britain, while Jefferson hoped to pursue neutrality without issuing a proclamation that would alienate France. Given neutrality's long history in European diplomacy and Enlightenment philosophy, Jefferson's insistence that the final proclamation not contain the word "neutrality" (using "impartial" instead) was a calculated move on his part to soften its effect on Franco-American relations.[32] He believed that America's noninvolvement in this war, as well as the availability of its free trade, would give the United States leverage with warring countries, particularly France.[33] The exclusion of the word "neutrality" also had diplomatic ramifications. It suggested a "strict" neutrality that favored Britain while also suggesting a higher implementation threshold than "impartial" did.[34] In the end, a carefully crafted statement emerged that accommodated the cabinet's differing viewpoints, with Washington achieving his ultimate goal: a unanimous declaration of America's noninvolvement in European hostilities.

The proclamation issued on April 22, 1793, epitomized compromise—no one in the cabinet was completely happy with the finished product, but it contained enough provisions to satisfy the competing viewpoints.[35] The document acknowledged the "David and Goliath" struggle that existed between France, on the one hand, and Austria, Prussia, Sardinia, Great Britain, and the United Netherlands, on the other, then declared that the United States intended "with sincerity and good faith" to "adopt and pursue a conduct friendly and impartial toward the belligerent powers."[36] This statement formalized a frequent theme in Washington's recent correspondence: his desire to shield the young nation from a European war.[37] Having established the broad outlines of U.S. noninvolvement, the remainder of the proclamation "exhorted and warned" American citizens not to involve themselves in foreign matters and cautioned that, if they insisted on doing so, they would "not receive the protection of the United States, against such punishment or forfeiture" triggered by their participation. (Enforcing this provision would produce an enormous set of governing challenges for the Washington administration.) With this statement disseminated to the nation's governors and to diplomats in the United States and Europe, as well as appearing in the nation's newspapers, Washington's cabinet members returned to the unresolved issues from the query, particularly those dealing with America's treaty obligations to France.[38]

In the weeks that followed, Hamilton, Jefferson, and Randolph tackled these outstanding questions with great gusto.[39] With both men generally in agreement, Knox happily deferred to Hamilton to present their joint opinions. On the opposing side were Jefferson and Randolph, who crafted individual replies to the remaining issues.[40] Their lengthy responses offered these men a chance to demonstrate their superior command of European history, earlier treaties, and Enlightenment writings on international law such as Hugo Grotius's *De Jure Belli ac Pacis* ("The Law of War and Peace") and *Mare Liberum* and Vattel's *Law of Nations*. The Enlightenment ideas Hamilton, Jefferson, and Randolph had studied in college proved particularly valuable because they offered a vision of free trade as a positive good rather than merely a tool of warfare.[41] More importantly, each cabinet member saw a golden opportunity to set the future direction of American foreign policy toward Europe. Although Jefferson submitted his written responses first, Hamilton had already presented his detailed opinions on these questions at the inconclusive April 19 cabinet meeting. As Jefferson and Randolph drafted their answers, their responses addressed the eleven outstanding issues as well as Hamilton's views on them.[42]

With France now a republic rather than a monarchy and at war with much of Europe, Hamilton saw an opportunity to shift America's European alliances away from France and toward Britain.[43] As the author of the thirteen-point query, he knew exactly where to launch his assault: question three, using the arrival of the new French minister as the occasion to suspend or even renounce America's treaty obligations to that nation. In his lengthy rationale, cosigned by Knox, Hamilton systematically argued that the political turmoil and regime change in France justified America's withdrawal from earlier agreements, most notably the Treaties of Alliance and of Amity and Commerce. Since these had been made with the monarch, not with a republican government, he believed that France's shifting political institutions might force the United States into situations that were now undesirable and even dangerous. Invoking Vattel's argument of national self-protection, Hamilton concluded: "If then a Nation thinks fit to make changes in its Government, which render treaties that before subsisted between it and another nation useless or dangerous or hurtful to that other nation, it is a plain dictate of reason, that the *latter* will have a right to renounce those treaties; because *it* also has a right to take care of its own happiness."[44] Since he had used question three to vitiate America's treaty obligations to France, the other outstanding issues dealing with the 1778 alliance were rendered moot. Hamilton nonetheless offered a response to these questions, but his reply was shorter and did not warrant the cosignature of Knox.[45]

Not surprisingly, Jefferson and Randolph's responses offered Washington a very different understanding of America's diplomatic relationship to France, particularly its responsibilities under the 1778 treaties.[46] For starters, Jefferson dismissed the heart of Hamilton's argument that America's treaties with France were no longer valid simply because a republic had replaced a monarchy. Instead, Jefferson (and Randolph in his separate response) contended that these agreements had been with "the people who constitute a society or nation as the source of all authority in that nation" and that "the treaties between the United States and France were not treaties between the United States and Louis Capet, but between the two nations of America and France."[47]

Jefferson also took issue with Hamilton's interpretation of Vattel's *Law of Nations* as providing an "escape" clause from undesirable treaties. He argued that the treaty had to be more than "dangerous, useless or disagreeable," that instead Vattel believed that the "danger which absolves us must be great, inevitable and imminent."[48] With Jefferson (and Randolph) contending that the 1778 treaties were still in effect, they addressed U.S. commercial and military obligations under these agreements now that France was engaged in a new war. Neither man saw an immediate threat to either the United States or to American neutrality from the "guarantee" clause of the Treaty of Alliance, requiring America's military to defend French territories in the West Indies. Nor did they believe the Treaty of Amity and Commerce offered France special trading privileges in U.S. ports that had not been already guaranteed in other European agreements.[49] Both Jefferson and Randolph concluded that breaking these treaties posed greater dangers than maintaining them because France would interpret such action as an act of war, drawing America into the very conflict it was trying to avoid.[50]

One issue that did not generate lengthy dissertations from these men was question thirteen: whether it was necessary to call Congress into session to apprise them of the European situation. While Jefferson had originally favored involving the legislative branch, he now joined the other cabinet members in concluding that such a step was unnecessary.[51] Congress's lack of participation in the proclamation's formulation also explained Vice President John Adams's absence in the cabinet's discussions. Despite Adams's earlier role in drafting the template for neutrality, the Model Treaty of 1776, the vice presidency found its initial constitutional home in Congress (as president of the Senate) rather than in the executive branch.⁵² The decision of Washington and his cabinet to issue the proclamation without congressional consent resulted in the executive branch's further assertion of its dominance over foreign affairs. Eschewing Congress also provided a win for the politically savvy Washington, who, like other Federalists, believed in emboldening the presidency.⁵³

The first round of the cabinet's consensus on neutrality came to a conclusion on May 6, with the submission of Randolph's comments. Although he had allowed these men to offer lengthy exegesis on the treaties specifically and on international law generally, Washington had told Jefferson that "he had never had a doubt about the validity of the treaty, but that since a question had been suggested he thought it ought to be considered."⁵⁴ The president had recognized that a foreign-policy statement needed the support of his entire cabinet to be successful. During the formulation and subsequent implementation of U.S. neutrality, Washington shrewdly encouraged each cabinet member to offer his detailed opinions on each aspect of this policy to permit a sharing and then a resolution of the political disagreements that divided them. While they might not win every debate, the men could walk away from the discussion knowing their views had been heard and even incorporated. Even Jefferson conceded that the president's involvement in the discussions had prevented the final document from being "a mere English neutrality."⁵⁵ In honoring the treaties with France, at least for the time being, Washington chose the option least disruptive to the diplomatic status quo and more compatible with neutrality. Amid the intellectual fireworks that produced this consensus, Hamilton, Jefferson, and even Randolph each shared the naive belief that their words and ideas could influence European affairs, a premise that would be sorely tested as the United States worked to enforce the proclamation.

Despite the compromises that had produced the April proclamation, Hamilton and Jefferson remained committed to their philosophical positions and thus, during the summer of 1793, sought to curry political support in the nation's highly partisan newspapers. Liberated from the consensus building of Washington's cabinet, Hamilton wrote under the peaceful pseudonym "Pacificus," while Jefferson employed a surrogate to express his opposition.⁵⁶ Hamilton structured his seven-essay defense of the president's Neutrality Proclamation around the criticisms lodged by an earlier essayist, "Veritas."⁵⁷

The Veritas essays originated as three letters to President Washington, subsequently published in Philip Freneau's pro-Democratic-Republican *National Gazette*, based in Philadelphia.⁵⁸ All three epistolary essays focused on the unconstitutionality of the proclamation. The May 30 letter, published on June 1, accused the president of being surrounded by "double dealing," "monarchical mystery," and "court intrigue" in unilaterally issuing this proclamation without concern for the will of the people. Additionally, it attacked Washington's disregard for America's "duty" and "interest" to France under the 1778 treaties.[59] The June 3 letter, published on the fifth, challenged the constitutionality of the proclamation, arguing that it had "caused uneasiness" and reminding Washington that "popular opinion is the basis of our government."[60] The third and final essay, written on June 6 and published on the eighth, challenged the "legality of the proclamation," particularly the president's authority "to annul solemn treaties by proclamation." Veritas also took issue with what he saw as the administration's "shamefully pusillanimous" approach to Britain despite their numerous violations of American sovereignty. He also questioned the timing of the proclamation. Lastly, Veritas called on Washington to convene the "representatives of the people, who can alone express the national will," in order to produce a policy that "all branches of the government" support.[61] With the president under attack for the proclamation, and that criticism being amplified in a Democratic-Republican newspaper, Hamilton launched a counteroffensive on June 27 in John Fenno's pro-Federalist *Gazette of the United States*, also based in Philadelphia.[62]

Hamilton began the Pacificus series with a refutation of Veritas's criticism that the executive branch lacked the authority to issue the proclamation. He cited the president's explicit role as commander in chief of the army and navy as well as the executive's responsibilities for making treaties and appointing and receiving ministers. While the legislature participated in foreign affairs through advice and consent on treaties and ministers as well as its authority to declare war, these responsibilities were specific and not constant. Instead, it was the executive who served "as the organ of intercourse between the Nation and foreign Nations," as well as the preserver of the peace and the interpreter of treaties, until war is declared.[63]

Hamilton's response to Veritas's criticism regarding U.S. treaty obligations to France composed the bulk of the Pacificus essays, just as these issues had preoccupied the cabinet's discussions. In "Pacificus no. 2," Hamilton emphasized the *defensive* nature of America's 1778 alliance, explaining that "assistance" would be given to France "upon attack." With that country acting as the aggressor in the current war, America had no "offensive" obligations.[64]

In "Pacificus no. 3" Hamilton explored America's responsibilities under the "guarantee" clause of the Treaty of Alliance.[65] Once again, he emphasized the defensive nature of this provision: "it relates merely to defence [*sic*] and preservation of her American colonies." Secondly, Hamilton noted that the "disproportion" between the actions demanded by the guarantee clause and the lack of American naval resources to perform these tasks excused the United States from any defensive obligations to France in its current war. He then cited Vattel to support this point, quoting from *Law of Nations,* "'If a state which has promised succors finds itself unable to furnish them, its very inability is its exemption.'"[66] Hamilton concluded this essay with the contention that the revolutionary and offensive nature of France's current war, including the toppling of its monarchy, extended far beyond "the ordinary case of foreign war" envisioned in the 1778 treaties and further excused America from involvement.[67]

Hamilton used Pacificus essays four, five, and six to refute Veritas's notion that America owed France "gratitude" for its revolutionary assistance. In "Pacificus no. 4," he emphasized that the Neutrality Proclamation's promise of "friendly and impartial conduct to all nations" continued current treaty obligations to France without requiring the United States to become involved in its war.[68] In his conclusion to this essay, Hamilton explored the one-sided nature of "gratitude." In his view, this referred to "a benefit received or intended, which there was no right to claim." But if the person offering assistance receives immediate benefits, "there seems scarcely in such a case to be an adequate basis for a sentiment like that of gratitude." He argued that France gained immediate and tangible advantages in its alliance with the United States so the concept of gratitude did not apply.[69] In "Pacificus no. 5," Hamilton summarized France's motivation for entering into the American alliance: "embracing a promising opportunity to repress the pride and diminish the dangerous power of its [British] rival . . . by lopping off a valuable portion of its dominions." He also noted that France was not America's only revolutionary ally and that the "cause had also numerous friends in other countries."[70] In the penultimate Pacificus essay, Hamilton concluded that France's war "with all of Europe" did not concern the United States and that Americans ultimately "will support the government they established and will take care of their own peace," despite efforts to detach them from each.[71]

In his conclusion to the Pacificus series, Hamilton strongly defended U.S. interests and ideas as he responded to Veritas's concerns about the timing and necessity of the Neutrality Proclamation.[72] He explained that the proclamation became necessary when France declared war against the "commercial maritime nations" of Britain, Spain, and the Netherlands. France's war against nonmaritime adversaries like Prussia and Austria did not concern the United States because these nations did not participate in transatlantic trade. A war involving America's principal trading partners, however, required an immediate statement of neutrality to silence international expectations of military support, to protect

American shipping and agriculture, and to discourage U.S. citizens from enlisting or taking sides in the conflict.[73] In its protection of U.S. interests, Hamilton emphasized the Neutrality Proclamation's adherence to republican and constitutional principles. He reiterated the president's constitutional authority over foreign affairs but added that the executive spoke "in the name and on behalf of the United States," unlike European kings and princes who "speak of their own dispositions."[74] While America pledged to be "friendly and impartial" to all nations, the young republic also intended to put its interests first.[75]

Even before the appearance of the Pacificus essays, Jefferson had begun to distance himself from the proclamation and the consensus that had produced it. Relying on Madison as his confidential sounding board, the secretary shared his criticisms of the policy and offered an alternative approach.[76] On May 13, he complained that the proclamation failed to promote "a manly neutrality" that recognized the "liberal rights" of the warring nations. Jefferson's "bold" approach clearly referred to France's revolutionary principles of "liberté, egalité, and fraternité."[77] A month later he offered Madison another vision of how American neutrality should have been addressed: "it would be better to hold back the declaration of neutrality, as a thing worth something to the powers at war, that they would bid for it, & we might reasonably ask as a price, the *broadest privileges* of neutral nations."[78] Believing he had lost the battle of neutrality in the cabinet, the secretary of state sought victory on a different front—the arena of popular opinion.

Jefferson also bristled at the compromises that had produced what he considered to be an ideologically weak statement. In particular, he directed his ire at his putative Virginia ally in the cabinet for his eagerness to side with the Federalist bloc. To Jefferson's great frustration, Randolph's more moderate and less partisan views made him the cabinet's swing vote, while the secretary had hoped he would be a reliable supporter like Knox was to Hamilton. Writing to Madison, he offered a withering critique of Randolph's approach: "E.R found out a hair to split, which, as always happens, became the decision." Jefferson, who saw such equivocation as a weakness rather than a virtue, added, "he always contrives to agree in principle with one, but in conclusion with the other." His concluding assessment of Randolph underscored his frustration with the neutrality policy and the process that had produced it: "Everything my dear Sir, now hangs on the opinion of a single person, and that the most indecisive one I ever had to do business with."[79]

A summer of Pacificus essays proved too much for Jefferson, and he now looked for a way to move his private criticisms into the public arena.[80] Unable to write the responses himself for fear of disloyalty to Washington and public exposure as a partisan, he once more turned to the next best thing: his Virginia neighbor and ally, James Madison, who also served in a different branch of government. On July 7, the secretary of state implored the congressman "to take up his pen" and respond to the secretary of the Treasury's published essays in support of the Neutrality Proclamation. Unleashing his frustrations, he added, "Nobody answers him, & his doctrine will therefore be taken for confessed."[81] Over the next few weeks, as he lobbied a reluctant Madison to write the response, Jefferson also completed his separation from a proclamation he had once endorsed.

As Madison contemplated whether to respond to Pacificus, he confronted both the geographical and political distances that separated him from the debate. The representative spent the summer of 1793 at Montpelier, his home in Orange, Virginia, far removed from the political business of Philadelphia. As a member of Congress, Madison had not participated in the cabinet's discussions nor been officially notified about the proclamation. Amid all these challenges, he concluded that "the task would be in bad hands" but promised Jefferson, "I will feel my own pulse" before any decision on the request.[82]

As Madison immersed himself in the issues surrounding the proclamation, his principal objection focused on its constitutionality. In a letter to Jefferson, he questioned if the executive branch had the authority to offer a "declaration of the *Disposition* of the U.S. on the subject of war and peace." While he believed the president could offer "an injunction of a suitable conduct on the citizens" during wartime, the question of war or peace seemed "to be essentially and exclusively involved in the right vested in the legislature." Madison then added more pointedly, "Did no such view of the subject present itself in the cabinet?"[83] Of course it had, with Jefferson agreeing with the majority that the executive had the authority to issue the proclamation and that Congress did not need to be consulted. Nonetheless, in late June Jefferson distanced himself from the proclamation (and Hamilton's defense of it) when he embraced Madison's views on Congress's constitutional role. Jefferson wrote, "Upon the whole, my objections to the competence of the Executive to declare neutrality . . . were supposed to be got over by avoiding the use of that term," a position he had successfully promoted. He then continued his delicate balancing act by adding, "the declaration of the *disposition* of the U.S can hardly be called illegal, though it was certainly officious and improper."[84]

On July 22 Madison moved closer to drafting a response to Pacificus when he posed specific questions to Jefferson about the cabinet's deliberations. He asked, first, "how far concessions have been made on particular points behind the curtain"; second, how committed was the president to "some doctrines"; third, what insights "from the law of nations" informed the "construction of the treaties"; and fourth, "whether any call was made by Great Britain or any other belligerent power... prior to the proclamation." In concluding this letter, Madison explained the importance of this information: "If an answer to the publication be undertaken, it ought to be both a solid and prudent one," particularly since its audience will be "none but intelligent readers."[85] As a newcomer to the neutrality debates, Madison's broadly based questions permitted Jefferson to redefine the role he had played in the cabinet's April discussions.

As Jefferson answered Madison's questions, he continued to divorce himself from the administration's policy. In terms of the concessions "made on particular points behind the curtain," he told Madison, "I think it is better you should not know them." In other words, he did not intend to share the compromises, including his own, that had resulted in the proclamation. On Washington's commitment to certain doctrines, Jefferson wrote, the president "is certainly uneasy at those grasped at by *Pacificus*," although he did not specify which ones. His vague response simultaneously undercut the integrity of Hamilton's Pacificus essays while also raising questions about Washington's command of the complex issues involved. Jefferson's answers to the final two questions adhered more closely to the facts: Vattel's writings had served as the cabinet's principal guide on international law, and "no call was made by any *power* previous to the *proclamation*."[86]

At the end of July, Jefferson finally received good news from Montpelier. Madison wrote, "I have forced myself into a task of a reply," adding that it was "the most grating one I ever experienced" in large part due to a "want of counsel on some points of delicacy, as well as of information as to sundry matters of fact."[87] As Madison began work on his essays, an elated Jefferson played an active role behind the scenes advising him on their content, reviewing the drafts, and even submitting them to Philadelphia's *Gazette of the United States*, in which Pacificus had also appeared, for publication.[88]

With Madison willing to offer a public response to Pacificus, Jefferson could turn his full attention to completing his transition from pragmatic cabinet member to partisan leader. He and Hamilton had been at loggerheads over the Constitution's interpretation since 1790, when his rival had published his "Report on the Public Credit." Jefferson now used his opposition to the neutrality policy as an excuse to leave Washington's philosophically diverse cabinet. Soon after learning of Madison's willingness to counter Pacificus, an emboldened Jefferson submitted his resignation letter to the president on July 31, effective September 30, "to retire to scenes of greater tranquility."[89]

Anticipating his liberation from Washington's cabinet, Jefferson used his response to Madison's July 30 letter to complete his separation from the proclamation. First, he described his early opposition to the executive branch issuing any neutrality proclamation, recounting a conversation with Washington: "I had, at the time, opposed its being made a declaration of neutrality on the ground that the Executive was not the competent authority for that." Later in the letter, Jefferson described a hastily drafted document that he believed placed Washington in an awkward position: "The instrument was badly drawn, and made the president go out of his line to declare things which, though true, it was not exactly his province to declare." In a final blow to the compromises that had produced the proclamation, Jefferson discounted his role in the document's creation: "The instrument was communicated to me after it was drawn, but I was busy, and only run [*sic*] an eye over it to see that it was not made a declaration of neutrality."[90] Conveniently absent in his recounting was the April 18 query, the April 19 cabinet meeting, and his own lengthy submission from April 28 on the outstanding issues surrounding the neutrality policy.

Meanwhile, Madison found that responding to Pacificus's comprehensive defense of America's right to remain neutral in this European war left him with little room to maneuver. Jefferson, with his finger firmly on the political pulse, advised him to avoid "caviling about small points of propriety."[91] A summer of neutrality violations in U.S. ports had affirmed the wisdom of this proclamation. Instead of confronting all four of the major issues Hamilton had addressed, Madison trained his focus on a single issue: questioning the constitutionality of the proclamation. In his five "Helvidius" essays, Madison revisited the concern he had originally shared with Jefferson: that Congress possessed authority over issues of war and peace, not the president.[92] In "Helvidius no. 2," he succinctly presented the argument that informed all five essays: "The power to judge of the causes of war, as involved in the power to declare war, is expressly vested where all other legislative powers are vested, that is, in the Congress of the United States."[93] In emphasizing the constitutional responsibilities of Congress, Madison's views appeared patriotic and consistent with the Democratic-Republicans' support of the legislative branch over the executive, even if this issue had not been controversial during the cabinet's debates.[94]

Unfortunately for Jefferson, the Helvidius essays did not inflict the fatal blow to the neutrality policy that he had sought. One reason is that the opinions Pacificus expressed hewed closer to Washington's (and Jefferson and Randolph's) more measured approach to international affairs than the pro-British recommendations Hamilton had previously advocated. Despite the writer's pro-Federalist vision of government, Pacificus also promoted *America*'s vision in international affairs rather than the foreign-policy preferences of two bickering political coalitions. Lastly, and most importantly, a series of neutrality violations committed by the French, the British, and even U.S. citizens like Gideon Henfield and John Singleterry during the spring and summer of 1793 affirmed the wisdom of the administration's policy.[95] The urgent need to prosecute these threats to U.S. sovereignty and autonomy quickly superseded this partisan and ideological debate. Ironically, the word "neutrality," which Jefferson strenuously tried to downplay, became popularized during the Pacificus-Helvidius debates, even appearing in Jefferson's own correspondence.[96] Additionally, with the numerous summertime violations occurring in the nation's ports and reported in American newspapers, neutrality became the operative term to describe this policy.

Despite his frustration with neutrality's partisan overtones, Jefferson nonetheless recognized the importance of the United States avoiding European warfare. Several days after the proclamation's issuance, he had written to Madison: "I fear that a fair neutrality will prove a disagreeable pill to our friends, though necessary to keep us out of the calamities of a war."[97] Madison reached the same conclusion in May, writing to Jefferson: "Peace is no doubt to be preserved at any price that honor and good faith will permit."[98] Keeping America at peace trumped partisan preferences, even for them. Under Washington's leadership, the formulation of the Neutrality Proclamation established two enduring precedents for American diplomacy: first, that the executive branch led the way in setting U.S. international priorities, and second, that Americans spoke in a single voice in foreign affairs.

While the Helvidius essays did little to weaken the Neutrality Proclamation, their existence has exaggerated the role that partisanship and the disagreements between Jefferson and Hamilton played in its formulation. Further obscured in this binary configuration was Washington, who advocated for a neutral stance toward the European war and insisted on consensus support for this policy. Although both Madison and Jefferson carefully avoided alienating or disagreeing with Washington in public, they nonetheless engaged in a "whispering campaign" that questioned the president's ability to counter Hamilton's poor advice and to recognize the Treasury secretary's political machinations. Jefferson, in justifying a rebuttal to Pacificus, repeatedly portrayed a president who had agreed to a policy that he did not fully understand. Madison advanced this impression as well, writing, "I regret extremely the position into which the P. [president] has been thrown," adding, "it is mortifying to the real friends of the

P. that his fame and influence should have been unnecessarily made to depend in any degree on political events in a foreign quarter of the Globe."99 These rumors, although untrue, undercut the president's role in crafting a consensus on neutrality and fueled the partisan aura surrounding the proclamation.

Washington's refusal to let Jefferson resign in September 1793 offers a competing portrait of a president fully aware of the policy debates and the partisan intrigues surrounding him. In considering the request, Washington approached the subject with great care and respect. First, he honored Jefferson with a visit to his home, and during their conversation, he laid out a variety of reasons why his resignation should be delayed. Washington appealed to Jefferson's sense of duty, expressing "his repentance at not having resigned himself." He also flattered Jefferson and his diplomatic experience in Europe when he explained the difficulty in finding a replacement: "mere talents did not suffice for the department of state, but it required a person conversant in foreign affairs, perhaps acquainted with foreign courts."100

Washington, recognizing the need to maintain a geographical and ideological balance in his cabinet, shrewdly mentioned that "Mr. Madison would be his first choice" as Jefferson's replacement, although he acknowledged the congressman would probably not take the job.101 If he could not retain Jefferson, Madison's appointment offered the president the next best hope for taming political tensions within his administration. Lastly, Washington told Jefferson that his chief antagonist, Hamilton, had also expressed a desire to leave the administration, a departure that might make staying in the cabinet more palatable. In the end, Washington struck a compromise that satisfied both of their needs: Jefferson agreed to remain in the administration until December to "get us through the difficulties of this year," because "he was satisfied that the affairs of Europe would be settled" and "Congress will have manifested its character and its views."102 By extending Jefferson's tenure until the end of 1793, Washington hoped to limit his ability to undercut the neutrality policy as a partisan leader, at least for a little while longer.103

IN 1797 WASHINGTON complained to William Heath that, "instead of being Frenchmen or Englishmen in politics, they would be Americans—indignant at every attempt of either of these—or any other Power to establish an influence in our Councils, or that should presume to sow the Seeds of distrust, or disunion among ourselves."104 Even in retirement, he would remain committed to a foreign policy that put U.S. interests first and avoid the dangerous entanglements of European affairs.

During his second term as president, Washington sought a policy that not only shielded the young nation from the perils of European warfare but also possessed the support of the divergent philosophical and partisan voices that composed his cabinet. He wisely let these four men submit lengthy abstract treatises and then consolidated their ideas into a statement that epitomized compromise. While partisan opinions found expression in the Pacificus and Helvidius essays, these debates did not fundamentally change the substance or the effect of the neutrality policy. Instead, Washington's proclamation established the primacy of the executive branch in foreign affairs and affirmed the importance of the nation speaking in a single voice internationally. The building of the neutrality policy occurred brick by brick, with each cabinet member contributing materials to its construction, but it was its chief architect, George Washington, who deserves credit for the enduring edifice. His steadfast commitment to consensus would face even greater obstacles as he and his cabinet, including Jefferson, built a government capable of enforcing its far-reaching provisions. These enforcement concerns were not hypothetical. In early April 1793, the newly arrived French minister brazenly encouraged Americans to enlist as privateers for his nation's cause—and in direct violation of American neutrality.

CHAPTER 5

"To Keep This Country in Peace"

French Violations and Executive Actions

With the ink still drying on the Neutrality Proclamation, maritime citizens began to alert the national government that French privateering was occurring in America's ports and along its coast.[1] While cabinet members had put their full efforts into drafting a consensus statement based on Enlightenment ideas, they had paid little attention to enforcing it. During the hectic spring and summer of 1793, the Washington administration confronted a barrage of domestic and international challenges to the neutrality policy. Beyond a general desire to avoid European hostilities, the national government had no mechanisms in place to block French privateering, to prohibit U.S. citizens from serving on these vessels, or to respond to British complaints about ship seizures and losses. With the violations outpacing the government's ability to respond, Washington once again employed his strong political skills to corral his advisors' divergent views into comprehensive enforcement plans. Seeking consensus on the best ways to implement the proclamation, as he had done during its formulation, the president and his cabinet deliberated on and agreed to a series of groundbreaking policies that defined the responsibilities of nascent federal agencies. Through their painstaking crafting of an enforcement strategy, Washington and his administration built a neutral federal government, beginning with the executive branch.

The first steps toward implementing the Neutrality Proclamation proved largely institutional, relatively small, and surprisingly contentious. The cabinet officer with the greatest role in enforcing neutrality was the secretary of state. As constituted by Congress, this position bore responsibility not only for U.S. diplomacy but also supervised "state" matters, including communication with governors. Washington institutionalized the protocol of diplomatic channels when he instructed Secretary of State Jefferson to disseminate the proclamation to American and European diplomats and to state governors.[2]

The letters to the various ambassadors captured both the boldness of America's neutral stance and the young nation's insignificance in European affairs. Writing to the French, English, and Dutch ministers stationed in the United States, Jefferson began, "As far as the public gazettes are to be credited, we may presume that war has taken place among several of the Nations of Europe." He then announced America's preemptive policy of neutrality: "Disposed as the U.S. are to pursue steadily the ways of peace, and remain in friendship with all the nations, the president has thought it expedient, by proclamation..., to notify this disposition to our citizens..., the line of conduct for which they are to prepare." Acknowledging the lack of communication from Europe's warring nations, Jefferson added that this statement was issued "without waiting for a formal notification from the belligerent powers."[3] British minister George Hammond's cheeky response confirmed Europe's low opinion of America's international standing while also previewing the men's rocky relationship. Hammond first affirmed America's "friendly and impartial conduct towards the belligerent powers." He then noted, "but as you seem to be of the opinion, that, in order to give this measure immediate and complete operation, it is necessary for this government to obtain some more formal knowledge of the existence of hostilities than such as is to be collected from the public Gazettes," on February 1, 1793, France had indeed declared war against Britain and the Netherlands.[4]

Jefferson also wrote to the five U.S. ministers posted in Europe, distinguishing between those stationed in countries that were at war (France, Britain, and the Netherlands) and those that were not (Portugal and Spain).[5] To the diplomats based in warring countries, he instructed that they alert their host countries of America's desire "to preserve peace and friendship with all the belligerent powers."[6] For those in countries not at war, Jefferson regarded his message as both informational and preemptive: "Should the nation where you are, remain neutral, these papers will serve merely for your information: should they take part in the War, you will be pleased to make to them the same communication, which our ministers at Paris, London, and the Hague, are instructed to make."[7] The secretary of state's letters to Europe announced America's intention to pursue peace and friendship with all nations, rather than waiting for formal notification from the warring countries or risking involvement by default. These dispatches also underscored the U.S. government's minor role in international affairs.

The domestic unveiling of this policy also exposed the gap between the statement's boldness and the relative weakness of the American government in enforcing it. Jefferson shared the proclamation with the governors of the fifteen states (now including Vermont and Kentucky), declaring to each that the policy "will have the benefit of Your Excellency's aid towards their general and strict observance by the citizens of the State over which you preside."[8] Secretary of the Treasury Hamilton sent copies of the proclamation to the collectors of the customs stationed in the coastal cities, advising that "the building of vessels calculated and fitted for war is a circumstance which will merit particular attention."[9] While Washington's cabinet correctly identified the states and ports as the frontline for possible neutrality violations, these letters did not specify how governors and customs collectors were supposed to handle any transgressions.

In 1789 Congress had nationalized the U.S. Customs Service through the Tariff Act and the Duties on Tonnage Act and had also authorized fifty-nine customs districts across eleven states.[10] The Customs Service had the twin distinctions of employing the bulk of the national government's personnel and collecting the lion's share of its revenues. By 1792, the customs service had expanded into fourteen states and employed 146 officers and 332 subordinates. The top position of collector of the customs proved to be a desirable one because of its high pay; its influential role in a community, particularly in a busy port city such as Boston; and its ability to hire staff.[11] The Customs Service also distinguished itself in revenue collection. Of the $5.1 million the U.S. government brought in during its founding decade, $5 million (88 percent) came from customs alone.[12] While this agency had a clear role in revenue collection, its enforcement responsibilities remained murky.

Disagreements on the best ways to employ the customs collectors and the U.S. attorneys produced the first of many cabinet debates on the domestic enforcement of neutrality. The controversy began on May 4, when Hamilton recommended to Washington that the Treasury Department's collectors of the customs report all neutrality violations, "including the building of ships with gun ports," to the secretary of the Treasury.[13] Given the Customs Service's size and influence, not to mention Hamilton's authority over it, Jefferson's vehement opposition to this proposal was not surprising. First, Jefferson feared that "the collectors of the customs are to be made an established corps of spies or informers against their fellow citizens." Second, he saw Hamilton's proposal as an unconstitutional power grab by the Treasury Department since this agency bore no responsibility for issues of war and peace. In addition, giving Treasury oversight of neutrality violations would further increase the power of the government's largest department, "already amply provided with business, patronage, and influence."[14] Lastly, Jefferson believed that grand jurors and judges, rather than Treasury officials, should handle neutrality violations because legal matters fell under their purview.[15]

Jefferson was not alone in objecting to Hamilton's proposed circular. Washington expressed concern that the provision identifying "the building of ships with gun ports" as a neutrality violation might be misunderstood. He wrote to Hamilton, "I am not disposed to adopt any measures which may check Ship-building in this Country" and cautioned against "too promptly" adopting measures that are "not indispensably necessary."[16]

This disagreement over enforcement protocol and responsibilities ended the same way disputes over the policy's formulation had: with Attorney General Randolph crafting a compromise. Randolph proposed that the customs collectors report neutrality violations to the U.S. attorneys, who would then relay them to the attorney general.[17] In addition, the revised instructions would not contain language about ship construction.[18] This compromise took authority away from the Treasury secretary as well as the secretary of state, who also bore responsibility for supervising the nation's district attorneys and federal marshals.[19] Although the cabinet reached this agreement on May 10, Hamilton pushed back on efforts to curtail his department's authority when he delayed the release of this revised circular until August 9, an enforcement lapse of three months.[20]

Washington and his cabinet found themselves embroiled in a second enforcement dispute when they debated the best way to issue sea passports (or sea letters). While government officials and maritime citizens both agreed on the important role sea passports played in protecting America's neutral commerce, questions quickly emerged on how to handle these requests. In late April, Stephen Higginson, a prominent Boston merchant, wrote to Hamilton, "I wish there were sea Letters or other proper documents issued by the officer of the union, to serve as a uniform mode of evidence as to property."[21] William Ellery, the customs collector of Newport, Rhode Island, requested that Hamilton provide "such sea letters or passports as you may deem will be for the security of our navigation and commerce."[22] As the government began to fulfill these requests, questions abounded over what diplomatic format to follow, which federal official would issue these passports, and whether foreign-built but American-owned ships were eligible for these protective documents.

The concept of sea passports had its origins in the Treaties of Amity and Commerce that the United States had negotiated with France (1778), the Netherlands (1782), and Prussia (1785). If one party to the treaty was at war but the other was at peace, the latter could issue sea passports to protect its neutral commerce.

Despite their agreement on the overriding principle, each treaty contained a slightly different format for these passports. Such variations proved to be an abstract concern prior to 1793 because the United States had no reason to issue these documents to its merchant ships. But with Britain at war with U.S. treaty partner France, protecting American commerce became a top priority.[23] Seemingly minor issues assumed great importance because these sea letters provided the first line of defense in America's campaign to remain neutral.

During the first week of May, Washington's cabinet members, along with the Treasury Department's commissioner of the revenue, Tench Coxe, exchanged a flurry of letters in an attempt to resolve these outstanding issues.[24] Jefferson wrote a detailed opinion on May 3, in which he made a strong case that "passports shall be given not merely to the vessels *built* in the United States, but to vessels *belonging* to them." He added that American commerce would suffer irreparable harm if foreign-built ships were subject to seizure, for "homebuilt vessels" provided "the transportation of a very small part of this produce to market."[25] In the discussions over which passport format to follow, diplomacy carried the day. With the United States already issuing sea letters using the Dutch template, Washington and his cabinet decided to also include language from the French treaty of 1778 to avoid any diplomatic misunderstanding with France.[26] Lastly, despite his previous misgivings about the Treasury Department's reach, Jefferson agreed with Hamilton that the collectors of the customs in each port should issue these passports. The protection of American commercial ships began in earnest on May 13, 1793, with the distribution of 500 blank ship passports to the nation's customs houses, each bearing the signatures of the president and the secretary of state.[27] One measure of these passports' effectiveness in promoting neutral American commerce, particularly in the transportation of goods from the French West Indies, was Britain's decision that November to attack U.S. ships because such cargoes were seen as benefiting France's war effort.[28]

As Washington and his cabinet methodically and incrementally implemented the neutrality policy, a tsunami named Edmond Charles Genet made landfall in Charleston, South Carolina, on April 8 and upended their delicate efforts. During his ten-month posting as the French Republic's minister, Citizen Genet, as he styled himself, repeatedly challenged U.S. neutrality as he fulfilled the mandate of his revolutionary government and supplied his own interpretations along the way.[29] While his antics affirmed the wisdom of Washington's policy, his transgressions also exposed numerous enforcement difficulties that the administration had yet to consider.

FIGURE 5. Edmund Charles Genet (1763–1834), the troublesome minister from France whose antics affirmed the necessity and wisdom of the neutrality policy. (Wikipedia.com)

Genet's tenure proved to be controversial from the outset, thanks to the ambitious and unrealistic instructions the idealistic Girondins, who now ruled the French republic, gave him. First, Genet was encouraged to form a "national pact" with the United States to renew the commercial and political bonds that had linked the two nations. In addition, he was supposed to seek advance payment of America's Revolutionary War debts to support France's wartime economy, to foster expeditions into Spanish Louisiana and Florida, and to liberally interpret the privateering provisions of the Treaty of Amity and Commerce by offering French commissions to Americans willing to serve as privateers or as soldiers on expeditions against Spanish territory. Amid these blatant challenges to U.S. sovereignty, Genet was also told to respect the federal government and its authority.[30]

Armed with these ambitious instructions as well as 300 blank commissions, Genet further upended diplomatic protocol by arriving in Charleston rather than proceeding directly to the nation's capital of Philadelphia. He blamed a turbulent Atlantic journey for his premature disembarking. Nonetheless, the minister conveniently found himself in a port city that was strategically important to France's West Indian colonial trade and in a state that remained favorably disposed to his country's revolution.[31] Not surprisingly, Genet's first violation of U.S. neutrality occurred here, when he commissioned four American ships as privateers to support the French war effort. The names of these newly converted ships announced their revolutionary ideas—the *Republican*, the *Anti-George*, the *Sans-Culotte*, and the eponymous *Citizen Genet*—and their mission to harass and capture British vessels.[32] With the French republic's navy decimated by Britain's superior fleet, privateering represented a viable alternative wartime strategy.[33] While Genet emerged as its most visible proponent, other French captains and their ships engaged in this practice in American waters as well.[34]

Genet's southern detour meant that, for five weeks, he conducted business as France's minister before presenting his credentials to the president of the United States. As Genet slowly meandered northward, reports of his misdeeds seeped into Philadelphia from a variety of sources.[35] President Washington received a letter from two Norfolk, Virginia, merchants who reported that the privateer *Sans Culotte* had been outfitted with guns and contained a large number of Americans but very few Frenchmen among its crew.[36] Several days later a Federalist congressman, William Vans Murray, reported to Jefferson that the *Sans Culotte* had sailed north to Maryland's Eastern Shore and had captured a British ship, the *Eunice*.[37]

These rumors escalated into a full-blown diplomatic crisis on May 2, when British minister Hammond sent Jefferson the first of numerous memorials complaining of French privateering against British vessels. His May 2 letter reported that the French frigate *Embuscade* (the same vessel that had transported Genet to America) had captured the English merchant ship *Grange* in Delaware Bay near Philadelphia. Hammond, who enjoyed lecturing Jefferson, pointed out the obvious: the seizure had occurred in U.S. waters "in direct violation of the Law of Nations" as well as an "infringement on its [American] neutrality."[38] He further urged the U.S. government to "adopt such measures . . . for procuring the immediate restoration" of the ship "and for obtaining the liberation of her crew now illegally and forcibly imprisoned" on the *Embuscade*.[39] The involvement of American sailors, vessels, and ports in European warfare had been exactly what Washington (and his cabinet) had hoped to avoid in issuing the Neutrality Proclamation two weeks earlier.

Jefferson offered a vague but sympathetic response to Hammond's memorial, declaring that "the US being at peace with both parties, will certainly not see with indifference its territory or jurisdiction violated by either" and promised to investigate the matter.⁴⁰ As subsequent exchanges between Hammond and Jefferson made clear, the American government did not have either rules or enforcement mechanisms in place to prevent French privateering. It also did not have any means to prohibit Americans from serving on these ships or from offering their vessels to a European nation's war effort. On May 8, an impatient Hammond reminded Jefferson of his May 2 memorial and requested "as speedy an answer as may be convenient."⁴¹ That day he also submitted two more memorials that reported additional privateering violations, including the *Embuscade* capturing two other British ships (the *Four Brothers* and the *Morning Star*) as well as describing the commissionings that had occurred in Charleston under Genet's direction.⁴² As late as May 31, Hammond still had not received a definitive response from Jefferson on the return of captured British ships, inquiring of the secretary of state "at what time I may expect to receive the determination of this government upon it."⁴³ The British minister appeared to have a long wait ahead of him.

With Washington and his administration preoccupied with smaller questions over which federal officials should report privateering violations and how to issue sea letters, a few weeks passed before they focused on the specifics of Hammond's May 2 memorial concerning the *Grange*'s capture. At the heart of the discussion was whether the Delaware Bay constituted U.S. territory or international waters, as the French claimed. Jefferson, at the president's request, asked the attorney general to prepare a legal opinion on the extent of America's jurisdiction over the Delaware Bay. Randolph confirmed that this bay was U.S. territory and that the French seizure of a British ship in its waters violated American neutrality.⁴⁴ On May 15, Jefferson wrote to both the British and French ministers to convey this decision and to urge a restoration of the *Grange* to its owners.⁴⁵ On May 27, Genet, in a rare act of cooperation, agreed to this request, writing, "My brave brethren, the seamen of the *Embuscade*, have readily concurred in a measure which I represented to them as a proper mean to convince the American government of our deference and of our friendship."⁴⁶ The quick resolution of the *Grange* case offered the false impression that enforcing neutrality would be easy and uncontroversial. Instead, it represented only a small drop in the tidal wave of neutrality violations that would confront the administration.

Even before the successful resolution of the *Grange* case, Washington expressed concern that American ships and sailors were serving as French privateers and on May 14 convened the cabinet to formulate a more comprehensive response. Employing the consensus-based approach that had proven effective during the policy's formulation, the president and his advisors quickly identified their enforcement priorities. First, the administration sought to prosecute "certain citizens" who "have engaged in committing depredations on the property and commerce of some nations at peace with the United States" in order to stop Americans from serving on privateers. As the supervisor of U.S. attorneys, Jefferson instructed William Rawle of Pennsylvania "to take such measures for apprehending and prosecuting" these violators "according to the law."[47] Second, Secretary of War Knox directed governors to use their state militias "to detain the parties first aggressing until you could communicate the case to the president" to prevent situations like the capture of the *Grange* in U.S. waters or the commissioning of privateers in Charleston from happening again.[48]

Beyond these initial steps, thornier issues such as the restoration of ships in open waters and the banning of all privateering activities in American ports preoccupied the cabinet for the remaining weeks of May. The *Grange* had established the precedent of returning prizes captured in territorial waters. But did the U.S. government have a similar obligation for ships (typically British) seized in the open Atlantic, particularly if the privateer (typically French) had been outfitted in American ports? In separately submitted opinions, Hamilton and Knox argued that the United States should restore prizes brought into U.S. ports, regardless of where they were captured, "in order to avoid participation in the war."[49] Jefferson and Randolph countered that the two belligerents should expect privateering and the capture of prizes to occur in open waters during wartime, therefore the neutral United States had no involvement in such cases. Jefferson explained, "If the commission be good, then the capture having been made on the high seas, under a valid commission from a power at war with Great Britain, the British owner has lost all his right, and the prize would be deemed good even in his own courts."[50] Several days later, on May 21, Washington adopted Jefferson and Randolph's approach of not intervening in captures that had occurred on open waters, believing this stance to be the most compatible with American neutrality.[51]

With these smaller enforcement issues resolved, the president and his cabinet turned their attention to the overriding one: how best to prohibit French (and British) ships from manning, outfitting, and equipping privateers in American ports.[52] In Jefferson's notes from the cabinet meeting, titled "the *Citizen Genet* and Its Prizes," the secretary of state listed the many issues at play, including U.S. obligations under the Treaty of Amity and Commerce as well as the "touchiness" of Franco-American relations, particularly with the new minister's arrival and the popularity of the French cause. Nonetheless, Jefferson's minutes acknowledged that Article XXII's prohibition against France's enemies outfitting privateers into American ports did not translate into *permission* for France to engage in this practice. Similarly, Article XVII of the treaty allowed France to bring prizes into U.S. ports but did not offer any elaboration on what else was permissible. As they concluded their discussions, Washington's advisors contemplated several options: one, require French privateers to give up the prize and order the prize, the privateer, or both to leave, whichever was feasible (Hamilton and Knox); two, do not order or give away anything (Jefferson); three, order the privateer only away (Randolph). Demonstrating his savvy as a statesman, Washington selected Randolph's recommendation because it promoted American neutrality while avoiding provocative actions that could jeopardize this stance.[53]

Before announcing these policies to the French and British ministers, Jefferson took the additional step of asking Randolph to prepare a statement that defended America's right to prohibit the French from commissioning privateers in its ports. Genet's May 27 letter to Jefferson had contained a very generous interpretation of the 1778 Treaty of Amity and Commerce, an understanding that the French minister would repeatedly express in his prolific correspondence to the secretary of state. After citing French privateering rights under that treaty, Genet added that the U.S. citizens commanding and manning these privateers had "entered the service of France in order to defend their brothers and their friends."[54] In response to the minister's fulsome expectations, Attorney General Randolph provided Jefferson with a six-point statement that emphasized America's sovereign right to prohibit the commissioning of privateers and to ban U.S. citizens from serving on them, that a "vessel . . . illegally commissioned, and illegally manned . . ., should be put out of the protection of the U.S."[55]

On June 5, 1793, with the cabinet's decisions on privateering and Randolph's statement on U.S. sovereignty in hand, Jefferson, in his capacity as the nation's chief diplomatic officer, communicated the administration's enforcement policies to Ministers Genet and Hammond. He wrote to Genet, "after mature consultation and deliberation," the president has concluded that "the arming and equipping vessels in the Ports of the United States to cruise against nations with whom they are at peace, was incompatible with the territorial sovereignty of the United States," then added the directive that "the armed vessels of this description should depart from the ports of the United States." Acknowledging the arguments the French minister had included in his May 27 letter, Jefferson responded with an affirmation of America's sovereign rights and countered that "the granting [of] military commissions within the United States by any other authority than their own is an infringement on their sovereignty."[56] In confronting France's principal transgression against American neutrality, he and Washington's administration at large believed this letter would be enough to end French privateering.

Jefferson's June 5 letter to Hammond addressed the concerns the British minister had raised in his numerous memorials: stopping privateering against British ships and restoring captured vessels to their owners. Jefferson wrote that "the president, after a full investigation of this subject, and the most mature consideration," had found the privateering complaints "to be just," and his administration had taken "effectual measures . . . for preventing repetitions of this act." In terms of returning captured ships, the secretary of state reiterated his earlier argument that the seizures of British vessels by legally commissioned French privateers in international waters were acts of war between these two countries and did not concern the United States. While he acknowledged that the United States had not been prepared for the French privateering that began in Charleston, Jefferson explained that the United States was now taking steps "that the vessels, so armed and equipped, shall depart from our ports."[57]

With privateers ordered to leave American ports and the appropriate governing authorities (U.S. attorneys, governors, and customs officers) and diplomatic officials notified, Washington and his administration seemed well on their way to stopping additional transgressions and to upholding U.S. neutrality. Yet the reactions of the two European ministers demonstrated that the United States had crafted an unenforceable "paper policy." Genet remained committed to privateering in American ports, and Hammond intended to press the U.S. government to restore and even indemnify the British prizes French ships had captured. In Genet's defiant response to Jefferson, he reiterated France's right to outfit and equip privateers in U.S. ports. Demonstrating the dramatic flourish that characterized his diplomatic tenure, Genet wrote to Jefferson, "I have seen with pain . . . your letter of the 5th of this month." Genet then reaffirmed his understanding of France's privateering privileges: "The United States, friends of the French . . . , have permitted them to enter armed, and remain in their ports, to bring there—their prizes, to repair them, to equip in them, whilst they have expressly refused this privilege to their enemies."[58] Genet found authority for the current privateering activities by conflating two provisions of the Treaty of Amity and Commerce: Article XVII, which permitted French captains to bring their prizes into American ports (but did not authorize equipping, outfitting, or manning them), while Article XXII prohibited France's enemies from "fitting" prizes in those same ports or "to sell" or "to exchange" captured ships and their cargoes.[59] With the French so allowed to bring privateers into U.S. waters,

Genet further interpreted the "prohibition" against the signatories' enemies as "permission" for France to privateer in American ports.

In his June 17 reply, Jefferson refuted the authority that Genet claimed the Treaty of Amity and Commerce had provided. He wrote, "The XVIIth article... permits the armed vessels of either party, to enter the ports of the other, and to depart with their prizes freely." But, Jefferson countered, "the entry of an armed vessel into a port, is one act; the equipping a vessel in that port, arming her, manning her, is a different one, and not engaged by any article of the Treaty."[60] In fact, the right of French vessels to bring privateers into U.S. ports had been affirmed in a May 30 circular that Hamilton had sent to the customs collectors.[61] Genet, of course, was having none of this, and his vociferous commitment to his interpretation increasingly soured Washington and his cabinet on him.

With France continuing to privateer in American ports, Hammond remained equally committed to involving the U.S. government in the return of British prizes. The minister based his appeal on two loopholes in America's June 5 enforcement policy: first, claiming that the commissions of French privateers' commissions were invalid, because a foreign power lacked sovereignty in American ports, and second, arguing that the seizures had occurred in U.S. waters, based on the *Grange* decision. Hammond dedicated the summer to pursuing these points in federal court and elsewhere (as detailed below) in order to force a decision favorable to British interests.

With the United States lacking a navy to enforce the administration's June 5 policy, French privateering continued with abandon, and Genet remained its enthusiastic supporter. Two of the privateers he had commissioned in Charleston, the *Sans Culotte* and the *Citizen Genet*, proved to be particularly aggressive and prolific, as did the *Embuscade*, which had transported the French minister to America.[62] While the privateers' initial captures had launched America's enforcement policy, their later prizes, most notably the *William* and the *Little Sarah*, illustrated both the federal government's neutral aspirations as well as the domestic and international difficulties in enforcing them.

The *William*, a Scottish ship, was among the *Citizen Genet*'s many prizes. Its capture led to two landmark enforcement cases: first, the prosecution of an American serving on privateers, and second, Hammond's campaign to require the U.S. government to restore prizes captured in American waters. The *William*'s notoriety began on May 14, when a skeletal crew from the *Citizen Genet* transported the ship into Philadelphia to be condemned as a prize.[63] Leading this effort was the privateer's prize captain, an American mariner named Gideon Henfield, who, along with another American, John Singleterry, had been recruited to serve on the *Citizen Genet*.⁶⁴ Henfield had joined its crew based on the lucrative promise that he would be put in charge of the privateer's first prize.⁶⁵ (In one of his memorials, Hammond described the nefarious "houses of rendezvous" in Charleston where such transactions occurred.)⁶⁶ Upon Henfield and Singleterry's arrival in Philadelphia, U.S. Attorney Rawle arrested both men for violating American neutrality, pursuant to Jefferson's May 15 instructions. Preventing Americans from participating in the current Anglo-French war was a major goal of the Neutrality Proclamation, and Washington and his cabinet hoped this initial prosecution would set an example and stop future violations.

Not surprisingly, Citizen Genet (the minister, not the vessel) vehemently opposed the arrests of Henfield and Singleterry, sharing his opinions with Jefferson on the matter. Tangibly demonstrating his disrespect for U.S. sovereignty and the rule of law, Genet questioned their arrests in a series of letters. On June 1, he wrote, "I have this moment been informed, that two officers in the service of the republic of France . . . have been arrested on board the privateer of the French republic." Genet dramatically added, "The crime which my mind cannot conceive, and which my pen almost refuses to state, is the serving of France, and defending with her children the common and glorious cause of liberty." Then the French minister took the even bolder step of asking for Jefferson's intervention "and that of the President of the United States in order to obtain the immediate releasement [*sic*] of the abovementioned officers."⁶⁷

Jefferson's terse response wisely focused on the constitutional and legal impossibilities of Genet's request. First, he pointed out that "Mr. Henfield appears to be in the custody of the civil magistrate, over whose proceedings the executive has no control." Jefferson then added, "the act with which he is charged will be examined by a jury of his countrymen, in the presence of judges of learning and integrity." He also included a memorandum from Randolph, outlining the federal government's case against Henfield.⁶⁸ The attorney general listed three major reasons for Henfield's prosecution: first, he was a citizen of the United States and subject to its laws; second, his actions violated American treaties with the three powers (Great Britain, Prussia, and the Netherlands) at war with France because these agreements required the United States and its citizens to remain at peace; and third, Henfield's activities constituted disturbing the peace.⁶⁹ Jefferson's letter would not be the last time he explained to Genet the authorities and responsibilities of the federal government. Not easily dissuaded, Genet played an active role in defending Henfield's right (and that of other Americans) to serve on French privateers.

The *William* also figured in Hammond's campaign to involve the U.S. government in the restoration of captured British ships. The British minister encouraged the *William*'s owners (as well as the *Fanny*'s, a vessel seized by the *Sans Culotte*) to petition for restitution of their ships through the U.S. district court in Pennsylvania. Each case rested on two arguments: first, the *William* had been seized in U.S. territorial waters, specifically in the Chesapeake Bay, two miles from Maryland's shore.[70] Second, the petitions declared the French commissions invalid because a foreign power did not have the authority to privateer in America's neutral waters.[71] The *William*'s capture offered the federal government two opportunities to slowly assert its authority, with the U.S. attorney holding Henfield and Singleterry in jail for bringing this vessel into port, and the marshal of the district court assuming custody of the *William* (and the *Fanny*) as its owners awaited the federal judge's ruling.[72]

While Jefferson and Randolph worked to prosecute neutrality violations in the federal courts, Secretary of War Knox began to see a positive response to his May 24 order that governors detain ships suspected of privateering in their ports.[73] On June 9, Governor George Clinton of New York reported to President Washington "that a sloop was equipped, armed, and manned in this Harbor and ready to sail, and that there were reasons to suspect that she was intended to act as a privateer." Clinton added that he had "ordered a small detachment of militia on board with directions to detain her until you should be notified." The governor identified the ship as the American-owned *Polly*, but its French captain had renamed it the *Republican*, one of Genet's original four commissions.[74] Washington and his cabinet, seeking to establish a protocol for dealing with cases like this, directed Clinton to deliver the vessel to Richard Harison, the U.S. attorney in New York, to investigate the allegations of privateering.[75] Jefferson, in his role as supervisor of the U.S. attorneys, specifically instructed Harison to institute "such proceedings at law against the vessel and her appurtenances as may place her in the custody of the law, and may prevent her being used for purposes of hostility against any belligerent powers."[76] By holding and disabling the *Republican* through legal channels, the federal government sought to put an end to the arming and equipping of all privateers in American ports.

The government's temporary detention of both the *William* and the *Republican* further enraged Genet. Believing in France's fundamental right to privateer in U.S. waters, Genet launched an ill-advised tirade against the government's efforts to remain neutral. Writing to Jefferson on June 14, he declared the holding of these vessels to be "in contempt of the treaties which unite the French and Americans" and "in contempt of the law of nations." Dismissive of the government's policies, the French minister boldly directed Jefferson to "inform the President of the United States of these facts; to let him know that they [civil and judicial officers] have used his name in committing these infractions of laws and treaties." Genet concluded his letter with the demand that Washington provide immediate restitution, with damages and interests, for the French prize, the *William*, and the privateer, the *Republican*.[77] In response, Jefferson returned to familiar arguments, first refuting Genet's belief in France's right to privateer in American ports, then explaining that the judicial branch, not the executive, handled disputes over property.[78]

Despite Jefferson's confidence in the judiciary, the federal government's enforcement efforts endured a significant setback with the court's ruling on the *William*. On June 21, the U.S. district court judge in Pennsylvania, Richard Peters, released the *William* from custody, declaring a lack of jurisdiction "to decide in a matter growing out of the contests between belligerent powers."[79] Hammond, undeterred by this ruling, immediately turned to the executive branch for redress. Writing to Jefferson, the British minister expressed "no doubt that the executive government of the United States will consider the circumstances of this capture as an aggression on its sovereignty and will consequently pursue such measures . . . for procuring the immediate restoration to its rightful owners of the British Ship *William* thus illegally taken."[80] As Washington's cabinet scrambled to formulate a response to Hammond, Secretary of War Knox directed Governor Thomas Mifflin of Pennsylvania and his state militia to assume temporary custody of the *William* from the federal courts.[81]

The unwillingness of federal courts to exercise their statutory authority in admiralty cases such as that of the *William* placed an embarrassing obstacle in the government's enforcement efforts. While the Judiciary Act of 1789 had established that the U.S. district courts possessed "exclusive original cognizance of all civil causes of admiralty and maritime jurisdiction," Judge Peters, along with other judges in future cases, denied that the federal courts bore this responsibility.[82] This ruling left the federal government without admiralty authority at a time when foreign privateering was rampant. Without U.S. courts to detain prizes and resolve these disputes, Jefferson found himself in the awkward position of turning to the unreliable and unpredictable Genet for assistance.

On June 25 the secretary of state requested that ships captured in U.S. waters by armed French vessels "be detained under the orders of yourself [Genet] or of the Consuls of France in the several ports, until the government of the United States shall be able to inquire into and decide on the fact." In other words, the proverbial "fox" (French privateers) would be guarding the lucrative "hen house" (ports with captured prizes). Additionally, Jefferson instructed Genet that if a French consul was unavailable, the state governors would be responsible for detaining the vessels until a "consul may be called in."[83] Pursuant to Jefferson's request, Secretary Knox ordered the Pennsylvania state militia to transfer the *William* to Francois Dupont, the French consul in Philadelphia.[84]

The district court's failure to assume its admiralty responsibilities, coupled with the delegation of this role to a foreign minister, laid bare the federal government's impotence in enforcing neutrality. Jefferson, who had repeatedly explained America's constitutional rules and its national sovereignty to Genet, now had to cede some of that authority to an individual who had never respected it in the first place. Specifically, he sought Genet's help in resolving the question at the heart of Hammond's June 21 memorial: was the *William*'s claim of being "taken within the limits of the protection of the United States" legitimate? If so, he requested Genet "to give orders to the Consul of France at this port to take the vessel into his custody and deliver her to the owners"; if not, the minister should report this conclusion to Jefferson and await further instruction.[85]

With Jefferson (and the U.S. government) approaching Genet from a position of weakness, the normally obstreperous French minister was all smiles and cooperation. In his response, Genet declared, "The arrangement you propose, sir, suits us in every respect," adding, "I shall communicate them to the consuls and vice consuls of the republic." He even made the preposterous claim that the French diplomatic community considered "the first of our duties to respect all the rights of sovereignty of the United States."[86] Whether Genet would actually take any steps to resolve the twin cases of the *William* and the *Fanny* remained to be seen.[87] What was clear was that Jefferson's June 25 request had exposed the federal government's lack of enforcement powers, a revelation that would embolden Genet to intensify his campaign against its authority.

In the aftermath of the *William* ruling, the judicial branch proved to be the site of a second and even greater setback to the administration's enforcement efforts with the acquittal of Henfield.[88] Following his arrest in May for privateering, Henfield came to trial on July 22 at a special session of the Pennsylvania Circuit Court in the case *United States v. Henfield*. Recognizing the trial's significance, Attorney General Randolph and U.S. District Attorney Rawle worked together to prepare a strong case against him. Rawle, embracing his duties as district attorney, wrote a twelve-point indictment that built on the arguments contained in Randolph's May 30 memorandum. First, the United States had international treaties with several nations in which it pledged to remain peaceful. Since the Constitution considered these treaties to be the supreme law of the land, Henfield had violated U.S. law. Second, as an American citizen, Henfield had an obligation as a member of civil society to obey the laws of the United States. He could not merely "opt out" when he found a particular law onerous. Rawle's arguments proved persuasive enough to convince the Philadelphia-based grand jury to support the government's indictment. Further bolstering the government's case were the instructions to the jury from U.S. Supreme Court Justice James Wilson, one of the three presiding judges.[89] Wilson reinforced Rawle's arguments regarding the law of nations and a citizen's constitutional obligations, concluding "that a citizen, who, in our State of Neutrality, and without the Authority of the Nation, takes an hostile Part with either of the belligerent Powers, violates thereby his Duty and the Laws of his Country."[90] In establishing the legal basis for Americans remaining neutral, Randolph, Rawle, and Wilson also relied upon earlier instructions crafted by Chief Justice John Jay.[91]

Despite the federal government's united and seemingly formidable case against Henfield, his supporters mounted a spirited defense of his right (and that of other Americans) to privateer on behalf of France. Leading the charge was none other than the newly emboldened Citizen Genet, who had been the darling of Philadelphia's Democratic-Republicans since his triumphant arrival in May.[92] Still basking in the glow of numerous fetes in his honor and his newly acquired admiralty authority, Genet saw this case as his path to overriding the federal government's opposition to French privateering. With that goal in mind, he personally financed Henfield's team of prominent Republican lawyers: Peter Du Ponceau, Jared Ingersoll, and Jonathan Dickinson Sergeant.[93] These attorneys argued three major points in his defense: first, Henfield had renounced his U.S. citizenship when he boarded the privateer, so he was not violating any laws; second, the Treaty of Amity and Commerce with France did not prohibit Americans from serving on privateers; and third, perhaps most damning to the government's case, the Neutrality Proclamation lacked statutory authority. The fast-moving trial, which began on July 22 and produced an indictment five days later, ended dramatically on July 29, with the jury acquitting Henfield by a vote of 11 to 1.[94]

This verdict, occurring in the nation's temporary capital of Philadelphia, elated Genet and his supporters and stunned the administration. Genet immediately hosted a celebration in Henfield's honor, inviting Philadelphians to "meet Citizen Henfield." He also encouraged other "friends of liberty" to emulate Henfield and enlist on French privateers. With pro-Democratic-Republican newspapers such as Philadelphia's *National Gazette* covering and disseminating the verdict, news quickly spread up and down the Atlantic coast. Henfield's supporters in Boston and New York City, for example, saluted the mariner's activities and the "virtuous and independent jury of Pennsylvania" for affirming republican values.[95]

The *Henfield* verdict, of course, inflicted a devastating blow to a central objective of the administration's neutrality policy: preventing Americans from participating in a foreign war. The responses of Washington, Hamilton, and Jefferson revealed a great deal about their relationship to this policy. A concerned Washington pondered calling Congress into session to gain institutional support from the government's remaining constitutional partner.[96] Hamilton and Jefferson took a more partisan tack. Hamilton, who had been promoting the Neutrality Proclamation since late June through his Pacificus essays, now directed his fire at Genet in a new series under the pseudonym "No Jacobin," with the first essay appearing soon after the verdict.[97] Jefferson, seeking to spread his partisan wings and distance himself from the neutrality policy, penned his resignation letter to Washington on July 31, two days after Henfield's acquittal. The president shrewdly encouraged him to remain in the cabinet until the end of 1793.[98]

The long summer of enforcement challenges, exacerbated by these governing difficulties and rising partisan tensions in the cabinet, produced a full-blown crisis with the *Little Sarah* incident. The ordeal of the *Little Sarah* began on May 24, when this ship entered Philadelphia as a prize of the prolific French privateer *Embuscade* (which had previously captured the *Grange*).[99] A month after the *Little Sarah*'s seizure, Governor Mifflin wrote to Washington "that the Brigatine *Little Sarah* ... is fitting out as a privateer" and asked the president for direction in what "measures to be pursued."[100] By early July, the *Little Sarah* had been rechristened as the privateer *Petite Democrate*, had been outfitted with fourteen cannons, and was "lying in the river Delaware at some place between this city and Mud Island."[101]

What made the *Little Sarah* so significant was that its capture and conversion illustrated the failure of the federal government to ban privateering in its ports, including the nation's temporary capital. When an exasperated Washington wrote to Jefferson on July 11 "what is to be done about the *Little Sarah*," he was addressing both this specific case and the larger challenge of stopping privateering. The president had little doubt as to the culprit: "Is the Minister of the French Republic to set the Acts of this Government at defiance—with impunity? And then threaten the Executive with an appeal to the People?" Lamenting the failure to stop both privateering and Citizen Genet, he wrote, "What must the world think of such conduct, and of the Government of the United States in submitting to it?"[102] The *Little Sarah* launched Washington and his cabinet into a full-blown political and constitutional crises during the sweltering months of July and August 1793.

When the cabinet held its first meeting about the *Little Sarah* on July 8, the more moderating voices of Washington and Randolph were not present. Instead, the partisan tensions that had been simmering all along were on full display as Hamilton and Knox sought a more aggressive approach to stop French privateering. Reflecting a desire to weaponize American enforcement (and also to gain a partisan edge), they proposed the use of force to stop the repurposed *Little Sarah* from sailing. Specifically, Hamilton and Knox advocated "establishing a battery on Mud Island [in the Delaware River], under cover of a party of militia, with direction that if the brig *Sarah* should attempt to depart before the pleasure of the President shall be known concerning her, military coercion be employed to arrest and prevent her progress."[103] This proposal enjoyed the enthusiastic support of Governor Mifflin, but Jefferson opposed it.[104] Hamilton and Knox prepared a thirteen-point memorandum that elaborated on the need to use military force to stop "the unequivocal breach of neutrality." Jefferson countered with his own statement advocating a continuation of diplomacy rather than "the actual commencement of hostilities."[105] Hamilton and Knox's provocative proposal marked a dramatic departure from the ineffectual policy of asking privateers to voluntarily leave and reflected the administration's growing exasperation with France's aggressiveness and Genet's rising disrespect for U.S. sovereignty.

Washington's return to cabinet deliberations on July 12 inserted a moderating voice that had been absent at the earlier meeting. Instead of addressing the fortifying of Mud Island, an undertaking he opposed, the president sought to resolve the crisis through constitutional and diplomatic channels.[106] In an effort to understand "what shall be strictly conformable to the treaties of the United States and the laws respecting the said questions," Washington and the cabinet turned to their constitutional counterpart, the U.S. Supreme Court, for answers. While the court reviewed these issues, Jefferson wrote a joint letter to Hammond and Genet on July 12 requesting that the seven ships involved in unresolved privateering cases, including the *Little Sarah*, be detained until the president received the court's ruling.[107] Although Washington's approach avoided the hostilities associated with Hamilton and Knox's proposal, it nonetheless encountered obstacles. British minister Hammond scoffed at Jefferson's letter: "I cannot conceal from you my surprise at the requisition contained in it." He reminded the secretary of state that these vessels were outfitted to commit "hostilities on the subjects of Great Britain, or British property," and concluded, "I have no wit of control over any of them."[108] Genet, who had witnessed firsthand the American government's weakness, simply ignored Jefferson's request to detain the *Little Sarah* and instead ordered the ship to depart the Delaware River, an action that infuriated Washington and his cabinet.[109]

Despite earlier setbacks in the lower courts, Washington and his cabinet harbored great hope that advice from the Supreme Court would help the government resolve its current enforcement crisis. Returning to the consensus-based approach that had worked in the past, Hamilton, Knox, and Jefferson each drafted detailed questions for the court and then consolidated their submissions into a single document. Once again the ideas of the prolific Hamilton heavily influenced the final document because he had submitted the most questions (twenty two, compared with Jefferson's fourteen and Knox's twelve) as well as the most detailed. Interestingly, Randolph, the government's chief attorney, did not return to Philadelphia in time to submit questions or to participate in these discussions.[110]

After obtaining Washington's approval, Jefferson submitted the cabinet's twenty-nine questions to the Supreme Court on July 18 with the following instructions: "The President would therefore be much relieved if he found himself free to refer questions of this description to the opinions of the Judges of the supreme court . . . , whose knowledge of the subject would secure us against errors dangerous to the peace of the United States and their authority ensure the respect of all parties."[111] These comprehensive and carefully drafted queries, falling into three broad categories, cogently captured the enforcement challenges that threatened American neutrality. The first question tackled the broad theme of France's right to privateer based on its diplomatic agreements with the United States: "do the treaties between the U.S. and France give to France or her citizens a right, when at war with a power with whom the U.S. are at peace to fit out originally in and from the ports of the U.S. vessels armed for war, with or without commission?"[112] A second area of concern focused on America's obligations under the laws of neutrality and in its treaties with France and with its enemies to allow privateering in U.S. ports, including the selling of prizes, the outfitting of ships, and the establishment of consular courts. The final set of questions focused on the specific enforcement challenges occurring in the United States: restitution of captured ships, the distance of its water boundaries, the prohibition of Americans serving on privateers, and selling U.S.-built ships to the warring parties for merchandise. The document also offered an opportunity for the Supreme Court to affirm the free-trade principles that had inspired the Neutrality Proclamation: "Is the principle that free bottoms make free goods . . . to be considered as [a] now established part of the law of nations?"[113]

Despite the care the administration had taken in identifying the myriad enforcement challenges associated with neutrality, the Supreme Court proved more interested in asserting its institutional independence than resolving policy disputes. On July 12, when Jefferson, on behalf of the president, had asked the justices to come to Philadelphia on July 18 to address "matters of great public concern," he had not specified the topic to be discussed. On the seventeenth, Chief Justice Jay impatiently queried Washington as to when the court would know why they had been summoned.[114] While Jefferson's letter the next day amply answered Jay's question, the Court expressed "a reluctance to decide it, without the advice and participation of our absent Brethren."[115] With a quorum finally achieved, their response to the administration's questions proved to be more of a triumph for their constitutional role than for the enforcement of neutrality. On August 8, the justices informed the president that "lines of the separation drawn by the Constitution between the three departments of government" prevented them from offering advice to the executive branch.[116] While the federal judiciary would eventually find its constitutional voice on admiralty and neutrality cases, its record thus far was disappointing to the administration.

With the judiciary unwilling to act, Washington briefly contemplated turning to the remaining branch of government, the legislative as embodied in Congress, for assistance. Writing to the cabinet on August 3, the president queried "whether it be proper—or not—to convene the legislature at an earlier period than that at which it is meet, by law? And . . . at what time?" Washington specifically cited Henfield's acquittal and the administration's ongoing difficulties with Genet as reasons for involving Congress.[117] A day later he noted a decree from France's National Convention "authorizing their ships of wars and armed vessels to stop any neutral vessels loaded in whole, or parts with provisions, and send them into their ports" as an additional issue requiring congressional attention.[118] Jefferson once again emerged as the only cabinet member who supported calling Congress into session early. He argued that several legislative provisions were pending that would "enable the government to steer steadily through the difficulties daily produced by the war in Europe." In addition, "the legislature meeting a month earlier will place them a month forwarder" in their understanding of the unfolding events.[119] Countering Jefferson were Hamilton, Knox, and Randolph, who shared the belief that recent events did not qualify as "an extraordinary occasion" for convening the legislature. They also argued that meeting a month early did not offer that much extra time for Congress to discuss events, and the scheduling change would create logistical challenges in terms of communication and travel.[120] While Washington personally supported convening early, a lack of unanimity in his cabinet resulted in his dropping this proposal.[121] With Congress not scheduled to meet until December and the judicial branch slow to exercise its authority, the executive branch found itself with the sole responsibility for enforcing neutrality, at least for the time being.

After an exhausting three months spent reacting to a never-ending stream of privateering violations, Washington and his cabinet dedicated August to the formulation and issuance of systematic rules intended to stop infractions against American neutrality.[122] While these policies did not break new ground or reinterpret treaties, they did offer a comprehensive assertion of the federal government's authority over enforcing neutrality. Washington once again employed a consensus approach in crafting these policies as he solicited the opinions of all four cabinet members and incorporated their recommendations into rules that possessed their unanimous support.[123]

The first decision, titled "Rules on Neutrality" and dated August 3, went to the heart of privateering violations when it declared, "The original arming and equipping of vessels in the ports of the United States by any belligerent parties, for military service offensive or defensive, is deemed unlawful."[124] The subsequent seven points made a distinction regarding the outfitting of merchant ships (lawful) versus warships (unlawful), while giving vessels the benefit of the doubt when their purpose was unclear. Additionally, France's enemies were not allowed to outfit prizes made of French ships, in recognition of its 1778 treaty rights. Pursuant to earlier treaties, stranded or wrecked warships, including privateers, were permitted in American ports for humanitarian and emergency reasons. Lastly, these rules prohibited inhabitants of the United States from serving on privateers.

In an effort to uphold American neutrality and to calm British complaints, the administration's second policy decision took an aggressive stance against French privateering and its insubordinate minister. The second August 3 statement, titled "Cabinet Opinion on French Privateers," declared that "the Minister of [the] French Republic be informed that the President considers the United States as bound pursuant positive assurances, given in conformity to the laws of neutrality, to effectuate the restoration of, or to make compensation for, prizes which shall have been made of any parties at war with France subsequent to the fifth of June last by privateers fitted out of their ports." The policy continued that Genet "will cause restitution to be made of all prizes taken and brought into American ports" or, if this was not possible, the indemnification of these prizes, "to be reimbursed by the French nation." Lastly, the U.S. government intended to deny asylum to any privateers in order "to prevent the future fitting out of" these vessels in American ports.[125] This announcement reflected a dramatic departure from Jefferson's June 5 letters to Ministers Genet and Hammond, in which he had asked French privateers to voluntary leave American ports and had denied Hammond's request for the restoration and reimbursement of captured British ships.[126]

These policy decisions, of course, would be meaningless unless they were shared with the officials in charge of enforcing them. On July 29, Washington reminded the cabinet of the importance of customs collectors in reporting violations, writing, "It will not be amiss . . . to reconsider the expediency of directing the custom house officers to be attentive to the arming or equipping vessels—either for offensive or defensive war in the several ports to which they belong—and make report thereof to the governor, or some other proper officer."[127] While the process for customs collectors to follow in reporting neutrality violations had preoccupied the cabinet in May, a circular had never been issued to these officials. With Washington eager to systematically enforce neutrality, a recalcitrant Hamilton finally released this circular to the collectors of the customs on August 4. He instructed them to "have a vigilant eye upon whatever may be passing within the ports, harbors, creeks, inlets and waters of such district to contravene the laws of neutrality . . . and [to] give immediate notice to the governor of the state and to the attorney of the judicial district." Hamilton also disseminated the August 3 rules of neutrality in this circular.[128] Similarly, Secretary of War Knox shared the neutrality guidelines with state governors on August 7 and the French privateering rules on August 16.[129]

The final step of announcing these new enforcement rules was to share them with the British and French ministers. On August 7, Jefferson communicated the U.S. government's new policies on privateering and neutrality to Genet and Hammond, including the decision that France would be responsible for restoring or reimbursing captured British ships.[130] In a subsequent letter to Hammond, dated September 5, he reiterated America's intentions to offer either restitution or compensation for British vessels that had been captured either in U.S. waters or in its ports after June 5, 1793, in case France failed to do so. Additionally, even though the United States did not have a treaty with Great Britain dealing with trade, "it was the opinion of the president that we should use towards that nation the same rule" that the United States follows in its free-trade agreements with France and others.[131] In offering to indemnify British shipping losses, the government sought to resolve a festering diplomatic crisis with its principal trading partner that could potentially lead to war.

One of the principal goals of the Neutrality Proclamation was to keep Americans from participating in European hostilities. The lion's share of violations occurred on water and involved privateering. Yet there were a handful of individuals, including the governor of Virginia, who hoped to support France's war efforts on land. On September 15, 1792, a French military officer named Ferdinand Bayard wrote to Washington offering to raise a regiment of American troops and lead them into battle to aid the French republic, proclaiming: "The cause is a glorious one.... The American corps of volunteers, may be raised by individuals, to save government some inconveniences which may result from its interfering."[132] Not surprisingly, Washington never responded to Bayard's impudent offer.

The real shocker for Washington came from his revolutionary colleague and Virginia neighbor (and the state's current governor) Henry "Lighthorse Harry" Lee, who offered to fight on behalf of France. Lee, then struggling with depression after the death of his wife, sought a diversion that would utilize his military talents. He wrote to Washington, "Bred to arms I have always since my domestic calamity wished for a return to my profession, as the best resort to my mind in its affliction." Lee added: "Finding the serious turn which the French affairs took last year I interposed with the Marquis [Lafayette] to obtain me a commission in their army.... I am consequently solicitous for the best advice."[133] Washington had to respond to Lee because of the potential problems a U.S. citizen of such political stature, military reputation, and close association to the president volunteering to help the French could cause to America's fragile foreign policy. On May 6, Washington offered this carefully worded response to Lee: "I should ponder well before I resolved; not only for private considerations but on public ground."[134] The governor desisted. While Americans in Kentucky would eventually join French-led military units for action against Spanish Louisiana, the larger threat to neutrality continued to come from the sea, not the land.

The productive month of August included one more significant, but not entirely unexpected, enforcement decision: unanimous cabinet support for requesting the recall of the troublesome French minister, Citizen Genet. While this action had been contemplated as early as July, the administration drafted its case against Genet in mid-August and submitted it to the U.S. minister to France, Gouverneur Morris, a week later. The reasons for seeking Genet's recall were not difficult to fathom: authorizing French privateering; permitting French consuls to exercise exclusive admiralty authority over French prizes (a confusing point considering Jefferson's directive to Genet about the *William*); sending off the *Little Sarah*, in violation of instructions to the contrary; disrespecting the U.S. government, particularly the president; and supporting Americans serving on French privateers.[135] While the subsequent French decision to recall Genet represented a triumph of the federal government's authority and sovereignty, it also proved to be a time-consuming process that would include additional charges against the minister and eventually involve Congress, the federal courts, and a shuffling of diplomats.

AUGUST 1793 MARKED a dramatic turning point in the federal government's enforcement efforts. After struggling with blatant neutrality violations and a lack of comprehensive policies and procedures with which to respond, the executive branch took concrete steps to make American neutrality a reality. In a series of statements, Washington and his cabinet explicitly banned privateering in U.S. ports, reiterated the prohibition against Americans from serving on these ships and from participating in European warfare in general, and established procedures for indemnifying captured ships. The government also asserted its sovereignty in diplomatic matters by initiating the recall of Citizen Genet, the French minister who instigated many of these infractions. These enforcement efforts, of course, were not perfect, as evidenced by continued French violations and British complaints. Nonetheless, the recently constituted federal government asserted itself and defined its authorities for the first time in order to support Washington's goal of "keeping this Country in Peace."[136] Eventually, Congress and the courts would embrace their constitutional duties and strengthen the government's ability to enforce neutrality. But in its early days, as neutrality made the bumpy journey from Enlightenment concept to viable foreign policy, the executive branch took the lead in building a neutral nation. In doing so, the federal government came to promote and protect U.S. sovereignty and autonomy at home and abroad for generations to come.

CHAPTER 6

"A Rank Due to the United States"

Enforcing Neutrality across the Federal Government

A UGUST 1793 MARKED an important turning point for Washington and his administration in their enforcement of neutrality. Having reached unanimous decisions on how to handle privateering and privateers, the president and his cabinet operated from a position of increasing confidence as they confronted new challenges to U.S. sovereignty from France and Britain. The involvement of the government's other two branches in enforcing neutrality further strengthened their position. By 1794, Congress emerged as an eager constitutional partner through its passage of laws to protect the nation's shipping and defend its coastal ports. The courts continued to struggle with their role and authority, particularly in neutrality cases, but eventually found their constitutional voice in a landmark 1794 Supreme Court ruling. When the executive branch formulated and enforced neutrality, Washington insisted on consensus within his cabinet to ensure that it had the administration's full backing in order to be successful. With this policy now gaining tangible support across the federal government, the nation affirmed its sovereignty by speaking in a single diplomatic voice, both at home and abroad.

AS AUGUST 1793 came to a close, the last item on the administration's enforcement docket concerned a diplomatic controversy: the fate of the troublesome Citizen Genet. Employing the consensus approach that had proved effective in the Neutrality Proclamation's formulation and in its initial implementation, Washington solicited the cabinet's opinions about Genet individually and then crafted their ideas into a unanimous statement. While the minister's transgressions had been piling up since his arrival in the United States in April 1793, July 23 marked the first time the administration discussed requesting an end to his tenure. Washington's comments to the cabinet left little doubt where he stood.

"We must shortly determine what was to be done with Mr. Genet," he declared, offering two guiding principles for his advisors to keep in mind: affirming U.S. friendship with France while "insisting on the recall of Genet."[1] After a summer spent responding to the minister's outrageous actions and demands, the normally reticent Washington had reached his breaking point. He commented to Jefferson on July 27 after receiving one communication, "Another insulting letter, written in French, by the French minister." Washington, of course, did not read or speak French (Jefferson and later Randolph provided translations). Through his prolific correspondence, Genet had found an additional way to antagonize the president of the United States.[2]

Amid the many delicate compromises associated with the Neutrality Proclamation's formulation and implementation, Genet's removal proved to be particularly volatile. First, his privateering activities directly violated America's neutral stance and threatened its sovereignty and authority as an autonomous nation. Allowing his actions to go unpunished was simply not an option if the United States hoped to attain the international and domestic respect it sought. Second, France remained a valuable ally, and the recall of its minister needed to focus on his transgressions while avoiding a diplomatic crisis that could threaten American neutrality and even lead to war. Third, Genet's indiscretions placed him at the center of the partisan disagreements that Washington had largely managed to keep at bay through earlier compromises. Any statement on the minister's misdeeds could have easily favored Hamilton's Federalist supporters or disparaged Jefferson's Democratic-Republicans, with the controversy's larger national significance getting lost in the partisan crossfire. As the administration took the unprecedented step in American history of asking for the recall of another country's diplomat, the United States' status as an autonomous and sovereign nation faced a monumental test.

Despite these strong personal and partisan tensions, the cabinet agreed quickly and unanimously that Genet's tenure must end. What proved controversial was determining how to proceed with requesting his dismissal and deciding what justifications to provide to the French government. The administration chose to convey the message through established diplomatic channels rather than taking the more provocative step of writing directly to the leaders of the French republic. The U.S. minister to France, Gouverneur Morris, would present the recall request to the French governing body, the Executive Council, and would also share Genet's inflammatory correspondence. The cabinet also agreed to notify Genet of this action, although Jefferson had initially dissented on this point because he did not want to further agitate the unpredictable minister.

Amid these agreements, partisanship intruded. Hamilton wanted to share the recall statement with the American public in order to undercut domestic support for the French republic and even redefine America's diplomatic relationship with France.³ With some of the parameters set (and now one unresolved), the four cabinet members turned their attention to drafting the crucial letter that would explain the reasons for Genet's removal.

While Genet's privateering activities and his disrespect for the U.S. government's authority offered ample justifications for his recall, his support among Democratic-Republicans added a partisan wrinkle to an otherwise airtight case. Since his arrival in Philadelphia, Genet had been the darling of a pro-French political coalition who celebrated the new minister, the French Revolution, and the newly established republic. Genet, who found himself "in the midst of perpetual fetes," erroneously believed these public and partisan outpourings translated into tangible American support for France's revolutionary wars. He also profoundly misunderstood how the federal government operated, with Jefferson repeatedly explaining the Constitution's separation of powers and the unique responsibilities that each branch possessed.⁴ These two misinterpretations led Genet to believe he could defy the executive branch's decisions on neutrality and privateering because he thought Congress possessed ultimate authority on these matters. Even more controversial, he intended to make an appeal to the American people, if necessary, to overturn the government's neutral stance.⁵ If Genet proceeded with his foolish plans, Hamilton saw a golden partisan opportunity to discredit the Democratic-Republicans as well as the French cause by publicly announcing the minister's recall.⁶

Despite Hamilton's designs on composing the letter to Minister Morris, the responsibility for drafting it fell to Jefferson as the nation's chief diplomatic officer. The secretary of state approached Genet's dismissal with understandable ambivalence. On the one hand, he possessed great hopes for the French Revolution and its republican aspirations. Nonetheless, he had witnessed firsthand Genet's deficiencies as a diplomat and the threat he posed to American neutrality. Writing privately to Representative Madison in July 1793, Jefferson offered this blistering critique: "Never in my opinion, was so calamitous an appointment made, as that of the present minister of F. [France] here. Hotheaded, all imagination, no judgment, passionate, disrespectful & even indecent towards the P. [president] in his written as well as verbal communications, talking of appeals from him to Congress, from them to the people, urging the most unreasonable & groundless propositions, & in the most dictatorial style."⁷ Jefferson's decision to submit his resignation letter to Washington amid the Genet recall underscored his competing roles as partisan leader and chief enforcer of American neutrality. Of course, Washington asked him to postpone his departure until the end of the year, meaning the task of penning the rationale for the minister's dismissal would fall to Jefferson.[8]

In the end, Genet's appeal to the American people never materialized, nor did a spontaneous uprising of public support for him or the French cause take place. Instead, resolutions from towns and cities poured into Philadelphia expressing support for American neutrality, with some specifically denouncing Genet's behavior. An August 14 resolution from Kent County, Delaware, declared: "Resolved unanimously, That the citizens now convened do approve of the Proclamation of Neutrality issued by the President of the United States; and that in their opinions, it was prudent and well timed."[9] During August, similar resolutions came from coastal cities such as New Haven, Norfolk, and New York.[10] With the partisan time bomb defused, Washington backed Jefferson's and Randolph's separate recommendations that the recall be done quietly through diplomatic channels without a public announcement. With the obstacles in the cabinet resolved, Jefferson dedicated the next several weeks to drafting the letter to Morris, incorporating the suggestions of Washington, Hamilton, and the other cabinet members.[11]

The final version of Jefferson's letter, weighing in at twenty handwritten pages and echoing the Declaration of Independence, began with a brief history of America's desire for neutrality during the current war. It then shifted into an indictment of Genet's systematic violation of this stance in six detailed sections: first, Genet's assertion of "his right of arming in our ports, and of enlisting our citizens and that we have no right to restrain him or punish them"; second, his unwillingness to recognize America's admiralty authority over prize cases occurring in U.S. ports; third, the minister's lack of respect for a British merchant ship defending itself against illegal seizure because he incorrectly believed that the ship should be considered a hostile privateer; fourth, his insistence that French privateers had the right to sell their prizes in American ports; fifth, the minister's frustration that the "English take French goods out of American vessels" despite these seizures being "one of those deplorable and unforeseen calamities" of war; and sixth, Genet's acting as if he were a "co-sovereign of the [American] territory" and exercising the powers of the U.S. government as he "arms vessels, levies men, gives commissions of war, independently of them, and in direct opposition to their orders and efforts." The secretary of state also specifically mentioned the French minister's decision to allow the *Little Sarah* to sail away despite explicit orders from the U.S. government to detain the ship.

In concluding his instructions to Morris, Jefferson stressed, "our friendship for the nation [France] is constant and unabating," but the French government must "replace an agent, whose dispositions are such a misrepresentation of theirs."[12]

With Jefferson's draft completed, the cabinet and Washington met several times to review and revise this letter. On August 23, they unanimously agreed to send it to Morris under Jefferson's signature.[13] The secretary of state delivered these materials to a trusted ship captain, William Culver of the *Hannah*, for its transatlantic journey.[14] Jefferson shrewdly delayed telling Genet of his recall until September 7 so the minister could not intercept its transmittal.[15] The request for Genet's recall represented a bold affirmation of the federal government's neutrality policy, but now the waiting began. With a one-way trip across the Atlantic taking at least six to eight weeks, it would be several months before the administration would know if France would honor the U.S demand. In the meantime, the specific problems Genet had caused and the additional controversies he would generate provided Washington and his cabinet with ample opportunities to extend the executive branch's enforcement of neutrality.

One outstanding issue dealt with establishing the United States' ocean boundaries. On June 29, 1793, Jefferson had requested Genet's assistance in determining where the British ships *William* and *Fanny* had been captured, with the minister promising to help.[16] In September, Jefferson learned that the French consul stationed in Philadelphia had died, which meant that these cases had been languishing in his office since the summer. Genet's negligence and the consul's death put these unresolved jurisdictional issues back into American hands.[17] With the hope of resolving the *William* and *Fanny* cases and future ones like them, the administration issued three landmark enforcement decisions establishing America's coastal boundary. On November 8, Jefferson announced to the foreign ministers based in the United States, including Genet, that the administration had established the nation's coastal boundary as "one sea-league or three geographical miles from the sea shores." Acknowledging that a nation's coastal boundary might be as wide as "the extent of human sight, estimated at upwards of 20 miles," or as small as "the utmost range of a cannon ball, usually stated at one sea league," Jefferson explained that the United States had chosen the lesser distance because it was more consistent with current treaties. Using the newly established policy to resolve the case of the *Fanny*, the November 8 letters also concluded that, since the vessel was captured "four or five miles from land," the United States bore no responsibility for its indemnification.[18]

With the country's coastal boundaries defined, Jefferson's November 10 letter recognized and authorized U.S. district attorneys "as the persons the most capable of discharging" the investigation of such jurisdictional cases "with knowledge, with impartiality and with that extreme discretion" necessary in international disputes.[19] He then obeyed his own instructions by referring the case of the *William*, seized closer to the U.S. coastline, to U.S. District Attorney Rawle for resolution.[20] The third policy decision, also issued on November 10, contained procedures for foreign ministers and their consuls to follow when belligerent ships were seized in U.S. territorial waters. First, the consuls should notify the governor of the nearest state, who should "immediately" alert the "attornies [sic] of their respective districts," who would investigate such cases. Jefferson's guidelines also emphasized the importance of consuls reporting seizures in a timely manner so busy district attorneys could interview maritime witnesses before they returned to sea. Also, "this prompt procedure . . . will enable the President by an immediate delivery of the vessel and cargo to the party having title, to prevent the injuries consequent on long delay," such as the spoilage of goods and loss of income.[21]

Through the assertion of its executive authority, the federal government defined the country's Atlantic boundary and instituted a policy for reporting and investigating ship seizures occurring within this jurisdiction. Already committed to indemnifying ships captured within its ports and its territorial waters, the U.S. government finally had a clear definition of what composed those waters. Following its newly established guidelines, the executive branch resolved its backlog of privateering complaints and addressed the new cases washing up on its shores almost daily. Many claims were deemed ineligible for compensation because of where the ships were seized. Several did qualify, including the *William*, whose long judicial ordeal finally ended in 1795, when its owners received damages of $1,580 from the federal government.[22]

During the fall of 1793, as the administration consolidated its enforcement efforts, officials discovered that Citizen Genet was not the only French citizen disrespecting American neutrality. The district attorney for Massachusetts, Christopher Gore, reported that Boston's French vice consul, Antoine Duplaine, had recently commissioned an American ship, the *Roland*, as a privateer, and it had subsequently brought an English prize, the *Greyhound*, into Boston harbor.[23] The French commission of the ship and its resulting privateering activities clearly violated neutrality. Yet these transgressions represented only part of the story. On August 21, with the owners of the *Greyhound* challenging its capture, the federal marshal took possession of that vessel, awaiting legal resolution of the case pursuant to the administration's instructions. That evening Vice Consul Duplaine took the bold step of dispatching "twelve armed marines" and their commander to seize control of the *Greyhound*, declaring it French property.[24] This "daring violation of the laws," as Jefferson described it, generated a swift response from Washington's cabinet.[25] They unanimously agreed to revoke Duplaine's exequatur and directed Gore to prosecute him.[26]

As the supervisor of U.S. attorneys, Jefferson laid out to Gore the administration's case against Duplaine. He emphasized a vice consul's "unfounded right" to exercise admiralty jurisdiction, "probably meaning to assert it by this act of force." These directives also clarified Duplaine's status as "a foreigner, clothed with a public character," and included Jefferson's reminder that "consuls are not diplomatic characters, and have no immunities whatever against the laws of the land." He concluded, "Consequently, Mr. Duplaine is liable to arrest, imprisonment, and other punishment, even capital, as other foreign subjects resident here." Jefferson informed the district attorney, "The president therefore desires that you will immediately institute such a prosecution against him, as the laws will warrant."[27] Gore responded on September 10 that he had arrested Duplaine, who had posted a bond of $1,000 to guarantee his appearance before the next circuit court.[28]

The Duplaine case also provided an opportunity for the federal government to remind all French consuls and vice consuls operating within the United States of the limits of their powers. Addressing this cohort on September 7, Jefferson noted that "several of the Consuls of France are exercising, within the United States a general admiralty jurisdiction," including assessing the validity of prizes. (The failure of the U.S. courts to exercise this authority had created an administrative vacuum that the French consuls eagerly filled.) He added, "Moreover that they are undertaking to give commissions within the United States, and to enlist, or encourage the enlistment of men, natives or inhabitants of these states, to commit hostilities on nations with whom the United States are at peace." Reminding these French nationals that such actions violated American laws, Jefferson asserted the government's right to revoke exequaturs and to prosecute and punish those consuls and vice consuls engaged in such activities.[29]

As the case made its way through the federal courts, Jefferson revoked Duplaine's exequatur as vice consul for New Hampshire, Massachusetts, and Rhode Island pursuant to his own September 7 instructions. On October 3, the secretary of state explained to him that, "as Vice-Consul of the republic of France, you have with an armed force, opposed the laws of the land.... [T]he President of the

United States has considered it as inconsistent with the authority of the laws ... that you should any longer be permitted to exercise the functions, or enjoy the privileges of vice consul in these United States."[30] Letters announcing this revocation were sent to the appropriate diplomatic officials, Morris and Genet. The federal government also published this statement in the nation's newspapers to send a clear message to the maritime community and to other consuls and vice consuls regarding the limits of French authority in U.S. ports.[31]

Amid these decisive steps, the federal government's efforts to prosecute Duplaine proved more disappointing. Following Jefferson's instructions, District Attorney Gore prepared a case against the vice consul, but he failed to get a unanimous decision from the circuit court's grand jury. As Gore explained to Jefferson, "Eleven of the jury were for making the presentment, but more could not be convinced of its legality." Once again, the Neutrality Proclamation's lack of legal authority proved problematic: "they agreed that the facts were proved; but doubted of the law."[32] Despite this failure in the courts, the administration, by revoking his exequatar, successfully used its diplomatic authority to block Duplaine from further violating American neutrality as a vice consul.

Along with Genet's and Duplaine's activities in American ports, the administration soon learned that France's neutrality violations were not limited to privateering in the Atlantic. In late August, Jefferson received a letter from two Spanish diplomats who described a statement circulating in Louisiana "for the purpose of stirring up that province and making it independent from" Spain. Genet, of course, had authored this recruitment plea, with the hope of regaining Louisiana for France.[33] Several months later the same diplomats offered tangible evidence of his military preparations: four Frenchmen were "under authorization from the French minister, Mr. Genet, to head for Kentucky, and make as many recruits as they can along the way, of Americans and Frenchmen." Additionally, they were to travel by ship "on the Ohio and Mississippi [Rivers] to Louisiana to attack the first post in the province ... and to proceed to New Orleans," where they would be met by a French fleet.[34] Besides Kentucky, Genet was also offering commissions to U.S. citizens in South Carolina and Georgia in order to forcibly seize not only Spanish Louisiana but also East Florida.[35]

Alarmed by this news, Jefferson, at Washington's behest, alerted Kentucky's governor, Isaac Shelby, to stress "that they [agents for France] may not be permitted to excite within our territories or carry then any hostilities into the territory of Spain." He reminded Shelby that "these illegal expeditions" threatened the peace of the United States and urged him to use the state militia to put down any resulting rebellions, if necessary.[36] Jefferson also enlisted Secretary of War

Knox to write the governor that if the "course of laws ... should be ineffectual," he should use "military force" to prevent the French invasion of Louisiana.³⁷ Despite mounting evidence to the contrary, the shameless Genet published a declaration in a Philadelphia newspaper on December 27, 1793, denying any involvement in these activities: "the minister of the French republic, has not authorized the recruiting, formation, or assembling of any armed force or any military corps on the territory of the United States."³⁸ In early 1794, Edmund Randolph, having replaced Jefferson as secretary of state, received confirmation that Genet had successfully recruited over 2,000 Americans to invade Spanish Louisiana.³⁹

During the summer and fall of 1793, troubling reports of British assaults on American merchant ships demonstrated that France was not the only warring nation violating U.S. neutrality. While France's maritime transgressions had largely focused on enticing merchant ships to serve as privateers to bolster its navy, Britain adopted aggressive wartime policies that targeted the cargoes of American merchant ships to strip them of their neutral status. The British government's first order in council, dated June 8, 1793, and arriving in Philadelphia on September 12, identified wheat, flour, and meal as contraband and authorized the Royal Navy to detain and seize any ships headed to enemy ports with these items.⁴⁰ With the United States serving as a major supplier of grain to France, this policy resulted in the capture of at least fourteen American merchant ships en route to the European continent.⁴¹ On November 6, the British government issued a second order in council that extended this starvation policy to France's West Indian colonies and expanded the scope of goods included. It authorized "the seizure of all ships laden with goods the produce of any colony belonging to France or carrying provisions or other supplies for the use of any such colony."⁴² Because of the Caribbean's proximity to the United States, the November 6 order hit American shipping particularly hard, with 250 vessels seized, and 150 of those condemned. No longer in possession of their ships and cargoes, captains and seamen became stranded in the West Indies as they awaited the interminable adjudication of their cases.⁴³

Reports of ship seizures connected to the June 8 order reached Philadelphia in late summer, as Washington and his cabinet prepared for Congress's constitutionally mandated convening later in the year. These British polices stood as a direct assault on American neutrality, particularly their underlying philosophical doctrine that "free ships make free goods." But the outbreak of a yellow-fever epidemic in the nation's capital interfered with the administration's ability to respond to these encroachments and delayed its preparations for the upcoming congressional session in December. The likely source of the required infestation of female mosquitoes, which transmitted yellow fever, was the arrival of shiploads of refugees and their cargoes from the war-torn Caribbean island of Santo Domingo, present-day Hispaniola.[44] Philadelphia's population of 55,000, as did those of other American cities, absorbed about 2,000 Santo Domingans. By August, Philadelphians began to exhibit the disease's "colorful" symptoms, including yellow skin and black vomit.[45] Highly contagious, yellow fever cut a wide swath of infection across Philadelphia, resulting in staggering weekly death tolls during the months of September and October.

With the yellow-fever outbreak showing no signs of abating, Philadelphia's mayor urged residents to evacuate, and Washington and his cabinet complied. Attorney General Randolph sought higher ground and less contagious air in Germantown, Pennsylvania, while Hamilton, who had contracted the disease in early September, recuperated in a mansion outside of the capital.[46] By mid-September, Washington reluctantly relocated to Mount Vernon, at his wife's urging, to escape the "malignant fever," while Jefferson returned home to Monticello.[47] With the national government geographically scattered, Jefferson paid a visit to Mount Vernon on September 22 to resolve the growing backlog of governance issues.[48] One of the topics Washington raised was the temporary relocation of the nation's capital until the epidemic ended. Specifically, he asked the cabinet, as well as Representative Madison and others, whether the president possessed the constitutional authority to convene the upcoming Congress in a city other than the capital.[49] While Article II, Section 3 of the Constitution states, that the president "may, on extraordinary occasions, convene both Houses, or either of them," it does not specify whether this power extended to changing Congress's venue. The responses were unanimous: the president lacked the authority unless a positive law was passed. Madison explained: "From the best investigation I have been able to make in so short a time," summoning Congress "at a time and place to be named by" the president "seems to require an authority that does not exist under the Constitution and laws of the United States."[50] While Congress would eventually grant this authority, such a change would not be possible prior to the December 1793 session.[51]

As yellow fever raged into November, Randolph reported to Washington, "The mayor and the physicians dissuade people from returning yet, and especially in great numbers."[52] In response, the president and his cabinet took up temporary residence in nearby Germantown in order to conduct the government's business in a less geographically scattered manner. The administration's primary task was drafting Washington's annual address to Congress. While the Neutrality Proclamation and the subsequent challenges to it—privateering, Genet, and relations with France and Great Britain—dominated these discussions, the cabinet disagreed on the best way to explain the proclamation to Congress. They also debated whether to include other issues in this address, such as Indian affairs and the government's financial health.[53] Remarkably, despite the swirl of events surrounding American neutrality since the proclamation's issuance, Congress had not been officially notified of this policy. The president's message to the two chambers would need to comprehensively address what had transpired since April, including Genet's myriad privateering violations, designs on Spanish Louisiana, and the subsequent recall request. Along with Britain's orders in council, France and Spain posed additional diplomatic challenges, with the former rescinding its "free ships make free goods" policy for U.S. ships and the latter encroaching on U.S. territory along the Florida border and the Mississippi River.[54]

Over the course of several meetings in November and through the preparation of numerous drafts, the cabinet debated how best to share these problems with Congress while maintaining their partisan edge. Jefferson, of course, wanted to emphasize the Franco-American friendship, despite Genet's pending recall and France's May 9 policy of targeting neutral merchant ships traveling to enemy ports.[55] Hamilton and Knox, not surprisingly, chose the opposite tack: denounce France and praise Britain, despite that country's new hostile trade policies. At the November 28 meeting, Washington once again demonstrated his political savvy (and limitless patience) by approving a balanced approach that highlighted American difficulties with both countries.[56] By the time Congress gathered in December, the long epidemic was drawing to a close, as freezing temperatures killed off the infectious mosquitoes. During the interminable fall of 1793, yellow fever had claimed the lives of at least 4,000 Philadelphians and resulted in the distribution of over $36,000 in relief funds to survivors.[57]

Washington's annual address to Congress actually consisted of four separate speeches, all written by Jefferson but blessed by the cabinet. The first one most closely resembled a traditional annual address, or "State of the Union," with the speech emphasizing the year's highlights.[58] At noon on December 3, Washington entered the Senate chamber, accompanied by his cabinet and Chief Justice Jay, and addressed both houses of Congress.[59] His speech provided an update on the administration's policies of the past year, beginning with neutrality. Washington explained the need for the proclamation: "As soon as the War in Europe had embraced those powers, with whom the United States have the most extensive relations; there was reason to apprehend that our intercourse with them might be interrupted, and our disposition for peace, drawn into question." With Congress now officially informed of the neutrality policy, he invited the legislators in their "wisdom . . . to correct, improve or enforce this plan of procedure; and it will probably be found expedient to extend the legal code."[60] Acknowledging the weakness of the judicial branch in its handling of privateering cases, he also advised that "the jurisdiction of the courts of the United States . . . demand some further provisions." As he concluded this section of the speech, Washington clarified that neutrality did not mean pacifism: "There is a rank due to the United States among Nations, which will be withheld, if not absolutely lost by the reputation of weakness." Instead, "if we desire to avoid insult, we must be able to repel it; if we desire to secure peace, one of the most powerful instruments of our rising prosperity, it must be known, that we are at all times ready for war." To this end, the president reported that an inventory was being prepared of the nation's "arms and military stores."[61]

Washington presented three additional speeches that highlighted America's specific diplomatic difficulties with Europe and in the Mediterranean Sea. The second speech, delivered on December 5, updated the House and Senate on relations between the United States and France and Great Britain. While affirming France's "friendly attachment to this country," it also noted the National Assembly's hostile new policy of May 9 "making enemy goods lawful prize in the vessel of a friend, contrary to our treaty." The address also announced Genet's transgressions, including his "tendency . . . to involve us in war abroad, and discord and anarchy at home," and included the numerous letters leading to the request for his recall. Washington also highlighted Britain's aggressive actions against American shipping and its commerce, specifically that nation's "orders . . . to restrain generally our commerce in corn and other provisions to their own ports and those of their friends."[62]

The third and fourth messages to the House and Senate, both occurring on December 16, focused on challenges to American neutrality and U.S. sovereignty beyond the Atlantic. Washington's third speech highlighted Spain's territorial encroachments against the United States, including the disputed Florida border, where "the southern Indians" engaged in "hostilities" against Americans, and along the Mississippi River, where Spain had erected navigational barriers to U.S. trade.[63] Washington's other address that day dealt with the difficulties American ship captains encountered in the Mediterranean from the Barbary States, including the need to pay ransoms in order to free maritime citizens.[64] The challenges to neutrality the president described on December 5 and 16 would require future diplomatic missions and congressional actions to resolve.

Washington's composite address received enthusiastic responses from both houses of Congress. On December 7, the Speaker of the House of Representatives, Democratic-Republican Frederick Muhlenberg of Pennsylvania, praised the Neutrality Proclamation on behalf of his colleagues: "We accordingly witness with approbation and pleasure the vigilance with which you have guarded against an interruption of that blessing, by your proclamation."[65] In Washington's brief response to the House, he wrote, "It is truly gratifying for me to learn, that the proclamation has been considered, as a seasonable guard against the interruption of the public peace."[66] The Senate's response, delivered by its president (and the nation's vice president), John Adams, also affirmed the wisdom of the Neutrality Proclamation: "we therefore contemplate with pleasure, the proclamation by you issued, and give it our hearty approbation," adding, "we deem it a measure well timed, and wise."[67] In his reply to the Senate, Washington singled out "the decided approbation, which the Proclamation now receives from your house," and reaffirmed the importance of this policy to his administration.[68] With neutrality receiving the blessing of both houses of Congress, the legislative branch became an energetic constitutional partner in its implementation.

As the Third Congress began its work in January 1794, members eagerly embraced Washington's instructions to "correct, improve or enforce" neutrality through the passage of legislation designed to support it. Although the president's December addresses detailed trading violations against American ships from France, Britain, and the Barbary States, his description of British "vexations and spoliations" made a particularly strong impression on Congress as it considered a variety of remedies. This perspective had received additional credence on December 16, 1793, when Jefferson submitted his long-delayed valedictory "Report on Commerce" to Congress, originally requested in 1791. In this report, the outgoing secretary of state portrayed America's positive trading relationships with Spain, Portugal, France, the Netherlands, Denmark, and Sweden, in contrast to its negative experiences with Britain.[69] Jefferson summarized depredations against American commerce stemming from its orders in council: the Royal Navy's seizure of "800–900 vessels and nearly 40,000 tons of cargo" as well as the "proportional loss of seamen, shipwrights, and shipbuilding." In response to these hostilities, Jefferson proposed that the United States dramatically shift its trading relationships away from Britain and toward friendlier commercial partners, most notably France.[70]

With Jefferson concluding his tenure as secretary of state several weeks after submitting this report, the task of implementing these ideas fell to his friend and Democratic-Republican ally, Representative Madison. On January 3, 1794,

Madison introduced seven resolutions intended to increase America's commercial independence from Britain. The specific proposals included punitive measures: the imposition of import and tonnage duties and port restrictions on nations, including Great Britain, that did not have a commercial treaty with the United States, and the application of these funds to compensate American victims of the Royal Navy.[71] In addition, his resolutions encouraged domestic manufacturers, increased international trade with other nations, and sought to break Britain's monopoly on America's importation of manufactured goods.[72] With the House of Representatives controlled by Democratic-Republicans and the Senate equally divided between them and the Federalists, Madison's legislative proposals attracted more debate than decisions.[73]

Congressional anger toward Britain increased with the submission of Secretary of State Randolph's lengthy report "The Vexations and Spoliations on Our Commerce, since the Commencement of the European War" on March 5, 1794.[74] Unlike Jefferson's December 16 report that characterized America's European trading partners, with the exception of Great Britain, in a positive light, Randolph made clear that French "privateers harass our trade no less than those of the British," among its other transgressions. In addition, Randolph summarized the number of American shipping complaints: "the British were thirty-two; against the French twenty-six; against the Spanish ten; and against the Dutch one."[75] His report provoked a new round of outrage from members of Congress, who sought a more aggressive approach to defending U.S. maritime commerce.

On March 12 Congressman Theodore Sedgwick of Massachusetts, a Federalist, led the response with a legislative package emphasizing U.S. defense preparations. Among his proposals was the establishment of fifteen regiments of auxiliary troops, consisting of one thousand men, serving for two to three years, as well as presidential authority to call an embargo.[76] These initiatives borrowed generously from the recommendations of Treasury Secretary Hamilton, who had previously suggested them to Washington.[77]

As Madison's and Sedgwick's competing proposals awaited consideration in the House, Washington submitted another report to Congress on March 25 detailing assaults on American shipping, this time in the West Indies. The U.S. consul to French Martinique, Fulwar Skipwith, offered a devastating portrait of the Royal Navy's ruthless campaign against American commerce: "The ship *Delaware* with thirty three other American vessels have been condemned in the Vice-Court of Admiralty of Montserrat—about the same number have been also in St. Kitts, and upwards of one hundred and fifty more have been arrested and carried into the different ports of the English Windward Islands, and no doubt will share the same fate."[78] These captures, of course, had been authorized under the British government's November 6, 1793, order in council. With the two March reports detailing that country's unofficial war against a neutral United States, a furious Congress sprang into action.

Abandoning the competing proposals of Madison and Sedgwick (and Jefferson and Hamilton) for the time being, a unified Congress supported an immediate response to protect American shipping. Beginning on March 26, 1794, it ordered "that an embargo be laid on all ships and vessels in the ports of the United States . . . bound to any foreign port or place, for the term of thirty days," and directed the executive branch to enforce its provisions, including potential exemptions.[79] As the gatekeepers of the nation's ports, the Treasury Department instructed the customs collectors to take the lead in prohibiting ships from sailing, while the War Department, then lacking a standing navy, relied upon state militias, under the authority of the governors, to provide military support.[80] Treasury also fielded requests for noncommercial exemptions to this ban, including transporting political news (such as word of the embargo) or sailing out for humanitarian reasons.[81] In the latter case, numerous vessels applied for sea passports to rescue stranded American seamen whose ships had been seized in the Caribbean. One successful application stressed its adherence to the embargo's goals because "no goods, wares or merchandise of any kind or nature will be sent, and the boat so permitted shall bring back any American seamen that are there."[82] Another approved request involved two vessels sailing to Saint Domingue (Hispaniola) "to carry as passengers any habitants of that island wishing to return, along 'with their clothing, baggage and sea stores.'"[83]

With Congress extending the thirty-day embargo until May 25, the economic hardships on ship captains and seamen increased, as did the request for sea passports to escape these difficulties.[84] In a May 1 letter to Washington, Hamilton questioned whether the latest batch of passport applications was for humanitarian purposes or "a cover for carrying on mercantile speculations contrary to the true spirit of the embargo."[85] While the president approved the eight passports, he also agreed with Hamilton's suspicions: "I am so fully impressed with the necessity of discontinuing the issuing of them without some restrictions."[86] Although intended to protect America's transatlantic commerce, the embargoes harmed the maritime community's ability to earn a living and also proved increasingly difficult to enforce. The unpopularity of the embargo was confirmed on May 12, when a proposal to extend it until June 20 was overwhelmingly defeated in the House of Representatives 73 to 13.[87]

While the executive branch did its part to enforce the congressionally mandated embargoes, Washington came to realize that a more enduring solution would be needed to uphold American neutrality and to protect the nation's commerce. Rejecting Madison's unrealistic plans for redefining Anglo-American commerce and Sedgwick's belligerent proposals, he offered a third approach: the appointment of a special envoy to Britain to resolve America's trading difficulties. Randolph had originally suggested this idea, and by mid-April, Washington concurred, explaining, "my objects are, to prevent a war."[88] The next day he nominated Chief Justice Jay to serve "as envoy extraordinary of the United States, to his Britannic majesty."[89] This appointment was quintessential Washington: diplomatic, peaceful, and a reminder to Congress that the executive branch, not the legislature, initiated U.S. foreign policy.

Despite Congress's failure to redefine U.S. diplomacy, it proved more successful in passing a series of laws designed to protect American commerce and to ultimately promote neutrality. This prolific legislative output, relying on the Sedgwick-Hamilton recommendations as well as Knox's reports, included the Defence [sic] of Certain Ports and Harbors, the establishment of a Naval Armament, the erecting and repair of Arsenals and Magazines, the creation of a corps of artillerists and engineers to support and build these facilities, and an $80,000 appropriation to build a six-ship naval fleet, with the vessels including the USS *Constellation*.[90] Lastly, on April 19 the Senate approved Jay's appointment as special envoy 18 to 8, opening a new front in the implementation of neutrality, this time through international diplomacy.[91]

With congressional authorizations to strengthen the nation's coastal defenses in place, Secretary of War Knox devoted his energies to implementing these measures. First, he appointed engineers, including Pierre L'Enfant, to fortify the port cities of Philadelphia, New York, and Wilmington in consultation with their state governors.[92] Despite the federal government's efforts to lead the way in enforcing neutrality, it lacked the firepower to do so, and once again it turned to the states for assistance. As Knox explained to Washington, "The governors are commanders in chief of the militia of their respective states" and had been called upon in the previous year "in the name of the president of the United States to perform certain unpleasant duties relative to the preservation of our neutrality." He further requested that, as "a conciliatory and grateful measure" to the governors as commanders of the militia, they should be consulted on the fortification of their ports. Additionally, they should share their recommendations with the president and secretary of war. Lacking a strong military presence in the federal government, Washington had little choice but to agree to Knox's proposal.[93]

FIGURE 6. The USS *Constellation*, one of the six original warships that made up the U.S. Navy in the 1790s. (Wikipedia.com)

Among the military legislation was the Naval Armaments Act, which authorized the construction of the six vessels, with four mounting forty-four guns and the remainder thirty-six. In his plans for building the nation's first navy, Knox sought frigates that "combine the greatest possible force, with adequate strength, and swiftness of sailing, so as to render them equal or superior to any ships... belonging to the powers of Europe." In distributing them, Knox acknowledged that "the government is the government of the whole people," and he proposed that the busy ports of Charleston, Norfolk, Baltimore, Philadelphia, New York, and Boston each receive one of the warships.[94] On June 3, Washington nominated six officers who would serve as captains of the ships.[95] With the help of these newly appointed officers, Knox also submitted plans for the uniforms of the U.S. Navy, sparing no detail in each description. The specifics of each uniform made clear who held what rank: a captain wore a "full dress coat to be blue with long buff lapels," while a lieutenant's coat would be "blue with half lapels of buff." The lower-ranking midshipmen would wear a "plain frock coat of blue . . . without lapels," and marines would wear "plain short coats of blue, turned up with red." Amid these careful deliberations, Knox dismissed the captains' proposal for *"embroidery"* on the uniforms as an "expensive ornament for a Republican Navy."[96]

By June 1794, Washington could point to an impressive list of accomplishments in the enforcement of American neutrality. His four speeches to Congress in December 1793, based on compromises he forged within his cabinet, offered the rationale for neutrality as the wisest policy for the young nation to pursue. Additionally, the president presented further domestic and international challenges the government needed to tackle and encouraged the legislative branch to join in the effort. Amid partisan divisions in his administration and in Congress, Washington shrewdly sought a middle ground in its implementation because he saw neutrality as a *national* policy that promoted U.S. political and commercial interests while keeping the country at peace. With the enactment of laws to strengthen the nation's coastal defenses joining the administration's earlier bans on privateering, the paper proclamation began to develop a backbone and become a national priority.

The year 1794 marked another important turning point in the government's enforcement of neutrality, with the timid judicial branch finding its constitutional voice in the landmark case *Glass v. Sloop* Betsey.[97] With roots in Citizen Genet's notorious commissions, this case began in July 1793, when his prolific namesake, the *Citizen Genet*, captured the sloop *Betsey* and brought it into Baltimore as a prize. Exercising admiralty authority, the French consul affirmed the legality of the capture. The *Betsy*'s owners, hailing from the neutral nations of Sweden and United States, filed a suit in the U.S. district court in Maryland to overturn the French consul's ruling and ultimately recover their ship and its cargo. The district court judge, William Paca, accepted the French consul's authority over the matter, arguing "that the admiralty-courts of neutral countries have no such jurisdiction," only those of warring nations. When the owners appealed to the U.S. circuit court for Maryland, the presiding justice, William Paterson, upheld the lower court's ruling but paved the way for the case to appear before the Supreme Court.[98]

As the Supreme Court considered the fate of the *Betsey*, Chief Justice Jay (just before his appointment as special envoy to Great Britain) saw an opportunity to affirm the neutrality proclamation (which he had helped draft) to thwart France's war preparations and to exercise the admiralty authority that some European countries chose to cede to belligerents.[99] With this in mind, the court asked two central questions: first, did the district court have the authority to exercise prize jurisdiction, and second, did a foreign country have the authority to erect admiralty courts in the United States? In answering the first question, Jay located the judicial branch's authority in Article III, Section 2 of the Constitution, "to all cases affecting admiralty and maritime jurisdiction," with the district courts serving as the starting point for these cases, according to Section 9 of the 1789 Judiciary Act. Since the federal courts possessed sovereign authority over admiralty in the United States, Jay concluded, "the admiralty jurisdiction, which has been exercised in the United States by the consuls of France ... is not of right." In its unanimous ruling, issued on February 18, 1794, the Supreme Court returned the case of the *Betsey* to the district court for resolution and, more importantly, prohibited foreign countries from exercising admiralty authority in the United States.[100] With Jay's bold opinion, the Supreme Court finally exercised the jurisdiction over international law and commerce that the Constitution and the Judiciary Act had authorized. In turn, the district court assumed its newly recognized role in the case of the *Betsey*, which resulted in the release of the ship and the payment of $2,400 to its owners.[101]

In the aftermath of this landmark decision, the federal courts issued a series of rulings in prize cases that further clarified the U.S. government's jurisdiction over neutrality violations. Building on the precedent established in *Sloop* Betsey, these rulings also relied on existing treaty obligations as well as the role of U.S. citizens. Interestingly, all four cases originated in the privateering hotspot of Charleston. In 1794, the U.S. district court of South Carolina ruled in *Jansen v. Vrow Christina Magdalena* that federal courts have jurisdiction on "matters arising on the high seas," an authority that came from treaties with Holland, Prussia, Sweden, and the 1778 treaties with France.[102] In a ruling that repudiated the Henfield case, the Supreme Court in *Talbot v. Jansen* (1795) concluded that a U.S. citizen captaining an American ship had violated the nation's neutrality laws when he privateered for France.[103] That same year, in *Williamson v.* Betsey, the district court distinguished between a ship's previous national affiliation and its current one. This case concerned a former American privateer that had been dismantled and sold. Having been rebuilt in a French port and now possessing a French commission, the court ruled that this vessel did not violate American neutrality.[104] In 1796, the Supreme Court affirmed in *Moodie v. Ship* Phoebe Anne that a French privateer can enter an American port for repairs pursuant to the 1778 treaties with France (and consistent with the administration's August 3, 1793, policy).[105] Despite a slow start, the federal courts embraced their admiralty authority with gusto and contributed to the federal government's enforcement of neutrality.

Along with the *Sloop* Betsey ruling, the eventful months of 1794 also finally brought news from France concerning Genet's fate. Gouverneur Morris's October 18, 1793, letter to Washington, transported to Philadelphia by the trusted ship captain William Culver and arriving in mid-January 1794, announced "that your intentions are fulfilled" regarding Genet.[106] France's government had undergone dramatic changes since the minister's appointment, with the more aggressive Jacobins seizing power from the Girondins. The Reign of Terror had begun, with the execution of Marie Antoinette occurring the same week that the Jacobins approved Genet's recall.[107] In a second letter, dated November 12, 1793, Morris informed Washington that Genet's replacement would consist of a four person "commission," with Jean Antoine Fauchet serving as France's new minister to the United States.[108] In February 1794, Fauchet and his delegation arrived in Philadelphia, avoiding the detours and delays that had doomed Genet. On February 22, in an unexpected birthday gift to Washington, Fauchet presented his credentials to the president, bringing Genet's challenging ten-month tenure to an end.[109]

Genet's recall, however, came with several stipulations. In its October communications with Morris, the Jacobin government demanded that the minister be sent back to France as a "prisoner" and "should be punished." Morris clarified to the French government that the United States wanted his dismissal, not his head.[110] In February, Secretary of State Randolph officially affirmed that Genet's recall had satisfied the U.S. government's demands.[111] Washington, who had once described Genet as "entirely unfit for the mission on which he is employed," became his unlikely savior.[112] Instead of facing deportation to France and execution by guillotine, the deposed minister moved to New York State, married Cornelia Clinton, became a U.S. citizen, and lived happily as a gentleman farmer until his death in 1834.[113] Ironically, his now father-in-law, Governor George Clinton, had dealt with numerous privateering violations generated by his future son-in-law.

France's second stipulation dealt with the tenure of U.S. Minister to France Morris. As early as September 1793, the French republic had sought the ouster of Morris, who they considered hostile to their revolution.[114] With Genet's recall, French authorities saw their opening. Minister Fauchet, who Washington praised as "temperate and placid" and his predecessor's opposite "in all his movements," made the request in a conversation with Randolph on April 9.[115] France's diplomatic quid pro quo sent the administration into a political tailspin as it scrambled to find someone willing to accept the job. On April 29, Washington wrote to two prominent New Yorkers, Robert Livingston and Chief Justice Jay (who had not departed for Britain yet), to gauge their interest in this post, but both demurred.[116] The ever-eager Hamilton submitted a bipartisan list of twenty-eight names that included his political rivals Jefferson, Madison, and Randolph (perhaps to remove them from the national government), while Randolph offered five suggestions.[117] In the end, Washington selected someone who did not appear on any of these lists but who had close philosophical and geographical ties to Jefferson and Madison: James Monroe of Virginia.[118]

Born into the Virginia gentry in 1758, Monroe initially pursued a career in the Continental Army. His failure to raise a regiment, despite the rank of lieutenant colonel and the support of General Washington, resulted in his return to the College of William and Mary. He gained a lifelong friend and mentor in Jefferson (who was Virginia's governor at the time) when he studied law in his office. Monroe served in the Virginia House of Delegates as well as the nation's Confederation Congress, where he acquired another influential friend in Madison.[119] In appointing Monroe, given his close ties to Jefferson and Madison and his pro-French sentiments, Washington hoped to balance the partisan tensions associated with his nomination of the pro-British and Federalist Jay to London.[120] This bipartisan appointment, however, proved to be an embarrassment. Monroe failed to uphold American neutrality, and Washington was forced to recall him in 1796.[121] This setback in France, however, did not hinder his later political career, in part due to his powerful political allies. He later served as governor of Virginia, secretary of state and acting secretary of war during the War of 1812, and the nation's fifth president. Despite their earlier philosophical differences, Monroe's presidency saluted Washington's, as he also toured the nation to promote national unity and affirmed the ideas of the Neutrality Proclamation in the Monroe Doctrine, his statement of U.S. hemispheric autonomy and sovereignty.[122]

While Washington and his cabinet breathed a sigh of relief over the installation of the new French minister, his predecessor's antics continued to generate problems. Despite Jefferson's exhortation to Kentucky's governor to stop American citizens from participating in the invasion of Spanish Louisiana, a letter from one of the state's U.S. senators, John Brown, reported that these enlistments continued with impunity. Written on January 25 but reaching Randolph on February 27, Brown described the numerous military units that had been organized and were already engaged in attacking "Spanish dominions in Louisiana." Among the leaders of these regiments were Generals George Rogers Clark and Benjamin Logan, who were then leading 2,000 men down the Mississippi River. Another Revolutionary War veteran, Colonel John Montgomery, had raised 200 soldiers and had positioned them at the mouth of the Cumberland River to head off the Spanish. The senator lamented the surprising ease with which these and other regiments were being formed: "So popular is the undertaking here that I fear the government will want power, either to prevent it or punish the adventurers."[123]

In dramatic contrast with his controversial predecessor, Fauchet moved quickly to put an end to the invasion of Spanish territories and to affirm American neutrality. In a statement appearing in Philadelphia's *General Advertiser* on March 6, 1794, the minister proclaimed: "Every Frenchman is forbid [sic] to violate the Neutrality of the United States. All commissions or authorizations tending to infringe that neutrality are revoked and returned to agents of the French Republic."[124] Additionally, Arthur St. Clair, governor of the Northwest Territory, had delivered his own statement on December 8, 1793, directing the territory's inhabitants "to observe a strict neutrality towards Spain; and to abstain from every act of hostility against the subjects and settlements of that crown."[125] Yet despite Fauchet's and St. Clair's efforts, the volatile situation required a more sweeping pronouncement from the federal government.

On March 24, 1794, the administration issued a second neutrality proclamation in order to prevent a war on its western borders. Like its April 22, 1793, predecessor, the western proclamation was a collaborative effort, with each cabinet member offering his suggestions. The new attorney general, William Bradford, wrote the final version, as Randolph had previously done for the original. It also did not include the word "neutrality," in a nod to the philosophical compromise that had resulted in the first statement. The western proclamation differed from its predecessor in one important regard: it placed Washington at the center of the document with the repeated use of the personal "I": "Whereas I have received information." This emphasis demonstrated the importance of neutrality to the president as well as his growing frustration with the violations of this policy, particularly by fellow Revolutionary War veterans.

The March 24 proclamation focused on the recruitment activities in Kentucky, where American citizens had "assembled an armed force for the purpose of invading and plundering the territories of a nation at peace with said United States." The statement warned that citizens engaged in unauthorized military activities did so "at their peril" and were admonished "to refrain from enlisting, enrolling, or assembling themselves for such unlawful purposes." Lastly, Washington directed "all court magistrates and other officers ... to exert the powers ... to prevent and suppress all such unlawful assemblages."[126] This second proclamation provided two important reminders. First, the United States faced threats to its sovereignty and autonomy not just along the Atlantic but also to its west and south. Second, there were still U.S. citizens eager to take up arms in a conflict that did not involve or concern their own country. Despite these dramatic developments in Spain's North American holdings, the 1794 Neutrality Proclamation has failed to garner the historical attention of its 1793 counterpart.[127]

Despite some setbacks, the first half of 1794 witnessed a succession of triumphs in the government's enforcement of neutrality, including congressional measures to protect American trade and ports, the judiciary's recognition of its admiralty authority, the successful recall of a disrespectful European diplomat, and the issuance of a western neutrality proclamation. The culmination of the government's comprehensive enforcement occurred in June, with the passage of the Neutrality Act of 1794.[128] With the abortive invasions of Spanish Louisiana and Florida fresh on his mind, Washington urged both houses of Congress to act. Writing on May 20, the president asked "for a stronger and more vigorous opposition" than existed under current law "to keep America in peace" and to prevent its citizens from participating in foreign wars.[129] Although divided along partisan lines, with the vice president breaking the tie in the Senate and the House voting only 48 to 38 in favor, Washington gained the law he was seeking.[130]

The sweeping Neutrality Act gave long-overdue legal authority to the proclamations and the policy decisions that composed the government's enforcement efforts. Containing ten sections, this law systematically addressed the array of neutrality violations the executive branch had encountered on both the land and sea since April 1793 while also offering legal remedies to resolve these challenges. Sections 1 and 2 embodied the original intention of both neutrality proclamations by making it illegal for American citizens to accept commissions from a foreign prince or state and by prohibiting all persons within the United States "from enlisting or hiring other persons to enlist in the service of any foreign prince or state." If an American were to accept such a wartime commission, he could be fined up to $2,000 and imprisoned for three years.[131] Sections 3 and 4 addressed privateering by banning "the fitting out and arming [of] vessels within the ports of the United States" for the purpose of supporting a war "against a prince or state with [which] the United States are at peace" as well as the augmenting ships of war within the jurisdiction of the United States.[132]

Section 5, building on the 1794 Neutrality Proclamation, prohibited the presence of military expeditions on American soil "to be carried on against the territory of a foreign prince or state with [which] the United States are at peace." Section 6 gave long overdue authority to the U.S. district courts to hear "cases of captures made within the territorial waters of the United States." The seventh section authorized the president to enforce these provisions with "the land or naval forces of the United States." The eighth provision, building on the administration's August 1793 privateering policy, authorized the president to order the departure of foreign vessels whose presence violated U.S. treaties. Section 9 addressed treason and piracy, while the final provision authorized this law until 1797. Its reauthorization that year and then permanent establishment in 1800 affirmed the wisdom and necessity of America's neutrality.[133]

THE YEAR 1794 proved to be a watershed in the implementation of American neutrality. No longer just an idealistic policy, it became the law of the land as the government's three branches embraced their constitutional responsibilities in support. The executive branch, having initiated the proclamation, led the way in its enforcement by energizing government officials, banning privateering, initiating lawsuits, defining the nation's coastal boundaries, and punishing errant foreign officials. But this ambitious stance required the full support of the entire federal government to be successful. Congress emerged as an eager partner, passing laws to protect American shipping and ports and to codify the neutrality doctrine. The courts also joined in its enforcement by finally embracing its constitutional and legal mandates to defend U.S. sovereignty on the high seas. Even the nation's maritime citizens began to see the value of neutrality as the government helped them recover their illegally seized ships and cargoes and to receive indemnification for their losses. Washington's vision of building a strong national government capable of promoting and protecting U.S. sovereignty and commercial interests through a policy of neutrality came to fruition during this productive year. With a united federal government successfully enforcing neutrality at home, Washington and his administration turned their attention to resolving international threats, with diplomatic missions to Britain and Spain as well as to points in the Caribbean and the Mediterranean Seas.

CHAPTER 7

"My Objects Are, to Prevent a War"

Enforcing Neutrality across the Globe

WITH THE SUCCESSFUL ENFORCEMENT of neutrality occurring at home, the U.S. government turned its attention to peacefully resolving the challenges to its policy across the globe. Washington's diplomatic initiatives followed the road map he had presented in his four-part address to Congress in December 1793.[1] In 1794, his administration launched a peaceful offensive as it concurrently posted envoys to London, Spain, the Caribbean islands, and the Barbary States of Algeria and Morocco. These appointments highlighted the numerous international incursions on U.S. neutrality and sovereignty, including boundary disputes on the North American continent and assaults on American commerce in the waters of the Atlantic, Caribbean, and Mediterranean. The mixed outcomes of these ensuing diplomatic discussions, with many issues taking over a decade to resolve, demonstrated that it was easier to enforce the neutrality policy at home than abroad. Nonetheless, these missions, and their eventual resulting treaties, possessed important legacies for the young nation. First, they announced Washington's commitment to promoting peace and asserting U.S. autonomy and sovereignty. Second, these agreements aided America's maritime citizens. Lastly, and most importantly, these pacts established the enduring precedent that the United States would place its needs first when engaged in international negotiations.[2]

WITH THEIR PROXIMITY to the United States, Europe's Caribbean colonies emerged as a top diplomatic priority as American shipping became ensnared by Anglo-French warfare. Prior to the outbreak of war in 1793, the Washington administration had appointed Fulwar Skipwith (1765–1839), a Virginia native and protégé of Jefferson, to serve as U.S. consul on the French island of Martinique.[3] In the contentious realm of eighteenth-century shipping and trading, consuls provided a cost-effective way for countries to protect their commercial interests abroad. Although appointed by the president and approved by the Senate, consuls lacked governmental or diplomatic status; they also did not receive a salary. Instead, they were well-connected businessmen who possessed an exequatur, a legal document permitting them to represent their fellow citizens in a foreign country. Operating under the direction of the U.S. State Department, consuls possessed responsibility for aiding and protecting American citizens, including sailors and captains, engaged in commerce overseas.[4] Skipwith primarily acted as an unpaid observer of events in Martinique, including reporting on revolutionary activities and recording American shipping losses. Largely powerless, the U.S. government had also advised him not to alienate France.[5]

By 1793, with France and Britain at war and the United States attempting to remain neutral, assaults on American shipping escalated, as did Skipwith's workload. Britain's orders in council, particularly those of November 6 targeting trade to and from France's Caribbean holdings, made American ships and their crews vulnerable to capture and imprisonment. In a March 7, 1794, report to Secretary of State Randolph, Skipwith explained that the British had seized "about two hundred and twenty sail of American vessels" and taken them into various British-controlled ports. As the U.S. consul in Martinique, Skipwith worked to aid the captured American sailors throughout the Caribbean, including procuring "a sufficiency of bread, beef and water to support them to their respective homes." He pointed out that without such assistance, many of these seamen "would have entered the foreign [government's] service."[6]

In addition to Skipwith's reports, Washington learned firsthand of American ship seizures from maritime citizens who petitioned the U.S. government for assistance. On May 6, 1794, John G. Wachsmuth and three other "citizens of the United States" described the "different losses they met with, by the captures of the following vessels and cargoes taken and carried by the British cruisers to the Island of Jamaica."[7] A week later Washington received a petition "from a committee appointed by numerous citizens of the United States holding claims against the French Republic." Their principal complaint was that they had not been paid for goods they had shipped to the French colonies of Saint Domingue and elsewhere.[8] The administration also became actively involved in the rescue of Joshua Barney, a ship captain and naval veteran of the Revolutionary War, whose ship, the *Sampson*, was seized by the British in Santo Domingo.[9] Randolph arranged for both transportation and a passport to bring Barney from Jamaica to Baltimore, although the U.S. government did not pay the $525 bill for the journey.[10]

FIGURE 7. Commodore Joshua Barney of Baltimore, Maryland, one of the many ship captains the U.S. government rescued from the Caribbean as part of its neutrality policy. (Maryland Historical Society; painted by Rembrandt Peale 1817)

Skipwith's efforts to aid Americans trapped throughout the Caribbean came to an abrupt end with Britain's capture of Martinique in March 1794. Unable to conduct consular or any other business on the war-torn island, Skipwith returned to the United States a month later. (His meandering journey to Philadelphia included the British navy seizing and impounding his ship.)[11] He quickly returned to consular and diplomatic duties, accompanying the newly appointed minister to France, James Monroe, to serve as consul general to the legation.[12] In May 1794, Congress authorized $900 to reimburse the "just and reasonable expenses incurred by Fulwar Skipwith, in relieving the wants, and facilitating the return of the seamen" seized in the British West Indies.[13] This payment underscored the critical assistance Skipwith had provided to Americans in the Caribbean and the enormous void his departure created.

The congressionally mandated embargoes of 1794 offered one strategy for protecting American shipping in the Caribbean by keeping the vessels at home. Washington, however, recognized the more urgent need to continue Skipwith's relief efforts, this time with a full-time representative possessing diplomatic authority.[14] In April 1794, the president named Philadelphia lawyer Nathaniel Cabot Higginson "as an agent on behalf of the United States, to proceed to the British West India Islands for certain purposes relating to the ships or vessels of the United States, which have been, or may be seized and sent into the ports of any of those islands."[15] In addition, Higginson received a warrant for $5,000 to cover his $2,000 salary as well as any expenses he might incur, including indemnifying ship losses. As special agent, he would be island-hopping across the British Caribbean, pursuant to Secretary of State Randolph's instructions to proceed "without delay to the Islands of Barbados, Tobago, Grenada, Martinico [sic], Dominica, Antigua, Montserrat, St. Christophers, San Domingo, Jamaica, and New Providence."[16] This diplomatic mission encountered an unexpected setback in its initial months when Higginson died soon after arriving in the British colony of Dominica.[17] Without an agent in the Caribbean to assist them, America's maritime citizens, their ships, and their cargoes remained in limbo, with no resolution in sight.

On December 5, 1793, Washington had explained to Congress that "the British government having undertaken, by orders to the commanders of their armed vessels, to restrain generally our commerce in corn and other provisions to their own ports" was one of the major reasons for American trading difficulties.[18] He, of course, was referring to the two orders in council. The first, dated June 8, 1793, labeled food stuffs heading to France, particularly grain, as contraband and aggressively repudiated the principle that America's free (that is, neutral) ships meant free goods. The second hostile British order, dated November 6 targeted American ships carrying goods from France's Caribbean colonies.[19] Even indirectly, British actions, such as a 1793 truce negotiated between Portugal and Algiers permitting Barbary pirates to cross the Straits of Gibraltar and enter the Atlantic, made American ships vulnerable to attacks.[20] With the British government's aggressive policies resulting in an undeclared war on U.S. shipping, Washington sought a peaceful solution through the nomination of Chief Justice Jay as a special envoy to Britain.[21]

In assuming the position of "extraordinary envoy," Jay was not replacing the current U.S. minister to Britain, Thomas Pinckney of South Carolina. Instead, his role focused exclusively on securing a commercial treaty with Britain. Jay, who remained chief justice of the U.S. Supreme Court, had amassed significant diplomat experience under the Confederation Congress, including serving as its secretary of foreign affairs, its minister to London, and a delegate to the 1783 Treaty of Paris negotiations. Washington hoped that his stature and experience would ensure the success of this complex and delicate mission.[22]

The detailed instructions Jay received captured the long list of U.S. grievances since 1783 as well as the young nation's almost naive hope that a treaty with Britain would resolve them. Hamilton and other prominent Federalists took the lead in drafting the guidelines of Jay's mission, with Secretary of State Randolph modifying and then submitting them to the envoy on May 6, 1794.[23] Consisting of six major sections, Randolph began the document by counseling Jay to avoid a "wound" to Pinckney's "sensibility" by assuming this role of envoy. He then stated bluntly that the United States hoped to avoid war, but at the same time, the nation intended "to assert with dignity and firmness of our rights and our title to reparation for past injuries." Of course, Randolph was referring to the numerous "vexations and spoliations" occurring under the British orders of June 8 and November 6, 1793. Specifically, Jay should seek "compensations for all the injuries sustained," while "captures will be strenuously pressed by you." Another area of concern were British attempts to compromise America's friendships and alliances with other nations, particularly France. Randolph reminded Jay of the neutral stance of the United States, being "free in our affections and independent in our government," and stressed "that our neutrality has been scrupulously observed."[24]

Randolph's instructions also focused on outstanding issues from the 1783 Treaty of Paris, a topic with which Jay already possessed great familiarity. The United States sought compensation for damaged property, including enslaved laborers, and also wanted Britain to abandon its North American forts because "one of the consequences of holding the posts has been much bloodshed on our frontiers by the Indians." A central component of Jay's mission concerned the negotiation of a commercial treaty with Britain that guaranteed "reciprocity in navigation"; "the admission of wheat, fish, salt meat, and other great staples, upon the same footing ... as British staples in our ports"; the affirmation that "free ships make free goods"; "security for neutral commerce"; "no privateering commissions to be taken out by the subjects" of either nation; and U.S. "consuls to be admitted in Europe, the West and East Indies." Randolph offered two important caveats for this potential treaty. One, "if a treaty of commerce cannot be formed upon a basis as advantageous as this, you are not to conclude or sign any such" agreement at all. A second deal breaker would be any provision that would "detach us from France" or "derogate from our treaties and engagements with France." Lastly, once Jay arrived in London, he should reach out to the diplomats from the League of Armed Neutrality nations—Sweden, Russia, and Denmark—who were considering reestablishing this alliance.[25] With high expectations surrounding this mission, Jay boarded a boat for Britain on May 12, 1794.[26]

For the next six months, Jay engaged in negotiations with Lord Grenville, the secretary for foreign affairs and an architect of the aggressive orders in council against American trade. Despite the obstacles Jay faced in convincing Britain to cease such hostile policies toward the United States, the government proved more receptive to his overtures than might be expected. The war with France had been draining the government of allies and resources, and remaining at peace with the United States presented an attractive option.[27] Of course, Jay would not get everything he sought, but Grenville took the negotiations seriously and even made some concessions. Jay succeeded in getting Britain to abandon its western military posts and to indemnify American shipping losses occurring in the current war. The biggest disappointments centered on free trade. Britain dismissed American neutrality through its refusal to affirm the principle "free ships make free goods" along with its continued policy of regarding foodstuffs as contraband.[28]

Amid these mixed results, Jay addressed two additional issues that were not in the original instructions: impressment of American sailors and shipping losses in the Caribbean. In discussions with Grenville, he raised the topic of the Royal Navy impressing American sailors and even succeeded in getting an anti-impressment provision in an early draft of the treaty. Although this article did not make it into the final version, the issue was not as controversial as it later would become, largely because the impressments were occurring in British ports and not from American ships. Over time, the Royal Navy became more aggressive in its capture of American seamen, including attacking American ships in open water and seizing their crews. With its disruption of American transatlantic commerce and its violation of U.S. sovereignty, shipboard impressment would be one of the primary causes of the War of 1812.[29]

The administration's Caribbean mission enjoyed an unexpected revival during Jay's negotiations, even though this topic had not been included in his instructions. Upon his arrival, Jay came to realize the value of sending an envoy to London with exclusive responsibility for resolving American shipping losses, particularly those in the Caribbean.[30] His recommendation coincided with a letter from Philadelphia's merchants, led by Thomas FitzSimons, who requested that a U.S. agent be sent to Britain to adjudicate their losses. (In the spring of 1794, FitzSimons's ship *Sally* had been captured in the Atlantic and condemned in British Bermuda.)[31] In response to Jay and FitzSimons, Washington appointed Samuel Bayard, a Philadelphia lawyer and U.S. Supreme Court clerk, to prosecute claims before British admiralty courts.[32] Following the instructions originally written for Higginson, Bayard arrived in London in December 1794 to pursue his first case: compensation for the *Sally*.[33]

With the negotiations completed on November 19, 1794, Jay and the finished treaty journeyed across the Atlantic to gain its approval from the federal government and the American people. The treaty arrived in Philadelphia on March 7, 1795, and Washington called the recently recessed Senate back into session on June 8 to begin their deliberations.[34] Controversy quickly swirled around the agreement officially known as the Treaty of Amity, Commerce, and Navigation. Democratic-Republicans had opposed Jay's mission at the outset, favoring a new approach that lessened U.S. dependency on Britain as a trading partner.[35] Washington and Randolph also made the fateful decision not to divulge its provisions to the public, and the Senate deliberated in secret. Its terms were officially revealed *after* its ratification on June 24, 1795, by a vote of 20 to 10, further fueling the partisan and popular backlash the congressional opposition had already ignited. Perhaps most problematic were the treaty's actual provisions, twenty-eight in all, which paled in comparison to Jay's lofty instructions.[36] The principle opposition to the agreement, of course, centered on Britain's unwillingness to respect the U.S. right to free trade and therefore, its neutral stance in the current war, a glaring contrast with the relationship America had with France in its Treaty of Amity and Commerce.[37]

Despite these shortcomings, Jay had made progress in several areas. First, Britain agreed to abandon its western military posts, beginning in June 1796, although critics contended that this departure should occur sooner. Second, American ships of all sizes would be allowed to trade in the East Indies, while vessels under seventy tons could trade in the British West Indies. The limits on West Indian trade, composing Article XII, became a rallying cry for the treaty's opponents (and even some of its supporters like Hamilton); the Senate asserted its authority by striking it from the ratified document.[38] Lastly, the agreement established several commissions to, among other things, identify the river that formed the Canadian boundary in Maine (Article V), to address prerevolutionary American debts owed to British merchants (Article VI), and to consider ship losses and cargo seizures occurring in the current Anglo-French war (Article

VII). Funding these commissions provided an additional opportunity for Congress to oppose Jay's Treaty, as it became known, with the House of Representatives engaged in a contentious debate over the $90,000 needed to support them. The appropriation was eventually approved by the narrow margin of 51 to 48.[39]

The panel established under Article VII, known as the "seizure" commission, essentially codified the Skipwith/Higginson/Bayard missions. During its tenure, this committee provided significant financial remuneration to American ships (and some British ones), demonstrating the value of the federal government's intervention on behalf of its maritime citizens. The commission consisted of five members: two British, two American, and one chosen randomly. Washington appointed two attorneys: Christopher Gore of Massachusetts, who had been serving as district attorney for that state, and William Pinkney of Maryland, a state politician.[40] Their British counterparts were John Nicholl and Nicholas Antsey, both experienced maritime lawyers. The fifth spot went to the American Revolutionary War veteran and painter Colonel John Trumbull. Although Trumbull had recently served as Jay's secretary at the treaty negotiations, he lacked legal and diplomatic experience, owing his appointment largely to the fact that he was already in London.[41] Article VII instructed the commissioners to address shipping losses that could not obtain adequate damages in the "ordinary course of judicial proceedings" or under the standards established in Jefferson's September 5, 1793, letter to George Hammond, where he had announced the U.S. policy of indemnifying foreign ships captured in American waters, including Britain's.[42]

The London-based commission began its work in 1796 by considering the cases of two American ships, the *Betsey* (not to be confused with the sloop *Betsey*), seized in the West Indies, and the *Sally*, captured in the Atlantic en route to France.[43] With American ships making up the bulk of the losses, the U.S. commissioners found themselves playing offense against Britain's defensive maneuvers. In the case of the *Betsey*, British commissioner Nicholl contended that the panel had no jurisdiction over the matter because the vice-admiralty ruling in Bermuda was final. The three American commissioners overruled their British counterparts and awarded the *Betsey*'s owners $28,000 for their losses. Nicholl made a similar argument in the case of the *Sally*, but instead of waiting to be outvoted, he and his co-commissioner abandoned the panel for three years to prevent the case from proceeding. The British commissioners eventually returned to the table and completed their work in 1804. During its nine-year existence, the Article VII commission heard over 600 cases and made awards totaling $6.8 million, with $6.7 million going to 553 American and $143,000 to twelve British shippers.[44] Philadelphia merchant FitzSimons, the owner of the *Sally* who had pushed for a U.S. commercial agent in London, received $5,200 for his loss.[45] (Likewise, during the Adams and Jefferson administrations, Skipwith, in his role as commercial agent in France, would pursue American claims against the French government, with mixed results.)[46]

Alongside these small victories, the opposition to Jay's Treaty had the ironic effect of demonstrating popular support for Washington's neutrality policy. Numerous resolutions poured into Philadelphia from coastal cities that were dismayed that the treaty had not done more to uphold American neutrality and to protect American shipping and seamen. Boston citizens opposed the treaty "because it surrenders all, or most of the benefits, of a commercial nature, which we had a right to expect, from our neutrality in the present European war."[47] Similarly, New York citizens proclaimed, "As a neutral, and commercial people . . . , the United States should never voluntarily consent to any article prohibiting *free* vessels from making *free* goods."[48] Citizens from Sussex County, Virginia, (located near the James River) complained that the treaty was "degrading to the [nation's] dignity because no adequate reparation is made by Britain for insulting our Flag, obstructing our commerce, imprisoning our citizens and impressing our seamen."[49] Through these petitions, port cities muscularly asserted the rights and respect the United States should enjoy with its trading partners, particularly Great Britain, and in doing so enshrined the concept of neutrality as an American priority.

Jay's inability to fully achieve his diplomatic instructions reflected less his failure as a negotiator and more the weak hand Americans held against the formidable British. Most historians have concluded that Jay's Treaty, for all its flaws, represented the best the United States could hope for in these negotiations.[50] The most enduring legacy of the agreement reflected Washington's pragmatism in appointing an envoy to Britain to head off warfare with this powerful nation. As the president had explained to Secretary of State Randolph in nominating Jay for this diplomatic mission, "my objects are, to prevent a war."[51] Through its promotion of American neutrality without bloodshed, this agreement represented a major achievement in Washington's international vision of peace and independence for the United States and demonstrated his underappreciated skills as a statesman.

In November 1794 Washington launched a second diplomatic mission to Europe, this one receiving a warmer welcome than its British counterpart. Interested in pursuing peace in Europe and North America, King Charles IV of Spain encouraged the president to appoint a U.S. envoy to resolve questions about the nation's western boundary along the Mississippi River. Washington had shared news of this overture in his December 16, 1793, address to Congress, including his appointment of commissioners to conclude a treaty dealing with the "subjects of boundary, navigation and commerce."[52]

The U.S. territories abutting Spanish Louisiana, particularly Kentucky, had long been a hotbed of military unrest, as Genet's abortive western campaign and the subsequent Neutrality Proclamation of 1794 had made clear.[53] At the same time, Spain had grown tired of European warfare and was seeking ways to break its military alliance with Britain through a peace treaty with France.[54] Their desire to avoid a North American war over the Louisiana territory, as well as concerns about British plans on that continent, further motivated Spain to seek a diplomatic solution to issues surrounding the Mississippi River.[55]

On July 26, 1794, the Spanish government formally requested the appointment of an American envoy: "His Catholic Majesty desires that the President send a person with full power . . . for a treaty of alliance to be independent of the circumstances and relationships of the [present European] war."[56] Although the United States already had two envoys in Madrid, William Carmichael and William Short, Spain dismissed them "as most addicted to France" and lacking the authority to successfully negotiate a treaty.[57] Seeking to accommodate this request, Washington once again engaged in diplomatic musical chairs to produce a candidate with the requisite stature. After both Jefferson and Patrick Henry declined to serve in this post, he nominated the U.S. minister to Britain, Pinckney, as the "envoy extraordinary" to Spain.[58] In his letter of introduction, the president assured King Charles IV that the South Carolinian possessed the "fidelity, probity, and good conduct" to "render himself acceptable to your Majesty."[59] Pinckney's instructions, supporting America's neutral aspirations of international peacefulness and territorial sovereignty, directed him to negotiate a treaty "concerning the navigation of the river Mississippi, and such other matters relative to the confines of their territories."[60] Pinckney's nomination sailed through the Senate unanimously on November 24, 1794, reflecting the country's less contentious relationship with Spain.[61]

The favorable environment that had produced Pinckney's mission resulted in an equally successful final agreement. Within the treaty's twenty-three provisions, Pinckney defined the boundaries of Spain's North American holdings and also secured the U.S. right of navigation on the Mississippi River. The treaty also gave the United States the "right of deposit" in the bustling Spanish port of New Orleans. This provision meant that America's maritime citizens could store and sell their merchandise in this commercially and geographically advantageous city without having to pay additional duties. Finally, the treaty established commissioners (similar to Jay's Treaty) to resolve spoliation cases emanating from assaults on Spanish and American shipping during the current war.[62]

While the treaty did not offer the generous free-trade provisions of the Franco-American Treaty of Amity and Commerce, the resolution of commercial and boundary issues along the Mississippi River settled longstanding tensions and gave the United States a crucial foothold for westward expansion.[63] Pinckney's Treaty, also known as the Treaty of San Lorenzo and the Treaty of San Ildefonso because of the migrating negotiation venues, was signed on October 27, 1795. Washington affirmed the "general approbation" for Pinckney's efforts when he shared the news that the Senate unanimously ratified the agreement on March 3, 1796.[64] With the approval of this treaty, the United States could point to two successful negotiations with European powers that affirmed its rights on land and sea.

The most expensive and longest-lasting negotiations of Washington's presidency (and beyond) occurred with the Mediterranean states of Algiers and Morocco. The independent empire of Morocco and the semiautonomous Ottoman regency of Algiers were home to aggressive and ruthless "corsairs," or pirates, who preyed on European and American shipping. Piracy ebbed and flowed in relation to the Portuguese navy's blockade of the Straits of Gibraltar, preventing these states from sending vessels into the Atlantic.[65] Not content to simply seize ships and cargoes, pirates also kidnapped seamen and demanded exorbitant ransoms for their release. If the ransoms were not paid, captured sailors would be sold into slavery and a life of hard labor in mines or in ship galleys. Such barbaric practices led European and American sailors to dub these Mediterranean nations the "Barbary States."[66]

The lifting of Portugal's blockade in 1785 had left American ships vulnerable to Algerian piracy, and in May and December of that year, the *Maria* and the *Dauphin*, along with twenty-one sailors, were captured in the open Atlantic. The cash-strapped Confederation Congress managed to raise $80,000 in order to purchase treaties with Algiers, Tunis, Tripoli, and Morocco and sent an envoy, John Lamb, to handle the negotiations. The dey of Algiers wanted more than half that sum, $48,000, merely to release the twenty-one American hostages, resulting in the collapse of Lamb's efforts.[67] The captured seamen languished in Algerian prisons until 1792, when thirteen of the surviving captives petitioned the U.S. government for help.[68]

Appointing a new envoy to the Mediterranean states launched an additional front in Washington's international campaign to promote U.S. sovereignty abroad and to protect the rights of its maritime citizens. As he had done in the three earlier annual messages to Congress, Washington used his fourth address in 1793 to announce his diplomatic goals in the Mediterranean region of "obtaining recognition of our Treaty with Morocco, and for the ransom of our Citizens and the establishment of peace with Algiers."[69] This formal notification to Congress built on efforts already underway by Secretary of State Jefferson, including the appointment of an envoy to Algiers as well as the disbursement of the $20,000 already appropriated to obtain a treaty with Morocco.[70] Tragedy once again slowed negotiations. The first envoy, John Paul Jones of naval fame, died before he even reached Algiers, as did his successor, Thomas Barclay. The third appointee, Colonel David Humphreys, a Revolutionary War veteran and current minister to Portugal, successfully reached Algiers and began the arduous task of negotiating the release of the American seamen.[71]

The diplomatic situation Humphreys entered in September 1793 had been further complicated by the recent peace treaty between Britain and Portugal, which reopened the Atlantic to Algerian vessels. By October, the pirates had captured eleven more American ships and imprisoned over a hundred seamen. This latest round of assaults angered Congress, which soon authorized establishing the U.S. Navy, consisting of six frigates to protect American shipping in the Mediterranean region and elsewhere.[72] Amid these challenges, Humphreys, with the assistance of Joel Barlow (1754–1812), fellow poet and U.S. consul to Algiers, represented the United States, while one of the American captives, James Leander Cathcart, acted on behalf of the dey of Algiers.[73] The resulting treaty, achieved in 1795, led to the release of the surviving American hostages. In exchange, the United States would pay $642,500, supply three naval frigates, and offer an annual tribute of $21,600 in naval supplies.[74] Although costly, this agreement encouraged settlements with Tunis and Tripoli for $107,000 and ensured a cessation in assaults, at least for the time being. The Washington administration's successful foray into Mediterranean diplomacy also included the required renewal of an earlier commercial agreement, the 1786 treaty with Morocco.[75] The 1795 treaty, like its predecessor, offered more symbolic value than economic benefits. Nonetheless, it reaffirmed the young nation's commitment to free trade and its promotion of U.S. autonomy and sovereignty across the globe, particularly in the turbulent Mediterranean.[76]

The president's annual address to Congress in December 1795, occurring exactly two years after he had announced these diplomatic missions, served as a victory lap for the administration's international accomplishments. An unusually ebullient Washington declared that more so than any other time, the current period of American "public affairs has afforded just cause for mutual congratulation." He then proceeded to list the successful treaty negotiations with Morocco, Algiers, Spain, and Great Britain. These agreements affirmed the wisdom of Washington's neutrality policy as well as his political skills in leading an international campaign to promote American neutrality, to protect the nation's maritime citizens, to avoid warfare, and to assert U.S. sovereignty as an independent nation. He concluded, "The extinguishment of all the causes of our external discord . . . on terms compatible with our national rights and honor, shall be the happy result," adding, "how firm and how precious a foundation will have been laid for accelerating, maturing and establishing the prosperity of our country!"[77]

One immediate challenge for Washington and his administration was the cost of international diplomacy. While the agreements with the Mediterranean states proved to be expensive, the other treaties also came with price tags. On March 31, 1796, Secretary of State Timothy Pickering reported to both houses of Congress the expenses associated with implementing the provisions of the accords. Jay's Treaty cost around $80,000, while Pinckney's Treaty was estimated to be $18,000, with the bulk of these costs associated with the ongoing commissions. The treaty with Algiers came in at a whopping $762,000.[78] These expenses, of course, did not include the monies needed to build a navy, erect coastal defenses, and fund the militias, also important pieces in the protection of America's maritime economy.

The costs associated with treaty making, of course, had important policy and partisan ramifications. These international burdens came at a time when the U.S. government was still struggling to pay off its Revolutionary War debts. Hamilton's 1790 "Report on the Public Credit" had recognized the need to place the young nation on a sound financial footing in order to ensure its "strength and security." Defending the nation's interests militarily, both in the West and in the Atlantic, had long been identified as crucial functions of the new government.[79] Washington's treaties demonstrated that financial resources were also needed to keep the nation in peace and promote its interests. These agreements, with their long-term financial and political ramifications, also contributed to the growth of the executive branch's power and influence. Washington's presidential successors, Jefferson and Madison, would rely on the nation's public credit to purchase Louisiana and to fund its war effort in 1812.[80] But as current leaders of the Democratic-Republican opposition, which favored a smaller national government and more congressional influence, the extension of Hamilton's financial approach into international affairs and the accompanying expansion of the executive branch's authority dismayed them.[81]

Washington's diplomatic efforts established the precedent of peacefully promoting U.S. interests abroad. But with America's weight in the world still relatively small, there were limits to what diplomacy could accomplish. When negotiations failed, Washington's successors turned to military force to garner the attention and respect of more powerful nations. In 1798, John Adams conducted a "Quasi-War" by arming American merchant ships to fend off French trading assaults.[82] In 1801, Jefferson deployed the fledgling U.S. Navy to the Mediterranean to address Tripoli's renewed attacks against American ships. And in 1812 Madison pursued war against Britain to stop its aggressive practices against American ships, including impressment.[83] The reliance on military force to promote and sustain U.S. priorities would open new chapters in the nation's diplomatic history.

THE YEAR 1794 was a momentous one in the implementation of U.S. foreign-policy goals. These priorities had been crafted a year earlier in the Neutrality Proclamation, which announced America's intention to remain friendly with warring nations but not to take sides in the growing conflict. In December 1793, Washington delivered one lengthy annual address to Congress and three shorter ones in which he outlined the foreign-policy initiatives he intended to pursue with Britain, France, Spain, and the Mediterranean "Barbary States" in order to promote and secure American neutrality. With the domestic implementation of this policy well underway, the administration turned its attention to its international enforcement, in conjunction with Congress. During this whirlwind year of diplomacy, the United States posted envoys to London, Madrid, the French Martinique in the Caribbean, and to the Mediterranean states of Algiers and Morocco to defend U.S. autonomy and to protect its citizens. While the resulting negotiations might have been longer, costlier, and less favorable than Washington, his administration, Congress, and the American people may have wanted, they could nonetheless point to a string of diplomatic successes that avoided war, compensated ship captains, liberated sailors, and raised the young nation's standing throughout the globe. With his skilled execution of this policy at both home and abroad, Washington successfully launched America's neutral stance and built a federal government capable of enforcing it.

Conclusion

"First in Peace": George Washington, Statesman

THE FINAL YEARS OF Washington's presidency were not happy ones for him. Despite substantial achievements in launching the republican government, including the successful implementation of the neutrality policy, Washington found himself exhausted from the demands of the job and frustrated with the increasingly personal attacks made by partisan newspapers. The politically diverse cabinet that had carefully crafted and methodically enforced neutrality through a series of delicate compromises no longer existed. In addition, the president confronted the missteps of two Democratic-Republicans in his administration, Edmund Randolph and James Monroe, whose partisan biases undercut his policies. Despite Washington's sense of disappointment and even failure, American neutrality helped launch the United States as an independent, sovereign nation, both at home and abroad, and served as an enduring cornerstone of U.S. foreign policy well into the nineteenth century. In crafting the proclamation and then implementing it through the federal government's three branches and across the globe, Washington demonstrated his mastery as a political negotiator and established his enduring presidential legacy as a statesman who kept the young nation at peace.

SEVERAL WEEKS AFTER announcing America's foreign-policy triumphs to Congress, Washington sounded a very different note in a letter to Gouverneur Morris, the former minister to France.[1] Written on December 22, 1795, he reiterated his neutrality policy: "It is well know that peace has been the order of the day for me, since the disturbances in Europe first commenced." Yet, the president lamented, "by a firm adherence to these principles, and to the neutral policy which has been adopted, I have brought on myself a torrent of abuse in the factious papers in this country." In particular, Washington focused on the Democratic-Republican opposition to Jay's Treaty. Although conceding that "a more favorable one were to have been wished," he argued that the final document had its merits and was not as unpopular or as terrible as its opponents contended.[2]

As Washington bemoaned rising partisanship, he only needed to look at his administration to see its corrosive effects. By early 1795, his cabinet had completely turned over. Lacking the range of views that had forged the neutrality policy, with Jefferson and Randolph on one philosophical side and Hamilton and Knox on the other, it now consisted of four new members, all Federalists.[3] Randolph's forced resignation in August 1795 transformed Washington's cabinet into a partisan entity and made explicit the deep political divisions among its original members that had been previously held in check. Randolph enjoyed the distinction of being Washington's longest-serving cabinet member, having held the posts of attorney general and then secretary of state. After Jefferson's departure, he was also the only Democratic-Republican remaining. His continued service to Washington in two critical positions made him a reliable, hardworking, and trusted advisor, even if he lacked the political and philosophical brilliance of Jefferson or Hamilton. News of Randolph's later political missteps hit Washington hard, particularly his desire to elevate governing above partisanship.[4]

Randolph's dramatic departure from the administration occurred for two reasons: first, because he committed misdeeds, and second, because his Federalists colleagues in the cabinet, notably Timothy Pickering and Oliver Wolcott, made sure Washington knew about them. In March 1795, a British ship had captured the *Jean Bart*, a vessel carrying French minister to the United States Fauchet's diplomatic dispatches to France. These papers were eventually handed over to the British minister to the United States, George Hammond, who then shared them with Secretary of the Treasury Wolcott. Three of the dispatches, the third, sixth, and tenth, contained incriminating partisan information about Randolph and the Whiskey Rebellion. In Dispatch 10, dated October 31, 1794, Randolph discussed the rebellion with Fauchet and its implications for Democratic-Republican politics. In Dispatch 3, written on June 3, Randolph reported to Fauchet that Washington's administration had "hastened the local eruption, to make an advantageous diversion, and to lay the more general storm which it saw was gathering." Perhaps most damaging to Randolph was Dispatch 6, written on September 5, in which the secretary of state attempted to raise money from Fauchet in order to promote pro-French policies within the administration.[5]

After Washington reviewed translations of these dispatches (helpfully provided by Secretary of War Pickering), the president summoned Randolph to explain his betrayal of administration policy. This meeting occurred on August 19, with Pickering and Wolcott also present. Randolph, unable to challenge the veracity of these documents, submitted his resignation to Washington later that day.⁶ While continuing to deny any wrongdoing, he was unable to successfully dispute the contents of Fauchet's dispatches.⁷

Another partisan disappointment confronted Washington, this one coming from France. In 1794, the president had reached across the widening partisan aisle and nominated Monroe to be the new minister to France. He saw this appointment as an opportunity to soothe partisan discord and to also send an envoy more favorable to the French. Monroe, of course, was the friend and neighbor of the two leading Democratic-Republicans, Jefferson and Madison. He was also a strong supporter of the French Revolution, in contrast to his predecessor, Morris, whose disdain for it had led Paris to ask for his recall.⁸ Washington nominated Monroe on May 27, and the new minister sailed a month later.⁹

While Monroe's mistakes marred his brief tenure as minister to France, he also entered a chaotic political situation. The Committee on Public Safety, which had presided over the Reign of Terror, still controlled foreign affairs, although the National Convention also claimed governing authority. Amid this political confusion, Monroe hastily presented his credentials to the National Convention. Immediately afterward, he delivered a speech stressing the bonds between the two republics, their similar governments, their commitment to rights, and their shared military struggle for independence, which France was still fighting.¹⁰ These remarks, particularly the linking of the American Revolution with France's current upheaval, undercut U.S. policy to remain aloof from the European conflict.

The excesses of this speech could be attributed to the excitement and confusion of the moment. But Monroe committed a more serious mistake when he placed his partisan preferences above U.S. policy. Concerned about the effects of Jay's Treaty on Franco-American relations, he shared a summary of its contents with the French government.¹¹ Washington was understandably livid when he received the news. In response, he urged Monroe not "to sow the seeds of distrust in the French nation, and to excite their belief of an influence, possessed by Great Britain"; most importantly, he urged his minister to "maintain" America's "strict neutrality."¹² Despite this admonition, Washington had already decided to recall Monroe. With Randolph no longer in the cabinet to defend the Virginian, Washington informed the new secretary of state, Pickering, that he sought a minister "who will promote, not thwart the neutral policy of the government."¹³ With the arrival in Paris of Monroe's successor, Federalist Charles Cotesworth Pinckney, in December 1796, the Washington administration no longer had a bipartisan cast.¹⁴

Although the political missteps of Randolph and Monroe added color to Washington's second term, they should not be allowed to obscure the greater achievements associated with the formulation and implementation of neutrality at home and abroad. First among these accomplishments was the administration's decision to avoid participating in the European conflict, despite pressure from France and Britain. This approach ensured that U.S. autonomy and sovereignty would be upheld. It also set the precedent that U.S. foreign policy should put American needs first and avoid cumbersome alliances.

With assaults on American shipping testing the strength of this policy, Washington and his administration made a series of powerful decisions to enforce neutrality. The United States banned privateering in its ports and instructed customs officers to report privateering violations, authorized U.S. district attorneys to prosecute them, and empowered state governors to use the militias, if needed, to enforce such measures. The U.S. government also defined its oceanic boundaries and agreed to indemnify foreign ships captured in these waters. Lastly, the administration took the bold step of requesting the recall of Citizen Genet, whose activities had done so much to undercut the country's neutral stance. All of these decisions were the product of consensus among Washington and his cabinet. As the policy's chief architect, the president approved every document, letter, and policy statement that emanated from his administration dealing with neutrality. As he steered the United States onto this course, Washington demonstrated his skills as a political negotiator as well as his commitment to peace.

With the convening of Congress in December 1793, Washington and his administration found a valuable constitutional partner that passed laws to expand the domestic enforcement of neutrality. His 1795 letter to Pickering summarized these legislative achievements: "the fortifications and defenses of several harbors," the building of six naval frigates, and "the erecting and repairing of arsenals and magazines."[15] Additionally, Congress passed several embargoes to protect American shipping from the British navy's assaults. Lastly, it codified the two neutrality proclamations into the Neutrality Act of 1794, which legally banned privateering in American waters and prohibited U.S. citizens from participating in foreign conflicts. The third branch of the government, the judiciary, was slower to define its constitutional role in the enforcement of neutrality, but under the leadership of Chief Justice Jay, the Supreme Court ultimately asserted its authority over admiralty cases.

As the assault on neutrality occurred on a global scale as well as in American waters, Washington launched diplomatic offensives intended to resolve these encroachments. By 1794, envoys could be found in London, Madrid, Lisbon,

Algiers, and the Caribbean promoting American neutrality and coming to the aid of U.S. ship captains and sailors whose vessels had been captured and condemned. Early in the Anglo-French war, some maritime citizens, such as Gideon Henfield, sought to profit from French privateering. While the U.S. government prohibited Americans from serving on foreign privateers, the administration successfully negotiated financial compensation for lost ships and cargoes, sending vessels to rescue stranded American sailors. Through these diplomatic agreements, the seafaring community came to see the value of the government's involvement in the protection of American shipping.

In September 1796 Washington issued a farewell address to "Friends, and Fellow Citizens" in which he summarized the major accomplishments of his presidency as well as his concerns for the future. This lengthy message, possessing a bipartisan tinge, was not a speech.[16] Instead, it appeared in a Philadelphia newspaper, the *American Daily Advertiser*, on September 19, 1796, as an "open letter" to the American people from "an old and affectionate friend."[17] In this valedictory, Washington highlighted the themes that had guided his presidency: promoting national unity, strengthening republican government, upholding the Constitution's principles, avoiding partisanship, and pursuing American neutrality. Washington explained that his 1793 Neutrality Proclamation served as the "index to the plan," then listed the various reasons the United States should "steer clear of permanent alliances, with any portion of the foreign world." First, these overseas conflicts stemmed from complex alliances and rivalries that had nothing to do with the United States. Instead, "such an attachment of a small or weak, towards a great and powerful Nation, dooms the former to be the satellite of the latter." Second, foreign entanglements were "one of the baneful foes of republican government." While he urged that the United States "observe good faith and justice towards all nations," he also stressed the importance "in extending our commercial relations to have with them as little political connection as possible."[18] As Washington said farewell to the nation, he declared neutrality to be the signature issue of his presidency, thus securing his presidential legacy as a skilled diplomat and prescient statesman.[19]

Washington's accomplishments in promoting and implementing neutrality can be seen in the foreign-policy decisions of his successors. Although the neutrality policy sent a strong message to the world that the young United States intended to be an autonomous and sovereign nation, international challenges persisted. John Adams confronted French assaults on U.S. ships during the Quasi-War of 1798, while Thomas Jefferson and James Madison dealt with Britain's continued attacks on American vessels, including the practice of impressment. The Convention of Mortefontaine in 1800 finally disentangled the United States from its treaty obligations with France, while a war with Britain in 1812 would be needed to resolve the longstanding trading problems with that nation.[20] And despite the large financial commitments, tensions continued with the Algerian pirates until a peace treaty was reached in 1815.[21] Amid these challenges, each president followed the path established by Washington: defend U.S. interests and avoid entanglements in foreign conflicts. The continued pursuit of American neutrality beyond Washington's administration demonstrated the wisdom and vision of this policy. Its longevity also showed that the partisan divide in foreign policy was never as great as it was in domestic affairs.

IN HINDSIGHT, the neutrality policy seems like a "no-brainer." Of course the young nation should remain aloof from European warfare and not become entangled in conflicts that did not concern the United States. Pursuing friendly commercial relationships with all nations, regardless of their political associations, also made sense. The significance of the Neutrality Proclamation lies in its explicitness. Through a written document, the United States announced to its citizens and the rest of the world its intention to remain neutral in the current European war. This policy gained added strength from Washington's steadfast commitment to its implementation, both at home and abroad. Working with a divided cabinet, the president pursued policy compromises designed to ensure the successful enforcement of neutrality. With the executive branch leading the way in foreign affairs, this policy eventually gained the support of the Constitution's other branches, Congress and the judiciary. American neutrality endured through the nineteenth century because this approach provided the best path for the young nation to participate, grow, and even thrive in the world.

At George Washington's funeral, Henry Lee, Virginia's governor and a Revolutionary War veteran, famously and succinctly eulogized the late president as "first in peace, first in war, and first in the hearts of the nation."[22] From the battlefield, Washington had witnessed deadly European rivalries firsthand. These experiences resulted in his deep commitment to American neutrality as president, when he pursued peace and established his enduring legacy as a statesman. Thanks to Washington's unique experiences with war *and* peace, the United States built a neutral government capable of ensuring this policy's success and the nation's longevity.

NOTES

Abbreviations

ASP   *American State Papers: Foreign Relations*, vol. 1
PAH   Harold C. Syrett and Jacob E. Cooke, eds., *The Papers of Alexander Hamilton*, 29 vols. (New York: Columbia University Press, 1961–87)
PGW-CS   W. W. Abbot et al., eds., *The Papers of George Washington, Confederation Series*, 6 vols. (Charlottesville: University Press of Virginia, 1992–[97])
PGW-PS   Dorothy Twohig, ed., *The Papers of George Washington, Presidential Series*, 20 vols. (Charlottesville: University of Virginia Press, 1987–[2019])
PTJ   Julian P. Boyd et al., eds., *The Papers of Thomas Jefferson*, 44 vols. (Princeton, NJ: Princeton University Press, 1950–[2017])

Introduction

1. *PGW-PS*, 12:396n1.
2. Leibiger, *Founding Friendship*, 153–154.
3. Throughout the nineteenth century and into the early twentieth century, presidents from Thomas Jefferson through Theodore Roosevelt issued neutrality statements or passed neutrality laws to discourage Americans from becoming embroiled in foreign wars. See Fenwick, *Neutrality Laws of the United States*, 31, 33, 39, 40, 43, 44, 45, 46, 48, 52, 53, 55, 56, 57, 58.
4. In the 1930s a series of neutrality acts were passed to prevent American involvement in what would become World War II. See Fenwick, *American Neutrality*, 34–35, 37, 40, 46–47. Reflecting scholarly and popular interest in the topic, a comprehensive four-volume examination of neutrality was also published around this time. See Jessup and Deak, *Neutrality*. On American isolation prior to World War II, see Dallek, *Franklin D. Roosevelt and American Foreign Policy*.
5. Two recent books dedicate a chapter to the neutrality policy, both seeing it as one of the governing challenges of the early national period. Berkin, *Sovereign People*, identifies the neutrality proclamation as one of four "crises" in the 1790s but does not provide an in-depth examination of its formulation or implementation. Chervinsky's *The Cabinet*, highlights the major issues Washington and his cabinet confronted in formulating the

policy, along with some of the implementation challenges. Her primary concern, however, is with the cabinet's dynamics in formulating this and other policies rather than offering a comprehensive examination of neutrality.

6. On early American diplomacy, see Bowman, *Struggle for Neutrality*; DeConde, *Entangling Alliance*; Gilbert, *To the Farewell Address*; Varg, *Foreign Policies of the Founding Fathers*; and Combs, *Jay Treaty*. On the War of 1812, see Hickey, *War of 1812*; and Stagg, *Mr. Madison's War*. The volume in the series Oxford History of the United States dealing with foreign policy, George C. Herring's *From Colony to Superpower*, gives little attention to the actual proclamation, focusing instead on the rivalry between Hamilton and Jefferson.

7. See Thomas, *American Neutrality in 1793*; and Hyneman, *First American Neutrality*.

8. For an introduction to a globalized approach to American history, see McMahon, "Toward a Pluralist Vision"; Manela, "United States in the World"; and Kupperman, "International at the Creation."

9. Gilje, *Free Trade and Sailors' Rights*, 14, 17.

10. Kulsrud, "Armed Neutralities to 1780," 423–447.

11. Madariaga, *Britain, Russia, and the Armed Neutrality of 1780*, 156, 157, 169, 171. See also Scott, *Armed Neutralities of 1780 and 1800*.

12. For British and American perspectives on eighteenth-century privateering, see Starkey, *British Privateering Enterprise*; and Swanson, *Predators and Prizes*.

13. On America's early efforts to be viewed as "treaty worthy," see Gould, *Among the Powers of the Earth*.

14. For an introduction to the "neglected" field of American institutional history, see Novak, "Myth of the 'Weak' American State," 752–772. See also Edling, *Revolution in Favor of Government*; Edling, *Hercules in the Cradle*; Rao, *National Duties*; Chervinsky, *The Cabinet*; and Balogh, *Government out of Sight*. On the building and subsequent downsizing of the federal bureaucracy in the nation's early decades, see White, *The Federalists*; and White, *The Jeffersonians*.

15. During the Revolution, the Americans embraced the Westphalian system of state sovereignty and territoriality in order to be considered "treaty-worthy" by potential allies. See Sadosky, *Revolutionary Negotiations*, 6; and Gould, *Among the Powers of the Earth*, 12.

16. Kaplan, *Colonies into Nation*, 187.

17. For an overview of the 1790s, see Wood, *Empire of Liberty*.

18. Wood, *Empire of Liberty*, 95, 140.

19. Gautham Rao's recent article offers a valuable introduction to the literature in this field. See "New Historiography of the Early Federal Government," 97–128.

20. See McCullough, *John Adams*; and Chernow, *Alexander Hamilton*.

21. See Edling, *Revolution in Favor of Government*; Edling, *Hercules in the Cradle*; and Rao, *National Duties*.

22. While discussions of Washington's presidency have tended to emphasize the policy and partisan debates between Hamilton and Jefferson, recent historians have

recognized Washington's political acumen, his policy preferences, and his leadership skills as president, including his strong commitment to the success of republican government. On Washington's reentry into public life, including his election as the nation's first president, see Larson, *Return of George Washington*. On his efforts to establish a republican ceremonial culture, see Moats, *Celebrating the Republic*; Breen, *George Washington's Journey*; and Kathleen Bartoloni-Tuazon, *For Fear of an Elective King*. For his presidential accomplishments, see Chervinsky, *The Cabinet*; and Leibiger, *Founding Friendship*.

23. On the formulation of the proclamation, most histories rely on Thomas, *American Neutrality in 1793*. His approach stresses the debate between Hamilton and Jefferson and overlooks Washington's influential role.

24. See "The Farewell Address," September 19, 1796, Fitzpatrick, *Writings of George Washington*, 35:231–237.

25. Jefferson's reasons are explained in greater detail in chapter 4 below. See also Chervinsky, *The Cabinet*, 199–200.

26. On western-boundary disputes between the British Empire and the American republic as well as Native Americans, see Taylor, *Divided Ground*. On Indian warfare in Ohio during the 1790s, see Calloway, *Victory with No Name*; and Sleeper-Smith, *Indigenous Prosperity and American Conquest*.

27. On the vital connection between interior agriculture and transatlantic shipping, see McCoy, *Elusive Republic*, 84, 85, 132, 238. On the global ramifications of slavery and cotton, including in the Atlantic, see Beckert, *Empire of Cotton*, 110, 121, 213, 467.

28. The Atlantic world has attracted a vast literature. A good place to start is Bailyn, *Atlantic History*. See also Edling, *Hercules in the Cradle*, 8, 13; and Gilje, "Commerce and Conquest in Early American Foreign Relations," 735–770. For a contrasting opinion that stresses westward territorial expansion as the more important factor, see Shankman, "Toward a Social History of Federalism," 615–653.

29. On Genet, see Ammon, *The Genet Mission*. On the widespread practice of colonial American privateering, see Carp, *Rebels Rising*; Gilje, *Liberty on the Waterfront*; Perl-Rosenthal, *Citizen Sailors*; and Vickers, *Young Men and the Sea*.

30. Wood, *Empire of Liberty*, 89.

31. Prince, *Federalists and the Origins of the U.S. Civil Service*; White, *The Federalists*.

32. On the revival of diplomatic history and the long overdue inclusion of the early republic in discussions of globalization, see Dierks, "Americans Overseas in the Early American Republic," 18–35.

33. On sailors abroad, see Perl-Rosenthal, *Citizen Sailors*; and Rouleau, *With Sails Whitening Every Sea*.

34. See Conroy-Krutz, *Christian Imperialism*; and Van, "Cents and Sensibilities," 72–89.

35. Chervinsky, *The Cabinet*, 4, 5, 6.

36. On the masculine world of letters, see Bushman, *Refinement of America* 90; and Shields, *Civil Tongues and Polite Letters*, 203, 310, 326.

37. Washington Catherine Macaulay Graham, January 9, 1790, PGW-PS, 4:551–554.

Chapter 1

1. Beckert, *Empire of Cotton*, 110.
2. On this transatlantic exchange of goods, ideas, technologies, and information, see Hancock, *Citizens of the World*, 29–36.
3. Carp, *Rebels Rising*, 7; Nash, *Urban Crucible*, 3, 54; Vickers, *Young Men and the Sea*, 7, 41.
4. Hancock, *Citizens of the World*, 132.
5. Carp, *Rebels Rising*, 27; Vickers, *Young Men and the Sea*, 79, 120, 132, 145; Perl-Rosenthal, *Citizen Sailors*, 28.
6. Carp, *Rebels Rising*, 19, 67.
7. Even George Washington was drawn to the sea, but his mother refused to let him join the Royal Navy, so he pursued a career in the army instead. See Flexner, *George Washington: The Forge of Experience*, 30; Vickers, *Young Men and the Sea*, 106, 112, 123, 145, 159; and Gilje, *Liberty on the Waterfront*, 68.
8. Gilje, *Liberty on the Waterfront*, 20, 71; Lemisch, *Jack Tar vs. John Bull*, 3–5.
9. Lemisch, *Jack Tar vs. John Bull*, 4. For a comprehensive overview of the rich cultural life of sailors, see Gilje, *To Swear like a Sailor*.
10. For frequent examples of weather-related challenges, see Preble and Green, *Diary of Ezra Green*, 17–28.
11. Perl-Rosenthal, *Citizen Sailors*, 21, 22, 24, 25.
12. Brunsman, *Evil Necessity*, 2, 48, 241, 245.
13. Vickers, *Young Men and the Sea*, 156, 157.
14. Gilje, *Liberty on the Waterfront*, 74, 83; Perl-Rosenthal, *Citizen Sailors*, 26.
15. Gilje, *Liberty on the Waterfront*, 69, 74. On the common vessels used in the American transatlantic trade, see Jarvis, *In the Eye of All Trade*, 122–125.
16. Colley, *Britons*, 62, 65, 71.
17. On Dutch dominance of the seventeenth-century Atlantic, see Koot, *Empire at the Periphery*. On Britain's expanding role in the eighteenth century, see Brewer, *Sinews of Power*, 168; and Colley, *Britons*, 79, 99.
18. See Rediker, *Between the Devil and the Deep Blue Sea*, 285; and Gilje, *To Swear like a Sailor*, 18–19.
19. Starkey, *British Privateering Enterprise*, 24–26.
20. In addition to diplomats, maritime nations posted consuls in port cities to promote their commerce and protect their merchant ships and sailors. Treaties with the host country determined the conduct of these foreign consuls. In 1784, for example, France had a consul general, four consuls, and five vice consuls in American ports. As the United States became an independent nation, it slowly formalized this practice, first through a consular convention with France and then in a 1792 law defining the rules and responsibilities of the American consular service. In the 1790s, the United States had twelve consuls and six vice consuls appointed in different European ports. See Patterson, "Department of State," 317, 318, 324, 325. See also Crowhurst, *French War on Trade*, 67.

21. On Britain's increased reliance on privateering and its growing legitimacy, see Hanna, *Pirate Nests and the Rise of the British Empire*, 200, 357–358, 366, 412, 420.

22. Jessup and Deak, *Neutrality*, 1:14–15.

23. Swanson, *Predators and Prizes*, 20.

24. Hancock, *Citizens of the World*, 244–245.

25. Gilje, *Liberty on the Waterfront*, 107; Nash, *Urban Crucible*, 170.

26. Several other European countries did not agree to this ban either. See Starkey, *British Privateering Enterprise*, 245, 251n3. See also Stark, "Abolition of Privateering."

27. The Consolato del mare first appeared as a published document in Spain in 1494, although its tenets had been governing trade on the Mediterranean for at least a century before. See Jessup and Deak, *Neutrality*, 4:1, 124–125; and Neff, *Rights and Duties of Neutrals*, 12, 18–19.

28. In the English translation, the specific rule stated, "If an armed ship or cruiser meet with a merchant vessel, belonging to an enemy and carrying a cargo, the property of an enemy, common sense will sufficiently point out what is to be done: it is, therefore, unnecessary to lay down any rules for such a case." Jessup and Deak, *Neutrality*, 1:124.

29. Three Anglo-French treaties included some variation of the phrase "free ships make free goods": the Treaty of Westminster (1655), the Treaty of St. Germaine-en-Laye (1677), and the Treaty of Utrecht (1713). See Neff, *Rights and Duties of Neutrals*, 29–32; and Jessup and Deak, *Neutrality*, 1:126.

30. Holland's treaties with Portugal and France in 1661 and 1662, respectively, also contained this phrase. See Fenwick, *American Neutrality*, 10; and Jessup and Deak, *Neutrality*, 1:40, 131.

31. Gilje, *Free Trade and Sailors' Rights*, 29. Eliga H. Gould cites the Treaty of Utrecht and the earlier Treaty of Westphalia (1648) as so influential as to be considered "public law" across Europe. The Westphalia accords created the rules that established the international community of diplomacy. Gould, *Among the Powers of the Earth*, 17; and Herring, *From Colony to Superpower*, 12–13.

32. Gilje, *Free Trade and Sailors' Rights*, 30.

33. The phrase "letter of marque and reprisal" originally referred to a license a sovereign would give to a subject to recover property losses incurred because of the actions of an enemy's army or navy. With the dropping of the term "reprisal," the "letter of marque" assumed a more aggressive role, serving as the commission sovereigns issued to authorize wartime privateering. See Starkey, *British Privateering Enterprise*, 20–22.

34. Starkey, *British Privateering Enterprise*, 21; Andrews, *Elizabethan Privateering during the Spanish War*.

35. Colley, *Britons*, 70.

36. Brewer, *Sinews of Power*, 197. On the Anglo-French wars that dominated the eighteenth century, see Colley, *Britons*, 79, 99.

37. Swanson, *Predators and Prizes*, 3, 5. For a detail discussion of seventeenth-century American privateering, see Chapin, *Privateer Ships and Sailors*, 20, 22, 24, 28, 33; and Jameson, *Privateering and Piracy in the Colonial Period*.

38. The North American counterparts of these two European conflicts were King William's War (1689–97) and Queen Anne's War (1702–13), respectively. See Brunsman, *Evil Necessity*, 28.

39. Swanson, *Predators and Prizes*, 6.

40. This war eventually merged into Europe's War of Austrian Succession, with King George's War serving as its North American counterpart. See Brunsman, *Evil Necessity*, 28.

41. Swanson, *Predators and Prizes*, 6; Perl-Rosenthal, *Citizen Sailors*, 34. See also Chapin, *Privateering in King George's War*.

42. Starkey, *British Privateering Enterprise*, 22, 23, 24; Ubbelohde, *Vice-Admiralty Courts*, 5, 6, 9, 15, 17.

43. Swanson, *Predators and Prizes*, 38.

44. Carp, *Rebels Rising*, 67.

45. Perl-Rosenthal, *Citizen Sailors*, 36, 37. During the nineteenth century, American privateering continued to be an important component of war, particularly during the War of 1812. During the Civil War, the Confederate States of America relied on privateers to weaken both the U.S. Navy and its coastal blockade. See Kert, *Privateering*, and Head, *Privateers of the Americas*. See also Scharf, *History of the Confederate States Navy*.

46. While many books have dealt with privateering over the centuries in different wars and among a range of countries, this discussion seeks to connect privateering to the U.S. government's desire for free trade and neutrality.

47. Perl-Rosenthal, *Citizen Sailors*, 37; Gilje, *Liberty on the Waterfront*, 76.

48. Nash, *Urban Crucible*, 165.

49. Nash, *Urban Crucible*, 167.

50. Gilje, *Liberty on the Waterfront*, 20.

51. Nash, *Urban Crucible*, 166, 177.

52. Carp, *Rebels Rising*, 67.

53. Nash, *Urban Crucible*, 165, 166, 167–168, 169.

54. Garitee, *Republic's Private Navy*, 9; Anderson, *Crucible of War*, xxvii, 11.

55. See Cohen, *Commodore Abraham Whipple*, 12, 13; Truxes, *Defying Empire*, 4, 5, 157; and Ubbelohde, *Vice-Admiralty Courts*, 23.

56. On the "Rule of 1756," see Neff, *Rights and Duties of Neutrals*, 65–68.

57. In the Treaty of Utrecht (1713), France and Britain had affirmed the right of free trade. See Gilje, *Free Trade and Sailors' Rights*, 29, 30.

58. Nash, *Urban Crucible*, 240–241.

59. Nash, *Urban Crucible*, 239.

60. Nash, *Urban Crucible*, 237.

61. Garitee, *Republic's Private Navy*, 7, 8.

62. *Account of the Voyages and Cruizes of Captain Walker*, 1–3. See also Swanson, *Predators and Prizes*, 67–68, 88, 133–134.

63. Nash, *Urban Crucible*, 182, 240–41, 246.

64. Nash, *Urban Crucible*, 177; Gilje, *Liberty on the Waterfront*, 110; Truxes, *Defying Empire*, 80, 81, 86, 157.
65. Perl-Rosenthal, *Citizen Sailors*, 34, 38, 55, 59.
66. Perl-Rosenthal, *Citizen Sailors*, 41, 52; Ubbelohde, *Vice-Admiralty Courts*, 24.
67. Perl-Rosenthal, *Citizen Sailors*, 38, 67.
68. Between 1651 and 1673, the British government enacted several trade and navigation acts intended to regulate how colonists shipped certain raw materials. First, valuable items such as tobacco and sugar could only be traded through England. Second, they established a system of duties, along with the appointment of royal customs-house officers to enforce and collect them. Third, these restrictions limited colonial trade to nations that were at peace with Britain. Skirting these laws within American port cities became standard practice. Truxes, *Defying Empire*, 225.
69. Brunsman, *Evil Necessity*, 2, 172, 173.
70. Brunsman, *Evil Necessity*, 228–229; Carp, *Rebels Rising*, 37.
71. Brunsman, *Evil Necessity*, 230–231, 237–238.
72. Truxes, *Defying Empire*, 225; Carp, *Rebels Rising*, 38–39.
73. Carp, *Rebels Rising*, 44, 45, 55.
74. Carp, *Rebels Rising*, 53.
75. McManemin, *Captains of the Privateers*, i.
76. Crawford, *Autobiography of a Yankee Mariner*, 140, 191.
77. Winslow, "Wealth and Honor," 16.
78. Not surprisingly, Massachusetts employed the most privateers, 626, followed by Pennsylvania with 500, and Maryland with 225. See Coggins, *Ships and Seamen of the American Revolution*, 74; McManemin, *Captains of the Privateers*, ii, 535–556; and Morgan, "American Privateering," 82, 83.
79. For a comprehensive overview of America's naval presence during the Revolution, see Volo, *Blue Water Patriots*. On these naval estimates, see Gilje, *Liberty on the Waterfront*, 106.
80. Perl-Rosenthal, *Citizen Sailors*, 48; Middlekauff, *Glorious Cause*, 534–535.
81. McManemin, *Captains of the Privateers*, iv; Morgan, "American Privateering," 84.
82. Gilje, *Liberty on the Waterfront*, 99, 102.
83. Broadside, Beverly, MA, September 17, 1776, Library Company of Philadelphia.
84. Gilje, *Liberty on the Waterfront*, 107, 110, 112, 114.
85. Perl-Rosenthal, *Citizen Sailors*, 99.
86. Perl-Rosenthal, *Citizen Sailors*, 4–5, 11; Brunsman, *Evil Necessity*, 182.
87. Crawford, *Autobiography of a Yankee Mariner*, 233–235.
88. Fanning, *Narrative of the Adventures of an American Navy Officer*, 13, 177.
89. Painter, *Autobiography*, 16, 21, 25, 47. For additional anecdotal accounts of privateering, see Maclay, *History of American Privateers*, and Petrie, *Prize Game*.
90. Clark, *George Washington's Navy*, 2, 4, 6, 229, 236.
91. John Parke Custis (1754–81) was one of Martha Washington's two surviving adult children. George Washington became his guardian and the administrator of the

substantial Custis estate when he married Martha in 1759. See Chase, *Papers of George Washington, Revolutionary War Series*, 1:15–16n. On the vessel's name, see Custis to Washington, October 1777, ibid., 12:73–74n. On the privateer's joint ownership, see Washington to Custis, November 14, 1777, ibid., 249–250.

92. Hutson, John Adams and the Diplomacy of the American Revolution, 27, 28, 31; Gould, Among the Powers of the Earth, 1, 2.

Chapter 2

1. In 1494 this code of laws and practices appeared as a published document in Spain, although its rules had been in use since the thirteenth century. See Jessup and Deak, *Neutrality*, 1:124n3. See also Gilje, *Free Trade and Sailors' Rights*, 15, 29.
2. Gilje, *Free Trade and Sailors' Rights*, 15, 16, 17.
3. Fenwick, *American Neutrality*, 9; and Gilje, *Free Trade and Sailors' Rights*, 18.
4. On transatlantic exchanges of information, see Knott, *Sensibility and the American Revolution*, 16, 17; and Rosenfeld, *Common Sense*, 10. On the economic exchanges, see also Hancock, *Citizens of the World*, 29–36.
5. For an introduction to the American Revolution's philosophical origins, see Wood, *Radicalism of the American Revolution*, and Pocock, *Machiavellian Moment*.
6. For an overview of Vattel's life (1714–67), see Béla Kapossy and Richard Whatmore, introduction to Vattel, *Law of Nations* (2008).
7. Vattel, *Law of Nations* (1872), lxiii.
8. Vattel, *Law of Nations* (1872), 125.
9. Vattel, *Law of Nations* (1872), 144.
10. Vattel, *Law of Nations* (1872), 332. For a further examination of the ideas of Grotius, Vattel, and others, see Tuck, *Rights of War and Peace*, 90, 91, 107, 191–195.
11. William Bradford to Madison, October 17, 1774, Hutchinson and Rachal, *Papers of James Madison*, 1:125–128.
12. "Reports on Books for Congress," January 23, 1783, Hutchinson and Rachal, *Papers of James Madison*, 6:62–115; Franklin to Charles-Guillaume-Frédéric Dumas, December 9, 1775, Labaree and Bell, *Papers of Benjamin Franklin*, 22:287–291.
13. At a cabinet meeting on April 18, 1793, Hamilton cited Vattel to support his argument that the 1778 treaty with France was not valid, an interpretation Jefferson disputed. See "Thomas Jefferson's Notes on a Cabinet Meeting," May 6, 1793, *PGW-PS*, 12:529–530.
14. Fenwick, *American Neutrality*, 11.
15. Chernow, *Alexander Hamilton*, 46.
16. Franklin to James Bowdoin, March 24, 1776, Labaree and Bell, *Papers of Benjamin Franklin*, 22:389–390.
17. Washington to Robert Cary & Company, October 6, 1773, Abbot et al., *Papers of George Washington, Colonial Series*, 9:343–345.

18. Chernow, *Alexander Hamilton*, 52; Allen et al., *Diary of John Quincy Adams*, 2:287 (September 12, 1787).

19. Jefferson to John Garland Jefferson, June 11, 1790, *PTJ*, 16:480–482.

20. Thomas Paine, in *Common Sense*, published in January 1776, pioneered the idea that diplomacy offered the pathway to American independence. See Kaplan, *Colonies into Nation*, 90. On the "Secret Committee," see Middlekauff, *Glorious Cause*, 396, 398; and Dull, *Diplomatic History of the American Revolution*, 59.

21. Lee's complete resolution of June 7, 1776, stated: "That these United Colonies are, and of right ought, to be, free and independent States, that they are absolved from all allegiance to the British Crown, and that all political connection between them and the State of Great Britain is, and ought to be, totally dissolved; that measures should be immediately taken for procuring the assistance of foreign powers, and a Confederation be formed to bind the colonies more closely together." See "Notes of Proceedings in the Continental Congress, June 7, 1776," *PTJ*, 1:299.

22. Richard Henry Lee regarded the Declaration of Independence as a foreign-policy statement because only with diplomatic recognition would America become an independent nation. See Gould, *Among the Powers of the Earth*, 113, 114; and Dull, *Diplomatic History of the American Revolution*, 52, 53.

23. Kaplan, *Colonies into Nation*, 90–91.

24. See Ferling, *John Adams*, 15, 155–156, 176–177, 186.

25. "Notes on Relations with France, March–April 1776," Butterfield, Gaber, and Garrett, *Diary and Autobiography of John Adams*, 2:236.

26. Middlekauff, *Glorious Cause*, 399; Dull, *Diplomatic History of the American Revolution*, 53, 54. On the American desire for commercial independence, see Hutson, *John Adams and the Diplomacy of the American Revolution*, 27, 28, 31.

27. "In Congress, June–July, 1776," Butterfield, Gaber, and Garrett, *Diary and Autobiography of John Adams*, 3:337–338.

28. Adams, along with Franklin, concurrently served on the committee writing the Declaration of Independence, with Jefferson charged with drafting that document. The committee of treaties also consisted of John Dickinson, Benjamin Harrison, and Robert Morris. See "Editorial Note on the Plan of Treaties," Labaree and Bell, *Papers of Benjamin Franklin*, 22:473–474; and Ferling, *John Adams*, 188.

29. The three Anglo-French treaties that Adams used for Articles XIV–XXX of the Model Treaty were the Treaty of Peace, Westminster, 1655; the Whitehall Treaty of 1686, also known as the American Treaty of Peace, Good Correspondence, and Neutrality; and the Treaty of Navigation and Commerce, accompanying the Treaty of Utrecht, 1713. See Taylor, Kline, and Lint, *Papers of John Adams*, 4:278n11. On the Acadian–New England neutrality referred to in the Whitehall Treaty, see Faragher, *Great and Noble Scheme*, 79–80, 86.

30. See Taylor, Kline, and Lint, *Papers of John Adams*, 4:263.

31. Stinchcombe, "John Adams and the Model Treaty," 69–84; "Editorial Note on the Plan of Treaties," Labaree and Bell, *Papers of Benjamin Franklin*, 22:473–474.

32. Stourzh, *Benjamin Franklin and American Foreign Policy*, 125.

33. For the final version of the Plan of Treaties, adopted by the Continental Congress on September 17, 1776, see Taylor, Kline, and Lint, *Papers of John Adams*, 4:290–300.

34. Stourzh, *Benjamin Franklin and American Foreign Policy*, 126.

35. "In Congress," March 23, 1776, Library Company of Philadelphia. Evans Microcard 15135.

36. Ferling, *John Adams*, 189, 190, 197.

37. Article XXII of the Treaty of Amity and Commerce had unexpected long-term ramifications when the United States declared its neutrality in 1793 and France wanted to be able to privateer in American ports. This article reads, "It shall not be lawful for any foreign Privateers, not belonging to Subjects of the most Christian King nor Citizens of the said United States, who have Commissions from any other Prince or State in enmity with either Nation to fit their Ships in the Ports of either the one or the other of the aforesaid Parties, to sell what they have taken or in any other manner whatsoever to exchange their Ships, Merchandizes or any other lading; neither shall they be allowed even to purchase victuals except such as shall be necessary for their going to the next Port of that Prince or State from which they have Commissions." Revolutionary France interpreted this prohibition as a *right* to privateer, even in the 1790s. For both the Treaty of Amity and Commerce and the Treaty of Alliance, see Bevans, *Treaties and Other International Agreements*, 7:763–780.

38. Middlekauff, *Glorious Cause*, 408, 409–410, 411; Dull, *Diplomatic History of the American Revolution*, 93, 94.

39. Spain established a unilateral treaty with France in 1779. See Dull, *Diplomatic History of the American Revolution*, 69.

40. Madariaga, *Britain, Russia, and the Armed Neutrality*, 151, 156, 157; Madariaga, *Catherine the Great*, 81, 82.

41. Bolkhovitinov, *Beginnings of Russian-American Relations*, 14; Montefiore, *Prince of Princes*, 210.

42. Madariaga, *Catherine the Great*, 81.

43. Madariaga, *Catherine the Great*, 82, 83; Madariaga, *Britain, Russia, and the Armed Neutrality*, 178.

44. Scott, *Armed Neutralities of 1780 and 1800*, 273–274.

45. The Declaration of Armed Neutrality of 1780 was not the first such agreement. Russia modeled their efforts on earlier armed-neutrality agreements from 1613, 1689, 1691, 1693, and 1756, with smaller countries such as Sweden, Holland, and Denmark participating in them. See Kulsrud, "Armed Neutralities to 1780," 3, 423, 428, 431, 433, 436.

46. Scott, *Armed Neutralities of 1780 and 1800*, 280, 285.

47. Madariaga, *Russia in the Age of Catherine the Great*, 483; Bolkhovitinov, *Beginnings of Russian-American Relations*, 14; Madariaga, *Catherine the Great*, 83.

48. Bolkhovitinov, *Beginnings of Russian-American Relations*, 13; Morris, *Peacemakers*, 166.

49. Scott, *Armed Neutralities of 1780 and 1800*, 406, 419, 420, 430, 433.

50. Scott, *Armed Neutralities of 1780 and 1800*, 282.

51. Madariaga, *Catherine the Great*, 83.

52. Washington to Rochambeau, March 21, 1781, Fitzpatrick, *Writings of George Washington*, 21:350; Hutson, *John Adams and the Diplomacy of the American Revolution*, 81.

53. Madariaga, *Catherine the Great*, 84; Madariaga, *Britain, Russia, and the Armed Neutrality*, 193; Hutson, *John Adams and the Diplomacy of the American Revolution*, 87.

54. Griffiths, "American Contribution to the Armed Neutrality of 1780," 2, 165.

55. Ferling, *John Adams*, 216.

56. Adams to the President of Congress, April 26, 1780. Taylor, Kline, and Lint, *Papers of John Adams*, 9:238–240.

57. Morris, *Peacemakers*, 199.

58. In late 1776 Congress authorized missions to Prussia, Austria, and Tuscany. Historians coined the phrase based on a letter Adams wrote to Robert Livingston on February 21, 1782: "militia sometimes gain victories over regular troops even by departing from the rules." See Stourzh, *Benjamin Franklin and American Foreign Policy*, 126; and Hutson, *John Adams and the Diplomacy of the American Revolution*, 87.

59. Adams to the President of Congress, September 16, 1780, Taylor, Kline, and Lint, *Papers of John Adams*, 10:156–158. See also Hutson, *John Adams and the Diplomacy of the American Revolution*, 81.

60. Adams to C. W. F. Dumas, October 4, 1780, Taylor, Kline, and Lint, *Papers of John Adams*, 10:252–254.

61. See Ferling, *John Adams*, 227; and Hutson, *John Adams and the Diplomacy of the American Revolution*, 81.

62. Prior to 1776, Franklin had amassed significant experience as a pro-British colonial agent and businessman in Great Britain. He first went there as a young man in 1726. He later returned for two long stints, first representing Pennsylvania from 1757 to 1762, then from 1764 to 1775 he added New Jersey, Georgia, and Massachusetts to his portfolio. The later period, of course, coincided with the American revenue crisis, and Franklin believed his strong connections to the British government would be sufficient to negotiate a political solution. His failure to do so profoundly altered his sympathetic view of the royal authorities, and he returned to America in 1775 with a profoundly different political outlook. His experiences abroad and his celebrity in Europe made him the obvious choice to lead America's diplomatic delegation to Paris in 1776. See Wood, *Americanization of Benjamin Franklin*, 29, 82, 93, 97, 104, 126, 136, 150, 151, 158, 169.

63. Franklin to the President of Congress, May 31, 1780, Labaree and Bell, *Papers of Benjamin Franklin*, 32:448–453.

64. Franklin to the President of Congress, August 9, 1780, Labaree and Bell, *Papers of Benjamin Franklin*, 33:160–166.

65. Stourzh, *Benjamin Franklin*, 160. For example, in 1782 Sweden asked to enter into a Treaty of Amity and Commerce with the United States. See "Instructions in

Re: Treaty with Sweden," September 28, 1782, Hutchinson and Rachal, *Papers of James Madison*, 5:167–168.

66. Washington to the President of Congress, December 15, 1780, Fitzpatrick, *Writings of George Washington*, 20:478.

67. Bolkhovitinov, *Beginnings of Russian-American Relations*, 18.

68. Scott, *Armed Neutralities of 1780 and 1800*, 324.

69. Morris, *Peacemakers*, 167, 187, 355.

70. Ferling, *John Adams*, 218, 239, 241–242.

71. President of Congress to Adams, December 29, 1780, Taylor, Kline, and Lint, *Papers of John Adams*, 10:447–448.

72. President of Congress to Franklin, December 20, 1780, Labaree and Bell, *Papers of Benjamin Franklin*, 34:188–189.

73. Adams to the President of Congress, December 25, 1780, Taylor, Kline, and Lint, *Papers of John Adams*, 10:435–436.

74. Stourzh, *Benjamin Franklin and American Foreign Policy*, 160, 161.

75. Like his diplomatic colleague Adams, Francis Dana (1745–1811) hailed from Massachusetts, attended Harvard, and was a lawyer by profession. He briefly served as a delegate to the Second Continental Congress in 1776 before traveling to Paris as Adams's secretary. Both men also shared a distrust of what they perceived as Franklin's excessive fealty to France. Adams demonstrated his trust in Dana by allowing his fourteen-year-old son to serve as his secretary. John Quincy Adams proved to be an asset in the Russian court because of his ability to speak French, the language of diplomacy, something Dana lacked. See Cresson, *Francis Dana*, 3, 11, 33, 65, 306, 385; and Nagel, *John Quincy Adams*, 25–26.

76. Cresson, *Francis Dana*, 140, 155, 167, 183, 202.

77. On Spain's seizure of a Russian ship, see Madariaga, *Catherine the Great*, 83. On Russia's unwillingness to antagonize Great Britain, see Bolkhovitinov, *Beginnings of Russian-American Relations*, 27. On Catherine's reluctance to recognize the United States, see Morris, *Peacemakers*, 160, 166.

78. Cresson, *Francis Dana*, 247, 301, 305, 319.

79. Hutson, *John Adams and the Diplomacy of the American Revolution*, 81, 88, 97.

80. Hutson, *John Adams and the Diplomacy of the American Revolution*, 98, 100.

81. These events occurred in April and June 1782, respectively. See Hutson, *John Adams and the Diplomacy of the American Revolution*, 102, 107, 111, 114. For the full text of the Dutch Treaty of Amity and Commerce, see Bevans, *Treaties and Other International Agreements*, 10:6–18.

82. Although less commonly known than the French and Dutch agreements, the United States also entered into a Treaty of Amity and Commerce with Sweden during the Revolution. In contrast to the arduous negotiations associated with its counterparts, the Swedish treaty came about rather easily. For starters, King Gustavus III and his diplomats in Versailles approached Franklin about a possible agreement. In response, the Continental Congress appointed him to handle the negotiations. On April 3, 1783,

Sweden and Franklin signed the final Treaty of Amity and Commerce, modeled after France's. See "Instructions in Re: Treaty with Sweden," September 28, 1782, Hutchinson and Rachal, *Papers of James Madison*, 5:167–168. For the full text of this treaty, see Bevans, *Treaties and Other International Agreements*, 11:710–722.

83. Oneida Nation to Governor Trumbull, 1777, Calloway, *World Turned Upside Down*, 162.

84. Calloway, *American Revolution in Indian Country*, 30, 31, 65.

85. Calloway, *American Revolution in Indian Country*, 38; and Sadosky, *Revolutionary Negotiations*, 129.

86. Calloway, *American Revolution in Indian Country*, 273, 278, 281, 290.

87. Robert Livingston, secretary of foreign affairs, wrote to Dana on October 22, 1781, "They consider the plan of the Armed Neutrality as the best proof of an enlarged and generous policy . . . granted by the wisdom of the Empress to the trade of the world." Adams and Dana also shared this optimistic view of Empress Catherine's neutrality policy. See Cresson, *Francis Dana*, 109, 270.

88. "Continental Congress Report on American Participation in a European Neutral Confederacy," June 12, 1783, *PAH*, 3:377–378n1.

89. Cresson, *Francis Dana*, 321.

90. The United States remained steadfast in its refusal to join European alliances. In 1794, Washington resisted overtures to join an armed-neutrality league with Sweden and Denmark. See Combs, *Jay Treaty*, 145, 148, 157. In 1800, France's revolutionary wars inspired Austria, Sweden, and Denmark to form a second League of Armed Neutrality. The British navy's destruction of the Danish fleet immediately rendered this agreement meaningless, unlike its more effective 1780 predecessor. See Chamberlain, *"Pax Britannica,"* 33; Scott, *Armed Neutralities of 1780 and 1800*, 531, 537, 544; and Piggott and Omond, *Documentary History of the Armed Neutralities*, 379.

91. For the provisions in the Treaty of Paris, see Morris, *Peacemakers*, 461–465.

92. Middlekauff, *Glorious Cause*, 592–595.

93. Three of America's free-trade agreements were with members of the League of Armed Neutrality of 1780: the Netherlands, Sweden, and Prussia. On the limited benefits of these agreements, see Gilje, *Free Trade and Sailors' Rights*, 42, 48–51; and Edler, *The Dutch Republic and the American Revolution*, 232. On the Moroccan treaty, see Field, *America and the Mediterranean World*, 33.

94. Sears, *George Washington and the French Revolution*, 183, 284.

95. By 1785, with little diplomatic work to do in Europe, Franklin returned to America, Adams moved to London to assume his ministerial duties, and Jefferson remained the sole American diplomat in Paris. See Ellis, *American Sphinx*, 78; and Ferling, *John Adams*, 275.

96. Hamilton (1755–1804), having served as an aide-de-camp to General Washington during the war, began his career in national politics in 1782 as a delegate from New York to the Confederation Congress. See Chernow, *Alexander Hamilton*, 152, 173.

97. Publius [Alexander Hamilton], "Federalist no. 11: The Utility of the Union in Respect to Commercial Relations and a Navy," in Shapiro, *Federalist Papers*, 55, 56.

98. U.S. Constitution, in Shapiro, Federalist Papers, 460.

Chapter 3

1. See Flexner, *George Washington: The Forge of Experience*, 30.
2. These European conflicts in North America include King William's War, Queen Anne's War, and King George's Wars. See Anderson, *Crucible of War*, 11.
3. Anderson, *Crucible of War*, xxi, 7, 11, 49; Flexner, *George Washington: The Forge of Experience*, 53; Lengel, *General George Washington*, 19, 34.
4. Lengel, *General George Washington*, 19.
5. Anderson, *Crucible of War*, 6, 7, 11, 53; Lengel, *General George Washington*, 25, 30, 32, 46, 49.
6. Anderson, *Crucible of War*, 289–290.
7. Anderson, *Crucible of War*, 292; Lengel, *General George Washington*, 51, 78.
8. Anderson, *Crucible of War*, 289, 371; Lengel, *General George Washington*, 77, 89.
9. Lengel, *General George Washington*, 77, 88, 89; Flexner, *George Washington: The Forge of Experience*, 227–228.
10. Middlekauff, *Glorious Cause*, 410–411. On April 12, 1779, Spain formed an alliance with France that excluded the United States. This Franco-Spanish agreement underscored Europeans' greater interest in Continental affairs than in American independence when choosing to participate in the American Revolution. See Dull, *Diplomatic History of the American Revolution*, 109.
11. Dull, *Diplomatic History of the American Revolution*, 59.
12. Ferling, *Ascent of George Washington*, 202–203.
13. Lengel, *General George Washington*, 306, 307, 308.
14. Washington to John Sullivan, September 1, 1778, Lengel, *General George Washington*, 308.
15. On Lafayette's and La Rouerie's entry into the American Revolution, see Middlekauff, *Glorious Cause*, 426; and Hume, *General Washington's Correspondence Concerning the Society of Cincinnati*, 431, respectively. See also Flexner, *George Washington in the American Revolution*, 215; and Freeman, *George Washington*, 4:450, 458.
16. Washington to Morris, July 24, 1778, Fitzpatrick, *Writings of George Washington*, 12:227–228.
17. On the French army coming to America, see Ferling, *Ascent of George Washington*, 202–203, 204; and Stinchcombe, *American Revolution and the French Alliance*, 134.
18. Lengel, *General George Washington*, 331–337; Stinchcombe, *American Revolution and the French Alliance*, 146.
19. Americans celebrated the victory and the Franco-American alliance with ringing church bells and toasts offered to the "United States," "Congress," "George Washington," "Rochambeau," and "Louis XVI." See Middlekauff, *Glorious Cause*, 595; and Stinchcombe, *American Revolution and the French Alliance*, 149–152.

20. See Fitzpatrick, *Writings of George Washington*, 23:246.

21. Dull, *Diplomatic History of the American Revolution*, 142; Myers, *Liberty without Anarchy*, 1, 148.

22. Myers, *Liberty without Anarchy*, 17–19, 62, 145, 155. Writing to Washington on March 14, 1784, La Rouerie complained about applications "from persons who ought to be sensible that they have no right to be admitted." Hume, *General Washington's Correspondence Concerning the Society of Cincinnati*, 113.

23. All four of these men were career military officers and members of the French aristocracy: Charles-Hector, comte D'Estaing (1729–94); Marie-Jean-Paul-Yves-Roche-Gilbert du Motier, marquis de Lafayette (1757–1834); Charles Armand Tuffin, marquis de La Rouerie (1750–93); and Jean-Baptiste-Donatien de Vimeur, comte de Rochambeau (1725–1807). See Hume, *General Washington's Correspondence Concerning the Society of Cincinnati*, 415, 428–429, 430–431, 444.

24. On the revolutionary officers' world view based in exclusivity, honor, and status as gentlemen, see Royster, *Revolutionary People at War*, 88, 210, 317, 345, 353. On the aristocratic liberal ideology that defined their approach to the French Revolution, see Harsanyi, *Lessons from America*, 8, 10, 11, 12, 18, 21.

25. Rochambeau to Washington, January 19, 1784, *PGW-CS*, 1:59.

26. Washington to Rochambeau, August 20, 1784, *PGW-CS*, 2:48.

27. La Rouerie to Washington, February 4, 1784, *PGW-CS*, 1:103. La Rouerie may have visited Mount Vernon in April 1784. See ibid., 104n3.

28. On Lafayette's original plans and his subsequent visit in August, see *PGW-CS*, 1:182, 2:28–29. Forty years later Lafayette embarked on a triumphant tour of the United States as a living symbol of the American Revolution. See Purcell, *Sealed with Blood*, 171–179.

29. *PGW-CS*, 2:28–29n3.

30. During his campaigns in Newport and elsewhere, Admiral D'Estaing had failed to apprise Washington of his movements. See Freeman, *George Washington*, 5:86, 503.

31. D'Estaing to Washington, December 25, 1783, Hume, *General Washington's Correspondence Concerning the Society of Cincinnati*, 39; D'Estaing to Washington, February 26, 1784, *PGW-CS*, 1:158.

32. Washington to Rochambeau, February 1, 1784, *PGW-CS*, 1:102.

33. On aristocratic liberalism, see Harsanyi, *Lessons from America*, 18, 21. On Washington's republican views, see Phelps, *George Washington and American Constitutionalism*, 29–30.

34. Along with official reports from the American ministers stationed in Paris, including Jefferson, William Short, and Gouverneur Morris, Washington received updates from the British historian Catherine Macaulay Graham and the Irish politician Edward Newenham. He also obtained translated versions of French newspapers and pamphlets. In 1793 Martha Washington purchased a six-volume history of the French Revolution. See Sears, *George Washington and the French Revolution*, 14, 68, 88; and Branson, *Those Fiery Frenchified Dames*, 65–66. John Adams also relied on private

sources to make diplomatic decisions. See Perl-Rosenthal, "Private Letters and Public Diplomacy," 283–311.

35. The connections between the American and French Revolutions are well established. The American Revolution helped bring about the French Revolution as the alliance's high cost triggered a financial crisis for Louis XVI and the American example offered the economically distressed French people a new civic model based in natural rights and republican government. Some recent works that connect the two revolutionary struggles include Branson, *Those Fiery Frenchified Dames*; Cleves, *Reign of Terror in America*; Dunn, *Sister Revolutions*; Newman, *Parades and Politics of the Street*; Waldstreicher, *In the Midst of Perpetual Fetes*; and Ziesche, *Cosmopolitan Patriots*.

36. On the American ceremonial culture that developed around these revolutions, see Branson, *Those Fiery Frenchified Dames*, and Newman, *Parades and Politics of the Street*. On the Federalists' initial support, see Elkins and McKittrick, *Age of Federalism*, 310. On the differences between the two revolutions, see Doyle, *Oxford History of the French Revolution*, 114–115; and Ziesche, *Cosmopolitan Patriots*, 11. For the increasingly partisan understandings of the French Revolution, see Newman, *Parades and Politics of the Street*, 120, 125, 127.

37. Palmer, *Age of Democratic Revolution*, 2:40; Harsanyi, *Lessons from America*, 18, 20, 21.

38. See Hume, *General Washington's Correspondence Concerning the Society of Cincinnati*, 415, 430–431, 444; Whitridge, *Rochambeau*, 300; and Sears, *George Washington and the French Revolution*, 9, 31–32, 50. See also Kramer, *Lafayette in Two Worlds*, 147.

39. Palmer, *Age of Democratic Revolution*, 1:461, 464, 481; Rochambeau to Washington, January 31, 1789, *PGW-PS*, 1:268.

40. La Rouerie to Washington, June 18, 1789, *PGW-PS*, 3:37, 38, 40.

41. Washington to La Rouerie, October 13, 1789, *PGW-PS*, 4:175–176. For the other mid-October letters, see ibid., 168, 184, 192.

42. On these tours, see Moats, *Celebrating the Republic*, 51–56; and Breen, *George Washington's Journey*, 159–206.

43. Rochambeau to Washington, April 11, 1790, *PGW-PS*, 5:326.

44. Washington to Rochambeau, August 10, 1790, *PGW-PS*, 6:231.

45. Gouverneur Morris (1752–1816), then an American businessman living in Paris, offered Washington a different assessment of his protégé's aspirations: "Unfortunately both for himself and his country he [Lafayette] has not the talents which his situation requires. This important truth known to the few from the very beginning is now but too well understood by the People in general. His authority depends on incidents and sinks to nothing in a moment of calm." Morris to Washington, December 1, 1790, *PGW-PS*, 7:4–5, 6.

46. Lafayette to Washington, January 12, 1790, *PGW-PS*, 4:567.

47. Symbols establishing Washington as the link between these two revolutions include the presentation of the Bastille key by Lafayette as well as the conferral of honorary French citizenship by the National Convention. See Flexner, *George Washington and the New Nation*, 313; and Ammon, *The Genet Mission*, 19–20.

48. Lafayette had originally chosen Thomas Paine to deliver the Bastille key to Washington, but Paine was unable to make the transatlantic trip. For the letter accompanying the key, see Lafayette to Washington, March 17, 1790, *PGW-PS*, 5:242–244n.

49. For Chateaubriand's comment, as well as his biography, see *PGW-PS*, 5:243n3, 8:492n2.

50. Doyle, *Oxford History of the French Revolution*, 110–111; La Rouerie to Washington, January 2, 1790, *PGW-PS*, 4:511.

51. The National Assembly of France to Washington, June 20, 1790, *PGW-PS*, 5:540, 541, 542n1.

52. Washington to the President of the National Assembly of France, January 27, 1791, *PGW-PS*, 7:292.

53. "To the United States Senate and House of Representatives," December 8, 1790, *PGW-PS*, 7:47.

54. Washington to Lafayette, March 19, 1791, *PGW-PS*, 7:598.

55. Washington to Lafayette, July 28, 1791, *PGW-PS*, 8:378–379.

56. Washington to Lafayette, September 10, 1791, *PGW-PS*, 8:515, 516n1.

57. Washington to Humphreys, March 16, 1791, *PGW-PS*, 7:583–584. David Humphreys (1752–1818) was a diplomat and poet. Washington appointed him as minister to Portugal in 1791. Prior to this posting, Humphreys had served Washington as an aide-de-camp during the Revolutionary War and a personal secretary. See Chernow, *Washington*, 120, 409, 454, 473, 592.

58. Washington to Morris, July 28, 1791, *PGW-PS*, 8:381.

59. Morris had been living in Paris since 1788 and had served as an informal emissary to London. In 1792, Washington appointed him minister to France. Morris would be recalled from this position in 1794 amid the controversy surrounding Citizen Genet's diplomatic mission to the United States. See Adams, *Gouverneur Morris*, 231; and Chernow, *Washington*, 656, 688, 718.

60. Washington to Morris, October 20, 1792, *PGW-PS*, 11:245.

61. Louis XVI to Washington, September 19, 1791, *PGW-PS*, 8:541.

62. Washington to Louis XVI, March 14, 1792, *PGW-PS*, 10:108.

63. Washington to Lafayette, November 21, 1791, *PGW-PS*, 9:218.

64. Doyle, *Oxford History of the French Revolution*, 157, 158, 174. On the remaking of French society, see Hunt, *Politics, Culture, and Class in the French Revolution*.

65. *PGW-PS*, 9:495nn1–2.

66. Lafayette to Washington, January 22, 1792, *PGW-PS*, 9:493.

67. Washington to Lafayette, June 10, 1792, *PGW-PS*, 10:447.

68. Washington to Lafayette, June 10, 1792, *PGW-PS*, 10:447.

69. Doyle, *Oxford History of the French Revolution*, 437.

70. Kramer, *Lafayette in Two Worlds*, 41–43.

71. Kramer, *Lafayette in Two Worlds*, 10, 48, 147. Other French nationals were more successful in escaping their country's revolutionary excesses and relocating to America in the 1790s. See Furstenberg, *When the United States Spoke French*, and Harsanyi, *Lessons from America*.

72. He also wrote to Jefferson, asking, "Can anything be said, or done, respecting the Marquis de Lafayette?" Washington to Thomas Jefferson, November 22, 1793, *PGW-PS*, 14:414–415.

73. Washington to William Frederick II of Prussia, January 15, 1794, *PGW-PS*, 15:75–76n2, 77n4.

74. Lafayette to Washington, October 6, 1797, Twohig, Chase, Runge, and Grizzard, *Papers of George Washington, Retirement Series*, 1:384–386. Washington wrote his last letter to Lafayette on December 25, 1798. See ibid., 3:280–285. On Lafayette's release, see Kramer, *Lafayette in Two Worlds*, 10.

75. *PGW-PS*, 3:40–41; Sears, *George Washington and the French Revolution*, 31–32.

76. Sears, *George Washington and the French Revolution*, 213.

77. Hume, *General Washington's Correspondence Concerning the Society of Cincinnati*, 415.

78. Whitridge, *Rochambeau*, 275, 300, 308, 320; Sears, *George Washington and the French Revolution*, 325.

79. The French National Convention to Washington, December 22, 1791, *PGW-PS*, 11:259n, 538.

80. On these revolutionary events, see Doyle, *Oxford History of the French Revolution*, 437.

81. News of France's declaration of war against Britain reached Washington and his cabinet in early April 1793. See Jefferson to Washington, April 1, 1793, *PGW-PS*, 12:395.

82. Washington to Humphreys, March 23, 1793, *PGW-PS*, 12:363.

83. For the Neutrality Proclamation of April 22, 1793, see PGW-PS, 12:472.

Chapter 4

1. Jefferson to Madison, July 7, 1793, *PTJ*, 26:444.

2. Hamilton's Pacificus essays were published in Philadelphia's *Gazette of the United States* between June 29 and July 27, 1793. Madison's responses appeared in the same publication between August 24 and September 18, 1793. See *PAH*, 15:33n1; Ketcham, *Selected Writings of James Madison*, 230–231n; and Hunt, *Letters and Other Writings of James Madison*, 1:611–654.

3. Many historians have viewed the formulation and implementation of the Neutrality Proclamation as one more example of the partisan contest dividing Hamilton and Jefferson. While these disagreements existed, that interpretation misses the consensus Washington achieved not only in drafting the policy but also in enforcing it. For the early example of this approach, see Thomas, *American Neutrality in 1793*. See also Elkins and McKittrick, *Age of Federalism*; Bowman, *Struggle for Neutrality*; Combs, *Jay Treaty*; Kaplan, *Colonies into Nation*; and Varg, *Foreign Policies of the Founding Fathers*.

4. The president requested this meeting the previous day. See Washington to the Cabinet, April 18, 1793, *PGW-PS*, 12:452–453.

5. Washington to Morris, March 25, 1793, *PGW-PS*, 12:380.

6. Kaplan, *Colonies into Nation*, 187. On the federal courts' enforcement of neutrality, see Brown, *Alexander Hamilton and the Development of American Law*, 85, 99–100; and Arlyck, "Courts and Foreign Affairs," 1–64.

7. Sadosky, *Revolutionary Negotiations*, 151, 153. On the transformation of the Department of Foreign Affairs into the Department of State, see Patterson, "Department of State," 318, 320.

8. The Department of State came first (July 27, 1789), followed by the Department of War (August 7, 1789), the Department of the Treasury (September 2, 1789), and the position of attorney general (September 24, 1789). See White, *The Federalists*, 118, 130, 145, 164, 166.

9. Kaplan, *Colonies into Nation*, 191–192.

10. See Sleeper-Smith, *Indigenous Prosperity and American Conquest*, and Calloway, *Victory with No Name*.

11. Gilje, *Free Trade and Sailors' Rights*, 51.

12. See *PGW-PS*, 12:396n1.

13. See Jefferson to Washington, April 1, 1793, and Hamilton to Washington, April 5, 1793, *PGW-PS*, 12:395–396, 412–414.

14. The debates between Hamilton and Jefferson have produced a vast literature. This discussion relies on Wood, *Empire of Liberty*, 95, 140, 162; and Elkins and McKitrick, *Age of Federalism*, 355.

15. By 1793, French refugees to the United States also brought news of the revolution's excesses, helping quell the earlier popular and political American enthusiasm for France. See Branson, *Those Fiery Frenchified Dames*, 80; and Furstenberg, *When the United States spoke French*.

16. On Washington's cabinet, see Chervinsky, *The Cabinet*.

17. Washington to Hamilton, April 12, 1793, *PGW-PS*, 12:447.

18. Washington to Jefferson, April 12, 1793, *PGW-PS*, 12:448.

19. Although Jay held the position of chief justice of the Supreme Court, he remained active in foreign affairs, having served as secretary for foreign affairs in the Confederation Congress as well as interim secretary of state prior to Jefferson's return from France. In 1794, Washington would appoint him special envoy to Britain. See Combs, *Jay Treaty*, 15, 122; and Patterson, "Department of State," 318.

20. Hamilton to Jay, April 9, 1793 (first letter), *PAH*, 14:297–299.

21. Hamilton to Jay, April 9, 1793 (second letter), *PAH*, 14:299–300.

22. Washington to the Cabinet, April 18, 1793, *PGW-PS*, 12:452–453.

23. Jefferson wrote: "Apr. 18. The President sends a set of Questions to be considered & calls a meeting. Tho' those sent me were in his own hand writing, yet it was palpable from the style, their ingenious tissue [sic] & suite that they were not the President's, that they were raised upon a prepared chain of argument, in short that the language was Hamilton's, and the doubts his alone." See *PAH*, 14:328n2.

24. One example would be Washington's 1789 query on presidential conduct. See *PGW-PS*, 2:245–247; and Moats, *Celebrating the Republic*, 37.

25. *PGW-PS*, 12:452.

26. In 1800 the Convention of Mortefontaine finally released the United States from its obligations to France under these treaties. See Elkins and McKittrick, *Age of Federalism*, 689.

27. The "guarantee" clause appears in Article XI of the Treaty of Alliance, while the privateering provisions are in Articles XVII and XXII of the Treaty of Amity and Commerce. For the texts of these accords, see Bevans, *Treaties and Other International Agreements*, 7:763–780. See also Thomas, *American Neutrality in 1793*, 62.

28. *PGW-PS*, 12:452.

29. "Minutes of a Cabinet Meeting," April 19, 1793, *PGW-PS*, 12:459.

30. Jay's draft proclamation clearly informed the final version. It stressed the U.S. desire to "cultivate and preserve the Peace they now enjoy" by not becoming involved in Europe's war and also advised Americans to stay out of the conflict. The draft contained two additional provisions that would have been offensive to Jefferson and the Democratic-Republicans: it addressed the abolition of France's monarchy and the lack of a replacement government, and it cautioned against "division and parties" offending foreign powers with their comments. See Enclosure, Jay to Hamilton, April 11, 1793, *PAH*, 14:307–310.

31. For the biographies of Knox (1750–1806) and Randolph (1753–1813), see Puls, *Henry Knox*, and Reardon, *Edmund Randolph*.

32. Elkins and McKittrick, *Age of Federalism*, 338–339.

33. See DeConde, *Entangling Alliance*, 88, 89, 187, 189, 190.

34. See Chervinsky, *The Cabinet*, 199–200.

35. Consistent with Jefferson's request that "neutrality" not appear in the final text, the April 22 statement appeared in the nation's newspapers as the "Proclamation." By late summer of 1793, the term "neutrality" became commonplace thanks, in part, to the numerous violations of this policy, including the Gideon Henfield case. Additionally, the summertime Pacificus essays popularized the use of this term to describe the April 22 proclamation. On Henfield's case, see *General Advertiser* (Philadelphia), July 30, 1793. On popular support for neutrality, see Young, "Connecting the President and the People," 435–466.

36. Neutrality Proclamation, April 22, 1793, *PGW-PS*, 12:472–473.

37. See Washington to David Humphreys, March 23, 1793, and Washington to Gouverneur Morris, March 25, 1793, *PGW-PS*, 12:363, 380.

38. See Jefferson to Jean Baptiste Ternant, George Hammond, and F. P. Van Berckel, April 23, 1793; Jefferson to Gouverneur Morris, Thomas Pinckney, and William Short, April 26, 1793; Jefferson to William Carmichael and David Humphreys, April 26, 1793; and "Circular to the Governors of the States," April 26, 1793, *PTJ*, 25:583–584, 587–588, 591.

39. Washington received extensive comments from his cabinet. Jefferson's arrived on April 28; Hamilton and Knox's on May 2; and Randolph's on May 6. See *PGW-PS*, 12:487–488, 504, 534–548. In addition, Hamilton and Jefferson sent lengthy enclosures with theirs. See *PAH*, 14:367–396; and *PTJ*, 25:597–619.

40. On the divisions in the cabinet, see *PGW-PS*, 12:453–454n.

41. Gilje, *Free Trade and Sailors' Rights*, 15, 16, 17.

42. *PTJ*, 25:606n.

43. This discussion has benefited from Harper, *American Machiavelli*, 107–111; and Peterson, *Thomas Jefferson and the New Nation*, 482–484.

44. Hamilton and Knox to Washington, May 2, 1793, *PAH*, 14:377.

45. Given the centrality of question three to Hamilton's overall opinions on neutrality, he had Knox cosign the twenty-nine-page response he sent to Washington on May 2. See Hamilton and Knox to Washington, May 2, 1793, *PAH*, 14:367–396. Hamilton addressed the remaining ten questions in a separate letter. See Hamilton to Washington, May 2, 1793, ibid., 14:398–408.

46. Despite Jefferson's ideological affinity with Randolph, the attorney general did not prove to be the reliable partisan ally Jefferson had wanted. On his frustration with Randolph's moderation, see Jefferson to Madison, May 13, 1793, *PTJ*, 26:26.

47. Jefferson to Washington, April 28, 1793, *PTJ*, 25:608–609; Randolph to Washington, May 6, 1793, *PGW-PS*, 12:534–547.

48. *PTJ*, 25:609–610.

49. Randolph provided the president a list of recent treaties that contained these privileges. These included an Anglo-French commercial treaty from 1788 as well as the U.S. Treaties of Amity and Commerce with the Netherlands (1782) and Prussia (1785). See Randolph to Washington, May 6, 1793, *PGW-PS*, 12:546.

50. *PTJ*, 25:617–618; *PGW-PS*, 12:546–547.

51. Thomas Jefferson, "Notes on a Cabinet Meeting," May 6, 1793, *PGW-PS*, 12:530. For Jefferson's reasons for wanting to notify Congress, both political and constitutional, see Thomas, *American Neutrality in 1793*, 67–68.

52. See Ferling, *John Adams*, 312–314, 337; and Bartoloni-Tuazon, *For Fear of an Elective King*, 163–164.

53. Wood, *Empire of Liberty*, 89.

54. Jefferson, "Notes on a Cabinet Meeting," May 6, 1793, *PGW-PS*, 12:530.

55. Jefferson to Madison, May 13, 1793, *PTJ*, 26:26. Some historians have focused on the "mere English neutrality" part of the quotation and have excluded the qualifier about Washington. For an example of this misreading, see Wood, *Empire of Liberty*, 184.

56. While issues of popular support and partisan opinions certainly surrounded the Neutrality Proclamation, particularly in the short run, the long-term struggles over neutrality centered on the enforcement challenges that accompanied this proclamation. For a discussion of the popular and partisan issues, see Young, "Connecting the President and the People."

57. See chap. 4, note 2. In early 1794, Hamilton added two more essays to the Pacificus series. These appeared in Philadelphia's *Dunlap and Claypoole's American Daily Advertiser* under the name "Americanus." See *PAH*, 15:669n1.

58. For these letters to Washington, see *PGW-PS*, 12:647–649, *PGW-PS*, 13:17–19 and *PGW-PS*, 13:34–37. On their publication, see *PGW-PS*, 12:649n5. Veritas's identity remains unknown and numerous theories abound. Jefferson suspected the author worked for Hamilton in the Treasury Department, while Genet (perhaps wishfully) thought it was Jefferson. See Jefferson, "Note on Alexander Hamilton and Veritas," June 12, 1793,

PTJ, 26:267–268. A recent author has identified Hamilton as Veritas. See Young, "Connecting the President and the People," 446n17.

59. Veritas to Washington, May 30, 1793, *PGW-PS*, 12:647–649.
60. Veritas to Washington, June 3, 1793, *PGW-PS*, 13:17–19.
61. Veritas to Washington, June 6, 1793, *PGW-PS*, 13:34–37.
62. Elkins and McKittrick, *Age of Federalism*, 284.
63. "Pacificus no. 1," June 29, 1793, *PAH*, 15:34, 37, 38, 39, 40.
64. "Pacificus no. 2," July 3, 1793, *PAH*, 15:34.
65. The "guarantee" clause appears in Article XI of the Treaty of Alliance. See Bevans, *Treaties and Other International Agreements*, 7:779.
66. Vattel, *Law of Nations*, book II, 32, as cited in *PAH*, 15:67.
67. "Pacificus no. 3," July 6, 1793, *PAH*, 15:65, 67, 68.
68. "Pacificus no. 4," July 10, 1793, *PAH*, 15:83. Hamilton was referring to the privateering provisions contained in Articles XVII and XXII of the Treaty of Amity and Commerce. See Bevans, *Treaties and Other International Agreements*, 7:769, 770.
69. "Pacificus no. 4," July 10, 1793, *PAH*, 15:84.
70. "Pacificus no. 5," July 13–17, 1793, *PAH*, 15:91, 95.
71. "Pacificus no. 6," July 17, 1793, *PAH*, 15:106.
72. "Pacificus no. 7," July 27, 1793, *PAH*, 15:130.
73. "Pacificus no. 7," July 27, 1793, *PAH*, 15:130, 131, 132.
74. "Pacificus no. 7," July 27, 1793, *PAH*, 15:135.
75. In late July through August 1793, the prolific Hamilton authored nine additional essays, under the name "No Jacobin," that dealt specifically with the French minister's violations of American neutrality. See *PAH*, 15:151n1.
76. With Jefferson in Philadelphia and Madison at home in Virginia, the two employed numerous strategies to ensure their correspondence remained private, including the use of a cypher to disguise the letters' contents and reliance on trusted personal messengers, rather than the postal service, to deliver them. At one point Madison had left his cypher back in Philadelphia and was unable to decode Jefferson's correspondence. See Madison to Jefferson, August 11, 1793, *PTJ*, 26:654.
77. Jefferson to Madison, May 13, 1793, *PTJ*, 26:25–26.
78. Jefferson to Madison, June 23, 1793, *PTJ*, 26:346.
79. Jefferson to Madison, May 13, 1793, *PTJ*, 26:26.
80. Adding to the pressure to respond was Hamilton's publication of a second round of pro-neutrality essays. On August 11, 1793, Jefferson complained to Madison, "*Pacificus* has now changed his signature to '*No Jacobin*.'" *PTJ*, 26:650.
81. Jefferson to Madison, July 7, 1793, *PTJ*, 26:444.
82. Madison to Jefferson, July 18, 1793, *PTJ*, 26:521.
83. Madison to Jefferson, June 13, 1793, *PTJ*, 26:273.
84. Jefferson to Madison, June 29, 1793, *PTJ*, 26:403.
85. Madison to Jefferson, July 22, 1793, *PTJ*, 26:549.
86. Jefferson to Madison, August 3, 1793, *PTJ*, 26:606.
87. Madison to Jefferson, July 30, 1793, *PTJ*, 26:585–586.

88. In reviewing the draft essays, Jefferson described himself as "charmed" by the final one. See Jefferson to Madison, September 8, 1793, *PTJ*, 27:61. On Jefferson submitting them for publication, see Madison to Jefferson, August 11, 1793, ibid., 26:655.

89. Jefferson to Washington, July 31, 1793, *PTJ*, 26:593.

90. Jefferson to Madison, August 11, 1793 (first letter), *PTJ*, 26:649–651.

91. Jefferson to Madison, August 11, 1793 (second letter), *PTJ*, 26:651.

92. The name "Helvidius" referred to an exiled Roman senator who eventually returned to the Senate to oppose Nero's tyrannical rule. See Ketcham, *Selected Writings of James Madison*, 230–231.

93. "Helvidius no. 2," August 31, 1793, Hunt, *Letters and Other Writings of James Madison*, 1:624.

94. Madison's responses also appeared in Philadelphia's *Gazette of the United States*, on August 24, 31, September 7, 14, and 18, 1793. See Ketcham, *Selected Writings of James Madison* 230–231n; and Hunt, *Letters and Other Writings of James Madison*, 1:611–654.

95. On the Henfield case, see *General Advertiser* (Philadelphia), July 30, 1793.

96. The opening line of the first Pacificus essay refers to the "Proclamation of Neutrality." See "Pacificus no. 1," June 29, 1793, *PAH*, 15:33.

97. Jefferson to Madison, April 28, 1793, *PTJ*, 25:619.

98. Madison to Jefferson, May 8, 1793, *PTJ*, 25:689.

99. Madison to Jefferson, June 19, 1793, *PTJ*, 26:324.

100. "Notes of a Conversation with George Washington," August 6, 1793, *PTJ*, 26:627.

101. On August 11, 1793, Jefferson wrote Madison, "the president is extremely anxious to know your sentiments on the proclamation," adding, "He has asked me several times." Despite a summer spent conspiring against the proclamation, Jefferson deflected the president's questions: "I tell him you are so absorbed in farming that you write to me always about ploughs, rotations, etc." *PTJ*, 26:653.

102. "Notes of a Conversation with George Washington," August 6, 1793, *PTJ*, 26:627–630.

103. Jefferson to Washington, August 11, 1793, and Washington to Jefferson, August 12, 1793, *PTJ*, 26:659–660.

104. Washington to Heath, May 20, 1797, Twohig, Chase, Runge, and Grizzard, *Papers of George Washington, Retirement Series*, 1:148–150. William Heath (1737–1814) had served as a major general in the Revolutionary War. On his life, see Wilson, *Heath's Memoir of the American War*.

Chapter 5

1. See Newton and Lindsay (two Norfolk merchants) to Washington, May 5, 1793, *PGW-PS*, 12:521–522n1.

2. On Washington's request that Jefferson disseminate the proclamation, see *PGW-PS*, 12:473n.

3. Jefferson to Jean Baptiste Ternant, George Hammond, and F. P. Van Berckel, April 23, 1793, *PTJ*, 25:583–584.

4. Hammond to Jefferson, April 24, 1793, *PTJ*, 25:583.

5. The ranks of U.S. diplomats in Europe reflected both republican values and budgetary constraints. The representative in France held the position of minister plenipotentiary rather than ambassador to avoid the costs of entertaining and the ostentations of court life associated with this higher-ranking position. Occupying a slighter lower diplomatic rung, the Americans posted in London, Madrid, and Lisbon held the title of chargé d'affaires, while the U.S. representative in Amsterdam was an agent. Remarkably, the United States did not appoint an official ambassador until 1893. See Herring, *From Colony to Superpower*, 58; and Dougall and Chapman, *United States Chiefs of Mission*, 160.

6. Jefferson to Gouverneur Morris, Thomas Pinckney, and William Short, April 26, 1793, *PTJ*, 25:591.

7. Jefferson to William Carmichael (in Spain) and David Humphreys (in Portugal), April 26, 1793, *PTJ*, 25:587–588.

8. Jefferson, "Circular to the Governors of the States," April 26, 1793, *PTJ*, 25:588.

9. "Treasury Department Circular to the Collectors of the Customs," April 23, 1793, *PAH*, 26:702–703.

10. Gautham Rao has described this legislation as "effectively Americanizing the British navigation acts." See *National Duties*, 53.

11. Recognizing Boston's importance as a port, Washington appointed Benjamin Lincoln as its customs collector. In addition to serving as a major general in the Continental Army and as secretary at war in the Confederation Congress, he had quelled Shays's Rebellion in 1786. On Lincoln's career, see *PGW-CS*, 1:187n. In other busy ports, many of the original customs collectors—such as John Lamb in New York City, Sharp Delany in Philadelphia, Otho Williams in Baltimore, and Isaac Holmes in Charleston—had a military background, had served as a customs collector prior to 1789, or had done both. On Lamb, Delany, and Holmes, see *PGW-PS*, 2:368n, 89n, and 8:270n, respectively. On Williams, see *PGW-CS*, 1:24n.

12. See Prince and Keller, *U.S. Customs Service*, 35, 36, 37, 38, 39; and Rao, *National Duties*, 53–54, 65, 69–73.

13. Hamilton to Washington, May 4, 1793, *PGW-PS*, 12:511n1.

14. Jefferson had reasons to be concerned about Hamilton's patronage abilities. By 1792, the Treasury secretary employed ninety people in his main office, while Jefferson had a staff of only six. See White, *The Federalists*, 122, 136.

15. Jefferson to Randolph, May 8, 1793, *PTJ*, 25:591–592.

16. Washington to Hamilton, May 7, 1793, *PGW-PS*, 12:549.

17. The Judiciary Act of 1789 created district attorneys for each of the states that had ratified the Constitution. These attorneys handled legal matters for the U.S. government in their respective district courts. They reported to the secretary of state rather than the attorney general, who was considered strictly a legal advisor to the

president and did not possess a cabinet agency. See Executive Office for U.S. Attorneys, *Bicentennial Celebration of the United States Attorneys*, 3, 4; and White, *The Federalists*, 166, 406.

18. Randolph responded to Jefferson's concerns on May 9, 1793. See *PTJ*, 25:700–702.

19. The Justice Department did not come into existence until 1870. In addition to housing the attorney general, the original State Department had other domestic duties, including processing patent applications, issuing copyrights, and overseeing the census. See Patterson, "Department of State," 318, 320, 322, 324.

20. *PGW-PS*, 12:511n1. For this circular, dated August 4, see *PAH*, 15:178–181. On the jurisdictional uncertainty, see Ammon, *The Genet Mission*, 100.

21. Higginson to Hamilton, April 28, 1793, *PAH*, 14:354.

22. Ellery to Hamilton, April 29, 1793, *PAH*, 14:356.

23. See *PTJ*, 25:647–648n.

24. Tench Coxe (1755–1824) was an economic nationalist who supported both Hamilton and Jefferson. See Cooke, *Tench Coxe and the Early Republic*.

25. "Opinion on Ship Passports," May 3, 1793, *PTJ*, 25:648.

26. After 1795, language from America's commercial treaty with Spain would be added to the ship passports. On the use of the Dutch template and the subsequent adoption of the French format, see Jefferson to Hamilton, May 8, 1793, *PTJ*, 25:680–681, 682n.

27. On May 9, 1793, Hamilton wrote to Jefferson, "It appears to me, as it does to you, that the position of the Collectors of the Custom will render them the most convenient channel of distribution for the passports." The Treasury Department's "Circular to the Collectors of the Customs," dated May 13–16, 1793, contained these blank passports and Hamilton's instructions for issuing them, including a prohibition against *foreign-owned* vessels receiving them. *PAH*, 14:429, 442–447.

28. The November order is discussed in greater detail in chapter 6. On the effectiveness of the passports, see Clauder, *American Commerce as Affected by the Wars of the French Revolution and Napoleon*, 69.

29. The title "citizen" announced a French republic of equals in which aristocrats and monarchs no longer reigned. While Genet (1763–1834) appears in many political histories of the early republic, Harry Ammon's study remains the definitive account. See Ammon, *The Genet Mission*, vii, 44.

30. See Ammon, *The Genet Mission*, 26.

31. Jackson, *Privateers in Charleston*, 1–3. South Carolina's governor, William Moultrie (1730–1805), who had served as a major general in the Continental Army, emerged as a leading advocate of France's revolution despite his Federalist affiliation and the Neutrality Proclamation. Believing that the Treaty of Amity and Commerce still applied, he aided Genet in commissioning these privateers and became a steadfast supporter of the French minister's other endeavors. See Bragg, *Crescent Moon over Carolina*, 5, 205, 254, 256, 279.

32. On Genet's seizures in Charleston, see Ammon, *The Genet Mission*, 44.

33. Perl Rosenthal, *Citizen Sailors*, 112. Britain also engaged in privateering, although on a much smaller scale and only targeting merchant ships in the Caribbean.

34. Jean Baptiste Carvin, commander of *L'Industrie*, and Citizen L'Ecuyer, captain of the *Marseilles*, are two such examples. See Jackson, *Privateers in Charleston*, 11; and Winslow, *"Wealth and Honor"*, 78.

35. On Genet's delayed arrival in Philadelphia, see Ammon, *The Genet Mission*, 45, 52, 59.

36. Newton and Lindsay to Washington, May 5, 1793, *PGW-PS*, 12:521–522. William Lindsay also held a government position as the lighthouse keeper and the collector of the customs for Norfolk. Ibid., 522n1.

37. Murray to Jefferson, May 9, 1793, *PTJ*, 25:698–700.

38. George Hammond had been Britain's minister to the United States since 1791. He enjoyed a close friendship with Hamilton, further straining relations with Jefferson. *PAH*, 10:374n1.

39. Hammond to Jefferson, May 2, 1793, *PTJ*, 25:637–638.

40. Jefferson to Hammond, May 3, 1793, *PTJ*, 25:644.

41. Hammond to Jefferson, May 2, 1793, *PTJ*, 25:683.

42. Hammond to Jefferson, May 8, 1793, *PTJ*, 25:685, 687.

43. Hammond to Jefferson, May 31, 1793, *PTJ*, 26:150.

44. Randolph to Jefferson, May 14, 1793, *PTJ*, 26:31–36.

45. Jefferson to Hammond, May 15, 1793, and Jefferson to Ternant, May 15, 1793, *PTJ*, 26:38–40, 42–44.

46. Genet to Jefferson, May 27, 1793, appears in *ASP*, 150 (English translation).

47. William Rawle (1759–1836) was a prominent Philadelphia lawyer. Washington appointed him as Pennsylvania's district attorney in 1791.*PGW-PS*, 7:250–251n. See Jefferson to Rawle, May 15, 1793, ibid., 12:588n2; and Genet to Jefferson, June 1, 1793, *ASP*, 151. Jefferson also informed Virginia governor Henry Lee that prosecutions were underway against Hooper for neutrality violations in Norfolk. *PTJ*, 26:76.

48. Knox to State Governors, May 23, 24, 1793, Palmer et al., *Calendar of Virginia State Papers and Other Manuscripts*, 6:377, 379.

49. Knox to Washington, May 16, 1793, *PGW-PS*, 12:595–598. See also Hamilton to Washington, May 15, 1793, *PAH*, 14:454–460.

50. Jefferson to Washington, May 16, 1793, *PTJ*, 26:51. See also Randolph to Washington, May 17, 1793, *PGW-PS*, 12:602–605.

51. On Washington's approval, see *PTJ*, 26:52n.

52. Amid these discussions, Genet officially presented his credentials to Washington on May 18, 1793.*PGW-PS*, 12:607n1.

53. See Jefferson, "Notes on the Citizen Genet and Its Prizes," May 20, 1793, *PTJ*, 26:71–73n; and "Cabinet Opinion on French Privateers," June 1, 1793, *PGW-PS*, 13:2.

54. Genet to Jefferson, May 27, 1793, *ASP*, 150–151.

55. Memorandum from Edmund Randolph, ca. May 28–30, 1793, *PTJ*, 26:137–138.

56. Jefferson to Genet, June 5, 1793, *PTJ*, 26:195–196.

57. Jefferson to Hammond, June 5, 1793, *PTJ*, 26:197–198.
58. Genet to Jefferson, June 8, 1793, *ASP*, 151 (English translation).
59. Article XVII read, in part, "It shall be lawful for the Ships of War of either Party & Privateers freely to carry whithersoever they please the Ships and Goods taken from their Enemies, without being obliged to pay any Duty to the Officers of the Admiralty or any other Judges; nor shall such Prizes be arrested or seized, when they come to and enter the Ports of either Party; nor shall the Searchers or other Officers of those Places search the same or make examination concerning the lawfulness of such Prizes, but they may hoist Sail at any time and depart and carry their Prizes to the Places express'd in their Commissions." Article XXII declared, "It shall not be lawful for any foreign Privateers, not belonging to Subjects of the most Christian King nor Citizens of the said United States, who have Commissions from any other Prince or State in enmity with either Nation to fit their Ships in the Ports of either the one or the other of the aforesaid Parties, to sell what they have taken or in any other manner whatsoever to exchange their Ships, Merchandizes or any other lading." See Bevans, *Treaties and Other International Agreements*, 7:763–780.
60. Jefferson to Genet, June 17, 1793, *PTJ*, 26:298.
61. Hamilton to Collectors of the Customs, May 30, 1793, *PAH*, 14:499.
62. See "Notes on the *Citizen Genet* and Its Prizes," May 20, 1793, *PTJ*, 26:71–73n; and *PGW-PS*, 12:651n1.
63. *PTJ*, 26:335n.
64. Captain Gideon Henfield (1753–1800) hailed from Salem, Massachusetts, and had commanded numerous ships during the American Revolution. John Singleterry was originally from Charleston, South Carolina, but then resided in Beaufort, North Carolina. On Henfield and Singleterry, see *PGW-PS*, 13:3n5, 36n7. While Henfield's prosecution served as the administration's test case, the outcome of Singleterry's case is not known. See Genet to Jefferson, June 1, 1793, *PTJ*, 26:159n1.
65. *PTJ*, 26:131n.
66. Hammond to Jefferson, June 7, 1793, *PTJ*, 26:216.
67. Genet to Jefferson, June 1, 1793, *ASP*, 151. See also Genet to Jefferson, May 27, 1793, *PTJ*, 26:130–131.
68. Jefferson to Genet, June 1, 1793, *ASP*, 151.
69. Randolph to Jefferson, May 30, 1793, *PTJ*, 26:145–146.
70. Hammond to Jefferson, June 21, 1793, *PTJ*, 26:335–336n.
71. See Hammond to Jefferson, June 7, 21, 1793, *PTJ*, 26:217.
72. Because of Jefferson's central role in enforcing neutrality, Hammond kept him apprised of these cases through a series of memorials. See Hammond to Jefferson, June 5, 7, 21, 1793, Boyd, *Paper of Thomas Jefferson*, 26:199–200, 217–218, 335–336.
73. See Knox to State Governors, May 24, 1793, Palmer et al., *Calendar of Virginia State Papers*, 6:379. Not all governors were eager to stop privateering in their ports. For example, Governor Moultrie of South Carolina permitted France to engage in these activities in Charleston's harbor. See Bragg, *Crescent Moon over Carolina*, 254, 256.

74. See Clinton to Washington, June 9, 1793, *PGW-PS*, 13:47–48. See also Ammon, *The Genet Mission*, 44.

75. "Cabinet Opinion on the *Polly (Republican)* and the *Catherine*," see June 12, 1793, *PGW-PS*, 13:63–65. Richard Harison (1747–1829) was a New York City attorney and Federalist. Washington appointed him as New York's district attorney in 1789. Jackson and Twohig, *Diaries of George Washington*, 5:505n.

76. Jefferson to Harison, June 12, 1793, *PTJ*, 26:261–262.

77. Genet to Jefferson, June 14, 1793, *ASP*, 152.

78. Jefferson to Genet, June 17, 1793 (two letters), *PTJ*, 26:297–302.

79. *PTJ*, 26:200–201n.

80. Hammond to Jefferson, June 21, 1793, *PTJ*, 26:297–302.

81. Mifflin to Washington, June 22, 1793, *PGW-PS*, 13:128.

82. In the case of the brigantine *Catherine*, Judge James Duane of the District Court of New York also held that the court lacked jurisdiction in international-sovereignty violations. Amid these uneven federal court rulings, the Supreme Court ultimately declared in February 1794, in the case *Glass vs. the Sloop* Betsey, that district courts possessed jurisdiction in these cases. On the Judiciary Act, see *PGW-PS*, 13:350–351n5. On the *Catherine*, see *PTJ*, 26:254n. For the *Sloop* Betsey ruling, see Scott, *Prize Cases*, 9–19.

83. Jefferson to Genet, June 25, 1793, *PTJ*, 26:358.

84. *PGW-PS*, 13:132n4.

85. Jefferson to Genet, June 25, 1793, *PTJ*, 26:398–399. The *Fanny* had experienced the same legal process as the *William*, and Jefferson made a similar request to Genet on its behalf.

86. Genet to Jefferson, June 26, 1793, *ASP*, 160–161.

87. In September Jefferson discovered that Genet had not follow through on his promises regarding the *William* and the *Fanny*. The minister's negligence forced the U.S. government to take tangible steps to specifically define America's water boundaries. Jefferson to Washington, October 3, 1793, *PTJ*, 27:190–192.

88. For a critique of James Wilson's overreaching instructions in the *Henfield* case, particularly due to the Neutrality Proclamation's lack of statutory authority, see Wilmarth, "Elusive Foundation," 184–189. Wilmarth contrasts Wilson's unsuccessful efforts to "enlarge the rights of the judiciary" in this case with John Marshall's effort to "secure" them in his landmark *Marbury v. Madison* (1804) ruling.

89. Supreme Court justices James Wilson and James Iredell, along with district court judge Richard Peters, composed this tribunal. See Goebel, *Antecedents and Beginnings to 1801*, 624.

90. James Wilson, "Charge to the Grand Jury," July 22, 1793, Marcus et al., *Documentary History of the Supreme Court*, 2:420.

91. See John Jay, "Instructions to the Circuit Court for the District of Virginia," May 22, 1793, Marcus et al., *Documentary History of the Supreme Court*, 2:380–391.

92. Waldstreicher, *In the Midst of Perpetual Fetes*, 133–136.

93. *PTJ*, 26:130–131n.

94. *PTJ*, 26:130–131n.

95. On the partisan celebrations that followed this ruling, see Bradburn, *Citizenship Revolution*, 115.

96. Washington to the Cabinet, August 3, 1793, *PGW-PS*, 13:323–325.

97. See chap. 4, note 2. The "No Jacobin" series ran from July 31 to August 28, 1793, in *Dunlap's American Daily Advertiser*, based in Philadelphia. See *PAH*, 15:33n1, 151n1.

98. For Jefferson's July 31 resignation letter and Washington's efforts on August 6 to keep him in the cabinet, see *PTJ*, 25:385, 627.

99. On the *Grange*'s capture, see Hammond to Jefferson, May 2, 1793, *PTJ*, 25:637–638.

100. Mifflin to Washington, June 22, 1793, *PGW-PS*, 13:126–127n1.

101. "Cabinet Opinion on the *Little Sarah*," *PGW-PS*, 13:180.

102. Washington to Jefferson, July 11, 1793, *PGW-PS*, 13:211–212.

103. "Cabinet Opinion on the *Little Sarah*," *PGW-PS*, 13:181.

104. Mifflin to Washington, July 8, 1793, *PGW-PS*, 13:191–194.

105. "Reasons for the Opinion of the Secretary of the Treasury and the Secretary of War," July 8, 1793, *PAH*, 14:74–79; "Dissenting Opinion on the *Little Sarah*," July 8, 1793, *PTJ*, 26:449–452.

106. Washington, of course, did not want to escalate the privateering crisis into an armed conflict and preferred for governors to "detect those projects in embryo and stop them when no force was requisite." He also feared that granting Mifflin's request would result in similar applications from other governors, and he doubted that "the executive had the power to establish permanent guards." "Notes of a Cabinet Meeting," July 15, 1793, *PTJ*, 26:508.

107. Jefferson to Genet and Hammond, July 12, 1793, *PTJ*, 26:487.

108. Hammond to Jefferson, July 13, 1793, *PTJ*, 26:496–497.

109. *PGW-PS*, 13:212n6.

110. On the cabinet's deliberations, see *PTJ*, 26:525. For the cabinet members' draft questions, see *PTJ*, 26:527–533.

111. Jefferson to the Supreme Court, July 18, 1793, *PTJ*, 26:520–521.

112. "Questions for the Supreme Court," July 18, 1793, *PGW-PS*, 13:243.

113. "Questions for the Supreme Court," July 18, 1793, *PGW-PS*, 13:243.

114. "Circular to the Justices of the Supreme Court," July 12, 1793, *PTJ*, 26:488, 525n. Jay, of course, had helped Hamilton draft the proclamation and the query that had guided the administration's discussions. See *PAH*, 14:297–299, 299–300, 307–310.

115. Justices of the Supreme Court to Washington, July 20, 1793, *PTJ*, 26:543.

116. In this ruling the court affirmed their constitutional role as a separate branch of government rather than being a mere legal advisor to the executive branch. Justices of the Supreme Court to Jefferson, August 8, 1793, *PGW-PS*, 13:392.

117. Article I, Section 4 of the Constitution originally required Congress to meet at least once a year, specifically stating that "such meetings shall be on the first Monday in December unless they shall by Law appoint a different day." Washington to the Cabinet, August 3, 1793, *PGW-PS*, 13:323–324, 367–368n7.

118. Washington to Jefferson, August 4, 1793, *PGW-PS*, 13:337–339.

119. Jefferson to Washington, August 4, 1793, *PGW-PS*, 13:340–341.

120. Hamilton to Washington, August 5, 1793, *PAH*, 15:194–196; Randolph to Washington, August 5, 1793, *PGW-PS*, 13:365–368. For Knox's August 5 opinion, see ibid., 196n4.

121. "Notes of Cabinet Decisions," August 6, 1793, *PTJ*, 26:627.

122. Reflecting Jefferson's fatigue as neutrality's chief diplomatic enforcer, these policy decisions coincided with his July 31 resignation letter. He hoped to leave the cabinet by the end of September, but Washington persuaded him to remain until December 31, 1793. See Jefferson to Washington, *PGW-PS*, 13:311–312.

123. On this process, see "Notes of a Cabinet Meeting on Neutrality," July 29, 1793, *PTJ*, 26:579–581.

124. "Cabinet Opinion on the Rules of Neutrality," August 3, 1793, *PGW-PS*, 13:325–326.

125. "Cabinet Opinion on French Privateers," August 3, 1793, *PGW-PS*, 13:327–328.

126. See Jefferson to Genet and Jefferson to Hammond, June 5, 1793, *PTJ*, 26:195–198.

127. Washington to the Cabinet, July 29, 1793, *PGW-PS*, 13:299.

128. "Treasury Department Circular to the Customs Collectors," August 4, 1793, *PAH*, 15:178–181.

129. Knox to Governors, August 7, 1793, Executive Correspondence, 1790–99, Pennsylvania Historical and Museum Commission, Harrisburg; Knox to Tobias Lear, August 17, 1793, *PGW-PS*, 13:475–477n1.

130. Jefferson to Hammond and Jefferson to Genet, August 7, 1793, *PTJ*, 26:633–635.

131. Jefferson to Hammond, September 5, 1793, *PTJ*, 27:35–36.

132. *PGW-PS*, 11:112–113.

133. Lee to Washington, April 29, 1793, *PGW-PS*, 12:493–494, 495n2. Lee was the father of Robert E. Lee, the future Confederate general. Lengel, *Inventing George Washington*, 12.

134. Washington to Lee, May 6, 1793, *PGW-PS*, 12:533.

135. Randolph to Jefferson, August 4, 1793, and "The Recall of Edmond Charles Genet," August 16, 1793, *PTJ*, 26:616, 685–715, 730–732, 747–748; "Cabinet Opinion on the Recall of Edmond Genet," August 23, 1793, *PGW-PS*, 13:530.

136. Washington to Hamilton, May 5, 1793, PAH, 14:414–415.

Chapter 6

1. "Notes on a Cabinet Meeting," July 23, 1793, *PTJ*, 26:554.

2. *PTJ*, 26:564n.

3. "Notes on a Cabinet Meeting," August 1, 1793, *PTJ*, 26:598, 689–690.

4. On numerous occasions, Jefferson explained the workings of the U.S. government to Genet. In a conversation on July 10, 1793, Jefferson clarified "that all the questions which had arisen between him and us belonged to the executive department, and if Congress were sitting could not be carried to them, nor would they take notice of them." He also pointed out that "the president is to see that treaties are observed." In an October

2 letter, Jefferson reprimanded Genet for his efforts to communicate with Congress: "By our constitution all foreign agents are to be addressed to the president of the US. No other branch of the government being charged with the foreign communications." See *PTJ*, 26:465, 27:175–176. When Genet wrote directly to Washington on August 13, 1793, Jefferson scolded the minister for not respecting diplomatic protocol: "It is not the established course for the diplomatic characters residing here to have any direct correspondence with him. The Secretary of State is the organ thro' which their communication should pass." *PGW-PS*, 13:436–437, 438n5.

5. Ammon, *The Genet Mission*, 52, 56, 58, 78, 80, 112.

6. "The Recall of Edmond Charles Genet," *PTJ*, 26:689–690. Federalists John Jay and Rufus King also corroborated the rumors that Genet intended to appeal directly to the people. See Ammon, *The Genet Mission*, 118.

7. Jefferson to Madison, July 7, 1793, *PTJ*, 26:444.

8. On Jefferson's attempted resignation and Washington's efforts to delay his departure, see Jefferson to Washington, July 31, 1793, and "Notes of a Conversation with George Washington," August 6, 1793, *PTJ*, 26:593, 627–630.

9. *PGW-PS*, 13:449.

10. *PGW-PS*, 13:389–390, 506–507, 591.

11. "The Recall of Edmond Charles Genet," *PTJ*, 26:689–690, 693–694, 694–696.

12. Jefferson to Morris, August 16, 1793, *PTJ*, 26:697–711.

13. The president and cabinet met on August 15 and 20, 1793, while Jefferson met with Washington on August 6. *PTJ*, 26:690, 730–731. On the letter's approval, see "Cabinet Opinion on the Recall of Edmond Genet," August 23, 1793, *PGW-PS*, 13:530–531.

14. On the letter's transmittal, see *PGW-PS*, 14:234n1.

15. "The Recall of Edmond Charles Genet," *PTJ*, 26:691. In his carefully worded letter to Genet, Jefferson wrote, "In order to bring to an end what cannot be permitted to continue, there could be no hesitation to declare in it the necessity of their having a representative here disposed to respect the laws and authorities of the country, and to do the best for their interest which these would permit." See Jefferson to Genet, September 7, 1793, *PTJ*, 27:52–53.

16. Jefferson to Genet, June 29, 1793 (two letters), and Genet to Jefferson, June 30, 1793, *PTJ*, 26:398–399, 400.

17. Jefferson shared this news with Washington on October 3, 1793. *PTJ*, 27:190–191.

18. Jefferson to Certain Foreign Ministers, November 8, 1793, *PTJ*, 27:328–329. Jefferson wrote a separate letter to Genet in order to specifically respond to his September 13 inquiry. See ibid., 330–331.

19. Jefferson to the District Attorneys, November 10, 1793, *PTJ*, 27:338–340.

20. Jefferson to Rawle, November 15, 1793, *PTJ*, 27:384–385.

21. Jefferson to Foreign Ministers in the United States, November 10, 1793, *PTJ*, 27:340–341.

22. On May 25, 1795, Secretary of State Randolph reported to Washington that the *William*'s case had been resolved. See *PGW-PS*, 18:175n3. In late 1793 and 1794, the administration deemed the ships *Hope* and *Conynham* ineligible for compensation but

restored the *Pilgrim*. On the *Hope*, see Jefferson to Hammond, December 26, 1793, *PTJ*, 27:620–622. On the *Conynham* and *Pilgrim*, see "Cabinet Meeting," March 27, 1794, *PAH*, 16:200–203n2.

23. "Cabinet Opinion on the *Roland*," August 31, 1793, *PGW-PS*, 13:587–590, 590n2. Christopher Gore (1758–1827) served as district attorney for Massachusetts from 1789 to 1796. A prominent Federalist, he would later become one of the state's U.S. senators and its governor. See Pinkney, *Christopher Gore*, 51, 101, 116.

24. Gore included the depositions he collected in a letter to Jefferson. See Gore to Jefferson, September 10, 1793, *PTJ*, 27:79–82.

25. Jefferson to Gore, September 2, 1793, *PTJ*, 27:13–14.

26. The "exequatur" referred to the recognition a government gave to a consul to operate in their country. If a consul could no longer legally perform the duties of that position, the revocation of this authority amounted to a termination. The United States defined the roles of "consuls, vice consuls, agents, and commissaries" in its Consular Convention with France on June 11, 1789. See *ASP*, 89. See also "Cabinet Opinion on the *Roland*," August 31, 1793, *PGW-PS*, 13:587.

27. Jefferson to Gore, September 2, 1793, *PTJ*, 27:13–14.

28. Gore to Jefferson, September 10, 1793, *PTJ*, 27:79.

29. "Circular to French Consuls and Vice-Consuls," September 7, 1793, *PTJ*, 27:51.

30. Jefferson to Duplaine, October 3, 1793, *PTJ*, 27:184–185.

31. Jefferson to Genet, October 3, 1793; Jefferson to Morris, October 3, 1793; and "Revocation of Duplaine's Exequatur," October 3, 1793, *PTJ*, 27:185–186, 186–187, 188.

32. Gore to Jefferson, October 21, 1793, *PTJ*, 27:261.

33. See De Viar and De Jaudenes to Jefferson, August 27, 1793, and Genet, "Address to Louisiana," *PTJ*, 26:771–773.

34. De Viar and De Jaudenes to Jefferson, October 2, 1793, *PTJ*, 27:176–180.

35. Ammon, *The Genet Mission*, 161. See also *PTJ*, 27:620n.

36. Jefferson to Shelby, November 6, 1793, *PTJ*, 27:312–313.

37. *PGW-PS*, 14:343n3.

38. *PTJ*, 27:620n.

39. *PGW-PS*, 15:289–292nn1–3.

40. Ritcheson, *Aftermath of Revolution*, 278.

41. Ritcheson, *Aftermath of Revolution*, 286. For the transmittal of this policy to Jefferson, see Hammond to Jefferson, September 12, 1793 (second letter), *PTJ*, 27:100–102.

42. Ritcheson, *Aftermath of Revolution*, 299.

43. Ritcheson, *Aftermath of Revolution*, 300.

44. See Mansfield, "Disease of Commerce," and White, *Encountering Revolution*, 34, 124.

45. Powell, *Bring out Your Dead*, vii–viii, 5.

46. *PGW-PS*, 14:202–203; Chernow, *Alexander Hamilton*, 449.

47. Washington to Lear, September 25, 1793, *PGW-PS*, 14:135.

48. *PGW-PS*, 14:153n1.

49. Washington to Randolph, September 30, 1793, *PGW-PS*, 14:152.

50. Madison to Washington, October 24, 1793, *PGW-PS*, 14:278.

51. In April 1794 Congress passed an "Act to authorize the President of the United States in certain cases to alter the place for holding a session of Congress." See *PGW-PS*, 14:153n2.

52. Randolph to Washington, November 10, 1793, *PGW-PS*, 14:355.

53. "Drafting GW's Annual Address, November 18–28, 1793," *PGW-PS*, 14:383–400. Washington received multiple drafts from Randolph, Hamilton, and Jefferson and even one from Knox. See also Jefferson, "Notes on a Cabinet Meeting on the President's Address to Congress," November 21, 1793, *PTJ*, 27:411–413.

54. On France's decree of May 9, 1793, see *PGW-PS*, 14:444–445. On difficulties with Spain, see "Thomas Jefferson's Notes for GW's Annual Address to Congress," *PGW-PS*, 14:399.

55. *PGW-PS*, 15:185n6.

56. "Notes of Cabinet Address on President's Address and Messages," November 28, 1793, *PTJ*, 27: 453-456.

57. Powell, *Bring out Your Dead*, 278, 283; White, *Encountering Revolution*, 76. The contemporary writer Charles Brocken Brown addressed the yellow fever epidemic of 1793 in his novel *Arthur Mervyn*, published in 1799.

58. Chernow, *Washington*, 618, 635, 702–703.

59. As recorded in Washington's papers, "At 12 o'clock, Washington, attended by his cabinet, proceeded to the Senate chamber, where finding both Houses assembled, he delivered to them the following speech." *PGW-PS*, 14:467n.

60. Accompanying Washington's speech were the supporting documents, including the proclamation and the cabinet opinions on "Neutrality" and on "French Privateers," both dated August 3. *PGW-PS*, 14:467nn1–3.

61. Washington to the U.S. Senate and House of Representatives, December 3, 1793, *PGW-PS*, 14:462–468 (quotes, 463–464).

62. Washington to the U.S. Senate and the House of Representatives, December 5, 1793, *PGW-PS*, 14:474–475.

63. Washington to the U.S. Senate and the House of Representatives, December 16, 1793, *PGW-PS*, 14:531–532.

64. Washington to the U.S. Senate and the House of Representatives, December 16, 1793, *PGW-PS*, 14:534.

65. With Virginia and Massachusetts claiming the presidency and the vice presidency, respectively, and New York the chief justiceship of the Supreme Court, Frederick Muhlenberg's selection as Speaker brought a geographical balance to the U.S. government. See Peters, *American Speakership*, 24–25, 30. See also U.S. House of Representatives to Washington, December 7, 1793, *PGW-PS*, 14:490.

66. Washington to U.S. House of Representatives, December 7, 1793, *PGW-PS*, 14:492.

67. In the nation's early decades, the vice president was considered a member of the legislative branch, not the executive. See Chernow, *Washington*, 593; and U.S. Senate to Washington, December 9, 1793, *PGW-PS*, 14:494–495n1.

68. Washington to the U.S. Senate, December 10, 1793, *PGW-PS*, 14:501.

69. *PTJ*, 27:532n, 567–578, 579–581.
70. *PTJ*, 27:532n.
71. Welch, *Theodore Sedgwick*, 124.
72. Brant, *James Madison*, 393.
73. Thomas, *American Neutrality in 1793*, 37n3.
74. Washington to U.S. Senate and House of Representatives, March 5, 1794, *PGW-PS*, 15:331–332.
75. Randolph to Washington, March 2, 1794, *PGW-PS*, 15:310–315.
76. Welch, *Theodore Sedgwick*, 125–126.
77. Hamilton to Washington, March 8, 1794, *PAH*, 14:130, 134–136.
78. Washington to the U.S. Senate and House of Representatives, March 25, 1794, *PGW-PS*, 15:450–451n1.
79. "Cabinet Meeting on Best Mode of Executing the Embargo," March 26, 1794, *PAH*, 16:198n1.
80. "Treasury Department Circular to the Collector of Customs," March 26, 1794, *PAH*, 16:199-200. Knox to the Governors of the Maritime States, March 26, 1794, *PAH*, 16:198n1. On March 28, 1794, Washington informed Congress that the state militias were responsible for enforcing the embargo. *PGW-PS*, 15:456n1, 463–464.
81. Hamilton to Washington, March 28, 1794, *PGW-PS*, 15:459.
82. "Cabinet Meeting on a Request for a Passport," April 1, 1794, *PAH*, 16:235n1.
83. Hamilton to Washington, April 25, 1794, *PGW-PS*, 15:652–653n1.
84. *PGW-PS*, 15:485.
85. Hamilton to Washington, May 1, 1794, *PGW-PS*, 16:2–3.
86. Washington to Hamilton, May 2, 1794, *PGW-PS*, 16:8–9.
87. *PGW-PS*, 16:92n11.
88. Randolph to Washington, March 14, April 6, 1794; and Washington to Randolph, April 15, 1794, *PGW-PS*, 15:348, 379–80, 603.
89. Washington to the U.S. Senate, April 16, 1794, *PGW-PS*, 15:608.
90. Hamilton's military recommendations to Washington (which Representative Sedgwick proposed as legislation) included the fortification of the nation's ports. In February and March 1794, Secretary of War Knox issued a series of reports to Congress entitled: "Fortifications," "Arsenal and Armories," and "Increasing the Army, and Calling into Service 80,000 Militia." *PGW-PS*, 15:337–338, 338n2. Knox reported these laws to Washington on June 5, 1794. Ibid., 16:192–193nn1–5.
91. *PGW-PS*, 15:609n2.
92. Knox to Washington, April 2, 1794, *PGW-PS*, 15:494–495nn1–2. L'Enfant, of course, would later design the nation's permanent capital of Washington, DC.
93. Knox to Washington, March 19, 1794, *PGW-PS*, 15:410–411n3.
94. Knox to Washington, April 15, 1794, *PGW-PS*, 15:597–600n1.
95. These nominations were approved the next day. See Washington to the U.S. Senate, June 3, 1794. See *PGW-PS*, 16:181–182.
96. Knox to Washington, July 25, 1794, *PGW-PS*, 16:428–430.

97. For an overview of the federal judiciary's role in the neutrality crisis, see Arlyck, "Courts and Foreign Affairs," 1–64.

98. Marcus et al., *Documentary History of the Supreme Court of the United States*, 6:300–301, 303, 306, 309.

99. Stahr, *John Jay*, 310–311.

100. Marcus et al., *Documentary History of the Supreme Court of the United States*, 6:309–310.

101. Marcus et al., *Documentary History of the Supreme Court of the United States*, 6:310n72.

102. See "Article 3, Section 2, Clause 1: Jansen v. Vrow Christina Magdalena," Document 39, Kurland and Lerner, *Founders' Constitution*, https://press-pubs.uchicago.edu/founders/documents/a3_2_1s39.html.

103. Scott, *Prize Cases*, 92–126.

104. Arlyck, "Courts and Foreign Affairs," 41n204.

105. Scott, *Prize Cases*, 147.

106. Morris to Washington, October 18, 1793, *PGW-PS*, 14:229, 235n1; *ASP*, 374–375.

107. Ammon, *The Genet Mission*, 156–157.

108. Morris to Washington, October 18, 1793, *PGW-PS*, 14:363–364n1. The Provisional Executive Council of France sent the official notification of Genet's recall and Fauchet's appointment to Washington on November 15, 1793. He shared this news with both houses of Congress on January 20, 1794. Ibid., 15:97.

109. Randolph to Washington, February 22, 1794, *PGW-PS*, 15:262–263nn1, 6.

110. Morris to Jefferson, October 19, 1793, *ASP*, 374–375.

111. Randolph to Washington, February 21, 23, 1794, *PGW-PS*, 15:255–256, 265–266.

112. Washington to Richard Henry Lee, October 24, 1793, *PGW-PS*, 14:274.

113. Ammon, *The Genet Mission*, 160, 172, 175, 179.

114. Jefferson informed Washington of "the dissatisfaction of the executive council of France with Mr. Morris our minister there" on December 11, 1793. *PTJ*, 27:504–506n.

115. The president compared Fauchet and Genet in Washington to Richard Henry Lee, April 15, 1794, *PGW-PS*, 15:601–602. On Fauchet's April 9 conversation with Randolph, see ibid., 16:144n1.

116. Washington to Jay, April 29, 1794, and Washington to Livingston, April 29, 1794, *PGW-PS*, 15:674–674, 676. Jay departed for Britain on May 12. Given the cost of sending diplomats to Europe, the U.S. government sometimes nominated Americans who were already abroad to fill these posts. For example, John Adams was in France for the Treaty of Paris negotiations when he was named as U.S. minister to Britain in 1785. See Estes, *Jay Treaty Debate*, 25; and Ferling, *John Adams*, 275.

117. Hamilton to Washington, May 19, 1794, and Randolph to Washington, May 19, 1794, *PGW-PS*, 16:93–94.

118. Washington to the U.S. Senate, May 27, 1794, *PGW-PS*, 16:143.

119. Cunningham, *Presidency of James Monroe*, 1–2.

120. Chernow, *Washington*, 716.

121. Cunningham, *Presidency of James Monroe*, 5–6.

122. On Monroe's northern and southern tours, see Moats, *Celebrating the Republic*, chapters 4–5. On Monroe's sometime excessive passion for republican government, see Poston, *James Monroe*.

123. Randolph shared John Brown's letter with Washington on February 27, 1794, a day after its arrival, *PGW-PS*, 15:289–292. John Brown to Randolph, January 25, 1794, *PGW-PS*, 15:291-293.

124. *PGW-PS*, 15:293n5.

125. *PGW-PS*, 15:236–237n2.

126. *PGW-PS*, 15:446–447.

127. The exception would be Ammon, *The Genet Mission*, 161–162, 165.

128. *PGW-PS*, 16:310n7.

129. Washington to the U.S. Senate and House of Representatives, May 20, 1794, *PGW-PS*, 16:97–98.

130. Ammon, *The Genet Mission*, 169.

131. *PGW-PS*, 15:293n5.

132. Fenwick, *Neutrality Laws of the United States*, 26–27. See also Thomas, *American Neutrality in 1793*, 278–279.

133. Fenwick, Neutrality Laws of the United States, 27.

Chapter 7

1. For these addresses, see Washington to the U.S. Senate and House of Representatives, December 3, 5, 16, 1793, *PGW-PS*, 14:462–467, 474–475, 531–532, 534.

2. Treaties were important vehicles to establishing a nation's sovereignty and authority, and these efforts helped established the United States as "treaty worthy." Gould, *Among the Powers of the Earth*, 12.

3. Cox, *Parisian American*, 13, 27–30, 155–156.

4. In 1792 Congress passed a law establishing guidelines for the conduct of consuls and vice consuls. Among its provisions was the requirement that these officials post a bond of at least $2,000 and no more than $10,000 to ensure their faithful performance. The United States posted consuls throughout Europe and the Caribbean, including London, Dublin, Liverpool, Marseilles, and Hispaniola. See *PTJ*, 20:401–404, 23:617–620.

5. Cox, *Parisian American*, 29–30.

6. *PGW-PS*, 15:451–452n1.

7. Wachsmuth et al. to Washington, May 6, 1794, *PGW-PS*, 16:31–33n1. Most of the vessels described in this letter were eventually released.

8. Stewart et al. to Washington, May 13, 1794, *PGW-PS*, 16:65–68.

9. On Barney's maritime adventures, see Footner, *Sailor of Fortune*.

10. Randolph to Washington, March 29, 1794, *PGW-PS*, 15:465nn1–2. See also Randolph to Hamilton, June 16, 1794, *PAH*, 16:490–491.

11. *PAH*, 16:417–418n1.

12. Cox, *Parisian American*, 45.

13. *PGW-PS*, 15:451–452nn1–2, 16:194, 196n12.

14. The cabinet signaled their support for this appointment on April 2, 1794. See *PGW-PS*, 15:497.

15. Washington to Hamilton, April 16, 1794, *PGW-PS*, 15:605.

16. Hamilton to Higginson, April 16, 1794, *PAH*, 16:288–289. For Randolph's instructions of April 11, 1794, see ibid., 289nn2–4.

17. Nathaniel Higginson (1766–94) was the son of Stephen Higginson, a prominent Boston merchant. See *PGW-PS*, 15:494n2.

18. *PGW-PS*, 14:475.

19. Combs, *Jay Treaty*, 140.

20. *PGW-PS*, 15:315n6.

21. Washington to U.S. Senate, April 16, 1794. Jay's nomination was approved on April 19 by a vote of 18 to 8. See Washington to Randolph, April 15, 1794, *PGW-PS*, 15:603, 608–609n2.

22. Washington appointed Jay as chief justice in fall 1789, a position he held until 1795. Stahr, *John Jay*, 197, 273. See also Williams, *Founding Family*, 303.

23. Estes, *Jay Treaty Debate*, 25.

24. "Instructions to Mr. Jay," May 6, 1794, *PAH*, 16:323–325n13.

25. "Instructions to Mr. Jay," May 6, 1794, *PAH*, 16:325–328n13.

26. Estes, *Jay Treaty Debate*, 25.

27. Combs, *Jay Treaty*, 145, 148.

28. Combs, *Jay Treaty*, 86, 145, 148, 151, 153.

29. Combs, *Jay Treaty*, 153, 155, 156.

30. *PAH*, 18:466n4.

31. Randolph to Washington, October 23, 1794, *PGW-PS*, 17:105–106n1, *PAH*, 18:466n4.

32. The president appointed Samuel Bayard (1767–1840) on November 3, 1794. *PGW-PS*, 17:129n1.

33. On these instructions, see *PGW-PS*, 17:223n1. On his arrival date, see *PAH*, 18:466n4.

34. Washington to the U.S. Senate, June 8, 1795, *PGW-PS*, 18:200–201. Combs, *Jay Treaty*, incorrectly cites this date as July 8.

35. For Madison's proposals, see Brant, *James Madison*, 393.

36. For the full text of the treaty, see *PGW-PS*, 18:759–780.

37. Combs, *Jay Treaty*, 128, 134, 153, 160; Estes, *Jay Treaty Debate*, 34.

38. Combs, *Jay Treaty*, 151, 152, 161, 163.

39. Combs, *Jay Treaty*, 186–187.

40. Washington to U.S. Senate, March 31, 1796, *PGW-PS*, 19:634–644. See also Pinkney, *Christopher Gore*, 70–72; and Ireland, *Legal Career of William Pinkney*, 20–21, 22–23.

41. Perkins, *The First Rapprochement*, 54.

42. Article VII of the Treaty of Amity, Commerce, and Navigation, *PGW-PS*, 18:766–767; Jefferson to Hammond, September 5, 1793, *PTJ*, 27:35–37.

43. Moore, *International Adjudications*, 4:179, 306–307.

44. Ireland, *Legal Career of William Pinkney*, 24–30.

45. Moore, *International Adjudications*, 5(2):87.

46. On January 1, 1804, Skipwith reported to Secretary of State James Madison that 103 American ships had been held during the 1793–94 embargo at Bordeaux, France. See Brugger, *Papers of James Madison, Secretary of State Series*, 6:273n2; and Cox, *Parisian American*, 155.

47. Boston citizens, July 13, 1795, *PGW-PS*, 18:329.

48. New York citizens, July 20, 1795, *PGW-PS*, 18:375.

49. Sussex County, VA, citizens, August 12, 1795, *PGW-PS*, 18:537.

50. See Estes, *Jay Treaty Debate*, 31.

51. Washington to Randolph, April 15, 1794, *PGW-PS*, 15: 603.

52. *PGW-PS*, 14: 531.

53. Bemis, *Pinckney's Treaty*, 173.

54. Spain ended its wartime alliance with Britain when it signed the Peace of Basle with France on July 22, 1795. Bemis, *Pinckney's Treaty*, 267–268.

55. Bemis, *Pinckney's Treaty*, 203, 205, 207, 275.

56. Bemis, *Pinckney's Treaty*, 207.

57. William Short, a protégé of Jefferson, had served as the chargé d'affaires in France before assuming his diplomatic posting in Spain. William Carmichael, who had assisted the U.S. peace mission in Paris, served as chargé d'affaires in Spain from 1784 until his recall in 1794. See Bemis, *Pinckney's Treaty*, 164, 167.

58. Thomas Pinckney (1750–1828) hailed from a politically prominent South Carolina family. In addition to his diplomatic career, he was a Revolutionary War veteran, congressman, and vice-presidential candidate. See Williams, *Founding Family*, 13, 145, 304, 313, 323, 337.

59. Washington to the U.S. Senate, November 21, 1794, *PGW-PS*, 17:194–195nn1–2.

60. *PGW-PS*, 17:194.

61. "Monday, November 24, 1794," U.S. Senate, *Journal of the Executive Proceedings*, 164.

62. The payments to American ships captured during the European war amounted to $127,000 and was paid out between 1798 and 1802. Moore, *International Adjudications*, 5(2):80–87.

63. For the full text of the treaty, see Bemis, *Pinckney's Treaty*, 277–279, 343–362.

64. Washington shared this news with Pinckney on March 5, 1796. See *PGW-PS*, 19:531.

65. Portugal resumed its blockade of Gibraltar in 1786. These restrictions remained in place until 1793, when Portugal and Britain entered into a peace treaty. Reopening the Straits of Gibraltar in 1793 had a devastating effect on American shipping. See Barney, *Prisoners of Algiers*, 97, 102–103.

66. Orren, *Power, Faith, and Fantasy*, 18–19.

67. Barney, *Prisoners of Algiers*, 1, 72, 73, 81, 83, 94.

68. By the end of 1792, twelve captives remained. Seven had died of either the plague or consumption, and two had been released through private means. Barney, *Prisoners of Algiers*, 86, 94.

69. Washington to the U.S. Senate and House of Representatives, December 16, 1793, *PGW-PS*, 14:534.

70. See Jefferson, "Report on Morocco and Algiers," December 14, 1793, *PGW-PS*, 14:535.

71. Barney, *Prisoners of Algiers*, 99–100.

72. The first three frigates, the *United States*, the *Constitution*, and the *Constellation*, were launched in 1797 but were never used in the Mediterranean region. Field, *America and the Mediterranean World*, 36–37, 42.

73. Ford, *Joel Barlow*, 11; Field, *America and the Mediterranean World*, 37–38.

74. This agreement included Americans captured in the 1793 attacks. See *PGW-PS*, 16:613n1.

75. Axelrod, *American Treaties and Alliances*, vi.

76. Field, *America and the Mediterranean World*, 37–38.

77. Washington to the U.S. Senate and House of Representatives, *PGW-PS*, 19:221–227.

78. *PGW-PS*, 19:630n1.

79. Edling, *Hercules in the Cradle*, 81, 82, 88.

80. Edling, *Hercules in the Cradle*, 83.

81. White, *The Federalists*, 217–219.

82. Wood, *Empire of Liberty*, 245.

83. On the U.S. war with Tripoli, see Field, *America and the Mediterranean World*, 49–67. On the War of 1812's start, see Wood, *Empire of Liberty*, 659.

Conclusion

1. See Washington to the U.S. Senate and House of Representatives, December 8, 1795, PGW-PS, 19:221–227.

2. Washington to Morris, December 22, 1795, *PGW-PS*, 19:278–284.

3. Jefferson was the first to resign, leaving in December 1793. Knox followed a year later, in 1794, while Hamilton remained until January 1795. Randolph abruptly resigned on August 19, 1795. *PGW-PS*, 14:652, 17:323, 466, 18:563. Randolph was Jefferson's immediate replacement as secretary of state. Timothy Pickering replaced Knox as secretary of war. Oliver Wolcott Jr. became secretary of the Treasury after Hamilton. And finally, Pickering moved from the War Department to State after Randolph resigned, with James McHenry replacing him at War. See Elkins and McKittrick, *Age of Federalism*, 625, 627, 630, 633.

4. Elkins and McKittrick, *Age of Federalism*, 431.

5. For a summary of these dispatches, see *PGW-PS*, 18:482–483n3.

6. See Washington's questions to Wolcott and Pickering, August 12–18, 1795, and Randolph to Washington, August 19, 1795, *PGW-PS*, 18:538–541n, 563–564n1. See also Lindsay M. Chervinsky's treatment of this episode in *The Cabinet*, 287–300.

7. After leaving the cabinet, Randolph published a pamphlet, *A Vindication of Mr. Randolph's Resignation* (Philadelphia, 1795).

8. Ammon, *James Monroe*, 113, 114, 118.

9. Washington to the U.S. Senate, May 27, 1794, *PGW-PS*, 16:143–144; Ammon, *James Monroe*, 116.

10. Ammon, *James Monroe*, 119–120.

11. Ammon, *James Monroe*, 142–145, 148–149.

12. Washington to Monroe, August 25, 1796, Fitzpatrick, *Writings of Washington*, 35:190.

13. Washington to the Secretary of State, July 8, 1796, Fitzpatrick, *Writings of George Washington*, 35:127.

14. Charles Cotesworth Pinckney (1746–1825) was the brother of Thomas Pinckney. He also enjoyed a distinguished career in American politics and diplomacy. See Williams, *Founding Family*, 12, 314, 322.

15. Washington to Pickering, November 20, 1795, *PGW-PS*, 19:171–172nn2–4.

16. Hamilton was the principal author of this address, although Madison had drafted an earlier version in 1792, at the end of Washington's first term. See Washington to Hamilton, August 25, 1796, *PAH*, 20:307–309. On the 1792 exchange between Washington and Madison, see *PGW-PS*, 10:399–403, 475–480. See also Leibiger, *Founding Friendship*, 161, 209–215.

17. Fitzpatrick, *Writings of George Washington*, 35:214n84, 236.

18. Fitzpatrick, *Writings of George Washington*, 35:233, 234, 236.

19. Washington retired to his beloved Mount Vernon in the spring of 1797, after John Adams's inauguration as the nation's second president. From his home, Washington wrote, "I am once more seated under my vine and fig tree and hope to spend the remainder of my days ... in peaceful retirement." He died two and half years later, on December 14, 1799, at the age of sixty-seven. See Chernow, *Washington*, 775, 809.

20. Elkins and McKittrick, *Age of Federalism*, 689.

21. Wood, *Empire of Liberty*, 242–243, 641–643, 647–648, 696–697.

22. Washington's funeral was held on December 18, 1799, four days after his death. See Chernow, *Washington*, 809, 811–812.

BIBLIOGRAPHY

Abbot, W. W., Dorothy Twohig, Philander D. Chase, Beverly H. Runge, and Frederick Hall Schmidt, eds. *The Papers of George Washington, Colonial Series*. 10 vols. Charlottesville: University of Virginia Press, 1983–[95].

Abbot, W. W., Dorothy Twohig, Philander D. Chase, Beverly H. Runge, Beverly S. Kirsch, and Debra B. Kessler, eds. *The Papers of George Washington, Confederation Series*. 6 vols. Charlottesville: University Press of Virginia, 1992–[97].

An Account of the Voyages and Cruizes of Captain Walker, Commander of a Small Squadron of Privateers Called the Royal Family. Boston, 1761. The Library Company of Philadelphia, microform. https://babel.hathitrust.org/cgi/pt?id=hvd.hnpix9&view=2up&seq=8.

Adams, William Howard. *Gouverneur Morris: An Independent Life*. New Haven, CT: Yale University Press, 2003.

Allen, David Grayson, et al., eds. *Diary of John Quincy Adams*. 2 vols. Cambridge, MA: Harvard University Press, 1982.

American State Papers: Foreign Relations. Volume 1.

Ammon, Harry. *The Genet Mission*. New York: W. W. Norton, 1973.

———. *James Monroe: The Quest for National Identity*. Charlottesville: University Press of Virginia, 1990.

Anderson, Fred. *Crucible of War: The Seven Years' War and the Fate of Empire in British North America, 1754–1766*. New York: Alfred A. Knopf, 2000.

Andrews, Kenneth R. *Elizabethan Privateering during the Spanish War*. Cambridge: Cambridge University Press, 1964.

Arlyck, Kevin. "The Courts and Foreign Affairs at the Founding." *Brigham Young University Law Review* 2017 (2017): 1–64.

Axelrod, Alan. *American Treaties and Alliances*. Washington, DC: Congressional Quarterly Press, 2000.

Bailyn, Bernard. *Atlantic History: Concept and Contours*. Cambridge, MA: Harvard University Press, 2005.

Balogh, Brian. *A Government Out of Sight: The Mystery of National Authority in Nineteenth-Century America*. New York: Cambridge University Press, 2009.

Barney, H. G. *The Prisoners of Algiers: An Account of the Forgotten American-Algerian War, 1785–1797*. New York: Oxford University Press, 1966.

Bartoloni-Tuazon, Kathleen. *For Fear of an Elective King: George Washington and the Presidential Title Controversy of 1789*. Ithaca, NY: Cornell University Press, 2014.

Beckert, Sven. *Empire of Cotton: A Global History*. New York: Alfred A. Knopf, 2014.
Bemis, Samuel Flagg. *Pinckney's Treaty*. New Haven, CT: Yale University Press, 1960.
Berkin, Carol. *A Sovereign People: The Crises of the 1790s and the Birth of American Nationalism*. New York: Basic Books, 2017.
Bevans, Charles I., ed. *Treaties and Other International Agreements of the United States of America, 1776–1949*. 13 vols. Washington, DC: U.S. Government Printing Office, 1968–76.
Bolkhovitinov, Nikolai N. *The Beginnings of Russian-American Relations, 1775–1815*. Cambridge, MA: Harvard University Press, 1975.
Bowman, Albert Hall. *The Struggle for Neutrality: Franco-American Diplomacy during the Federalist Era*. Knoxville: University of Tennessee Press, 1974.
Boyd, Julian P., Charles T. Cullen, John Cantanzariti, Barbara B. Oberg, and James P. McClure, eds. *The Papers of Thomas Jefferson*. 44 vols. Princeton, NJ: Princeton University Press, 1950–[2017].
Bradburn, Douglas. *The Citizenship Revolution: Politics and the Creation of the American Union*. Charlottesville: University of Virginia Press, 2009.
Bragg, C. L. *Crescent Moon over Carolina: William Moultrie and American Liberty*. Columbia: University of South Carolina Press, 2013.
Branson, Susan. *Those Fiery Frenchified Dames: Women and Political Culture in Early National Philadelphia*. Philadelphia: University of Pennsylvania Press, 2001.
Brant, Irving. *James Madison: Father of the Constitution, 1789–1800*. Indianapolis: Bobbs-Merrill, 1950.
Breen, T. H. *George Washington's Journey: The President Forges a New Nation*. New York: Simon and Schuster, 2016.
Brewer, John. *Sinews of Power: War, Money, and the English State, 1688–1783*. Cambridge, MA: Harvard University Press, 1990.
Broadside, Beverly, MA, September 17, 1776. Library Company of Philadelphia. Subscription required.
Brown, Charles Brocken. *Arthur Mervyn; or, Memoirs of the year 1793*. 1799. New York: Burt Franklin, 1970.
Brown, Kate Elizabeth. *Alexander Hamilton and the Development of American Law*. Lawrence: University of Kansas Press, 2017.
Brugger, Robert J., ed. *The Papers of James Madison, Secretary of State Series*. 11 vols. Charlottesville: University of Virginia Press, 1986–[2017].
Brunsman, Denver. *The Evil Necessity: British Naval Impressment in the Eighteenth-Century Atlantic World*. Charlottesville: University of Virginia Press, 2013.
Bushman, Richard L. *The Refinement of America: Persons, Houses, Cities*. New York: Alfred A. Knopf, 1992.
Butterfield, L. H., Leonard C. Gaber, and Wendell D. Garrett, eds. *The Diary and Autobiography of John Adams*. 4 vols. Cambridge, MA: Harvard University Press, 1964.

Calloway, Colin G. *The American Revolution in Indian Country: Crisis and Diversity in Native American Communities*. New York: Cambridge University Press, 1995.

———. *The Victory with No Name: The Native American Defeat of the First American Army*. New York: Oxford University Press, 2015.

———, ed. *The World Turned Upside Down*. Boston: Bedford–St. Martin's, 2016.

Carp, Benjamin L. *Rebels Rising: Cities and the American Revolution*. New York: Oxford University Press, 2007.

Chamberlain, Muriel E. *"Pax Britannica"?: British Foreign Policy, 1789–1914*. London: Routledge, 1988.

Chapin, Howard M. *Privateering in King George's War, 1739–1748*. Providence: E. A. Johnson Company, 1928.

Chapin, Howard M. *Privateer Ships and Sailors: The First Century of American Colonial Privateering, 1625–1725*. Toulon, 1926.

Chase, Philander D., ed. *The Papers of George Washington, Revolutionary War Series*. 26 vols. Charlottesville: University of Virginia Press, 1985–[2018].

Chernow, Ron. *Alexander Hamilton*. New York: Penguin Books, 2004.

———. *Washington: A Life*. New York: Penguin Press, 2010.

Chervinsky, Lindsay M. *The Cabinet: George Washington and the Creation of an American Institution*. Cambridge, MA: Harvard University Press, 2020.

Clark, William Bell. *George Washington's Navy: Being an Account of His Excellency's Fleet in New England Waters*. Baton Rouge: Louisiana State University Press, 1960.

Clauder, Anna C. *American Commerce as Affected by the Wars of the French Revolution and Napoleon, 1793–1812*. Clifton, NJ: Augustus M. Kelley, 1932.

Cleves, Rachel Hope. *The Reign of Terror in America: Visions of Violence from Anti-Jacobinism to Antislavery*. New York: Cambridge University Press, 2009.

Coggins, Jack. *Ships and Seamen of the American Revolution*. Harrisburg, PA: Stackpole Books, 1969.

Cohen, Sheldon S. *Commodore Abraham Whipple of the Continental Navy: Privateer, Patriot, Pioneer*. Gainesville: University Press of Florida, 2010.

Colley, Linda. *Britons: Forging the Nation, 1707–1837*. New Haven, CT: Yale University Press, 1992.

Combs, Jerald A. *The Jay Treaty: Political Battleground of the Founding Fathers*. Berkeley: University of California Press, 1970.

Conroy-Krutz, Emily. *Christian Imperialism: Converting the World in the Early American Republic*. Ithaca, NY: Cornell University Press, 2015.

Cooke, Jacob E. *Tench Coxe and the Early Republic*. Chapel Hill: University of North Carolina Press, 1978.

Cox, Henry Bartholomew. *The Parisian American: Fulwar Skipwith of Virginia*. Washington, DC: Mount Vernon, 1964.

Crawford, Michael J., ed. *The Autobiography of a Yankee Mariner: Christopher Prince and the American Revolution*. Washington, DC: Potomac Books, 2002.

Cresson, W. P. *Francis Dana: A Puritan Diplomat at the Court of Catherine the Great.* New York: Dial Press, 1930.

Crowhurst, Patrick. *The French War on Trade: Privateering, 1793–1815.* Southampton, UK: Scolar, 1989.

Cunningham, Noble E., Jr. *The Presidency of James Monroe.* Lawrence: University Press of Kansas, 1996.

Dallek, Robert. *Franklin D. Roosevelt and American Foreign Policy, 1932–1945.* New York: Oxford University Press, 1979.

DeConde, Alexander. *Entangling Alliance: Politics and Diplomacy under George Washington.* Durham, NC: Duke University Press, 1958.

Dierks, Konstantin. "Americans Overseas in the Early American Republic." *Diplomatic History* 42 (2018): 18–35.

Dougall, Richardson, and Mary Patricia Chapman. *United States Chiefs of Mission, 1778–1973.* Washington, DC: Historical Office, Bureau of Public Affairs, Department of State, 1973.

Doyle, William. *The Oxford History of the French Revolution.* New York: Oxford University Press, 2002.

Dull, Jonathan R. *A Diplomatic History of the American Revolution.* New Haven, CT: Yale University Press, 1985.

Dunn, Susan. *Sister Revolutions: French Lightning, American Light.* New York: Faber and Faber, 1999.

Edler, Friedrich. *The Dutch Republic and the American Revolution.* New York: AMS, 1971.

Edling, Max M. *Hercules in the Cradle: War, Money, and the American State, 1783–1867.* Chicago: University of Chicago Press, 2015.

———. *A Revolution in Favor of Government: Origins of the U.S. Constitution and the Making of the American State.* New York: Oxford University Press, 2003.

Elkins, Stanley, and Eric McKittrick. *The Age of Federalism: The Early American Republic, 1788–1800.* New York: Oxford University Press, 1993.

Ellis, Joseph J. *American Sphinx: The Character of Thomas Jefferson.* New York: Alfred A. Knopf, 1997.

Estes, Todd, *The Jay Treaty Debate, Public Opinion, and the Evolution of Early American Political Culture.* Amherst: University of Massachusetts Press, 2006.

Pennsylvania Historical and Museum Commission, Harrisburg. Executive Correspondence, 1790–99.

Executive Office for U.S. Attorneys, Issuing Body. *Bicentennial Celebration of the United States Attorneys.* Washington, DC: Executive Office of the U.S. Attorneys, 1989.

Fanning, Nathaniel. *Narrative of the Adventures of an American Navy Officer, who served during part of the American Revolution under the Command of John Paul Jones, esq.* New York: Printed for Author, 1806.

Faragher, John Mack. *A Great and Noble Scheme: The Tragic Story of the Expulsion of the French Acadians from Their American Homeland*. New York: W. W. Norton, 2005.
Fenwick, Charles G. *American Neutrality: Trial and Failure*. New York: New York University Press, 1940.
———. *The Neutrality Laws of the United States*. Washington, DC: Carnegie Endowment, 1913.
Ferling, John. *The Ascent of George Washington: The Hidden Political Genius of an American Icon*. New York: Bloomsbury, 2009.
———. *John Adams: A Life*. Knoxville: University of Tennessee Press, 1992.
Field, James A. *America and the Mediterranean World, 1776–1882*. Princeton, NJ: Princeton University Press, 1969.
Fitzpatrick, John C., ed. *The Writings of George Washington*. 39 vols. Washington, DC: U.S. Government Printing Office, 1931–44.
Flexner, James Thomas. *George Washington: The Forge of Experience, 1732–1775*. Boston: Little, Brown, 1965.
———. *George Washington in the American Revolution, 1775–1783*. Boston: Little, Brown 1967.
———. *George Washington and the New Nation, 1783–1793*. Boston: Little, Brown, 1970.
Footner, Hulbert. *Sailor of Fortune: The Life and Adventures of Commodore Barney, U.S.N.* New York: Harper and Brothers, 1940.
Ford, Arthur L. *Joel Barlow*. New York: Twayne, 1971.
Freeman, Douglas Southall. *George Washington: A Biography*. 7 vols. New York: Charles Scribner's Sons, 1948–57.
Furstenberg, Francois. *When the United States Spoke French: Five Refugees Who Shaped a Nation*. New York: Penguin, 2014.
Garitee, Jerome R. *The Republic's Private Navy: The American Privateering Business as Practiced by Baltimore during the War of 1812*. Middletown, CT: Wesleyan University Press, 1977.
General Advertiser (Philadelphia), July 30, 1793.
Gilbert, Felix. *To the Farewell Address: Ideas of Early American Foreign Policy*. Princeton, NJ: Princeton University Press, 1961.
Gilje, Paul. "Commerce and Conquest in Early American Foreign Relations, 1750–1850." *Journal of the Early Republic* 37 (2017): 735–770.
———. *Free Trade and Sailors' Rights in the War of 1812*. New York: Cambridge University Press, 2013.
———. *Liberty on the Waterfront: American Maritime Culture in the Age of Revolution*. Philadelphia: University of Pennsylvania, 2004.
———. *To Swear like a Sailor: Maritime Culture in America, 1750–1850*. New York: Cambridge University Press, 2016.

Goebel, Julius, Jr. *Antecedents and Beginnings to 1801*. Vol. 1 of *History of the Supreme Court of the United States*. New York: Macmillan, 1971.

Gould, Eliga H. *Among the Powers of the Earth: The American Revolution and the Making of a New World Empire*. Cambridge, MA: Harvard University Press, 2012.

Griffiths, David M. "An American Contribution to the Armed Neutrality of 1780." *Russian Review* 30 (April 1971): 164–172.

Hancock, David. *Citizens of the World: London Merchants and the Integration of the British Atlantic Community, 1735–1785*. Cambridge: Cambridge University Press, 1995.

Hanna, Mark G. *Pirate Nests and the Rise of the British Empire, 1570–1740*. Chapel Hill: University of North Carolina Press, 2015.

Harper, John Lamberton. *American Machiavelli: Alexander Hamilton and the Origins of U.S. Foreign Policy*. Cambridge: Cambridge University Press, 2004.

Harsanyi, Doina Pasca. *Lessons from America: Liberal French Nobles in Exile, 1793–1798*. University Park: Pennsylvania State University Press, 2010.

Head, David. *Privateers of the Americas: Spanish American Privateering from the United States in the Early Republic*. Athens: University of Georgia Press, 2015.

Herring, George C. *From Colony to Superpower: U.S. Foreign Relations since 1776*. New York: Oxford University Press, 2008.

Hickey, Donald R. *The War of 1812: A Forgotten Conflict*. Urbana: University of Illinois Press, 1989.

Hume, Edgar Erskine, ed. *General Washington's Correspondence Concerning the Society of Cincinnati*. Baltimore: Johns Hopkins University Press, 1941.

Hunt, Gaillard, et al., eds. *Letters and Other Writings of James Madison*. 4 vols. Philadelphia: J. B. Lippincott, 1867.

Hunt, Lynn. *Politics, Culture, and Class in the French Revolution*. Berkeley: University of California Press, 1984.

Hutchinson, William T., and William M. E. Rachal, eds. *The Papers of James Madison*. 17 vols. Chicago: University of Chicago Press, 1962–91.

Hutson, James H. *John Adams and the Diplomacy of the American Revolution*. Lexington: University Press of Kentucky, 1980.

Hyneman, Charles S. *The First American Neutrality: A Study of the American Understanding of Neutral Obligations during the Years 1792 to 1815*. Urbana: University of Illinois Press, 1934.

Ireland, Robert M. *The Legal Career of William Pinkney, 1764–1822*. New York: Garland, 1986.

Jackson, Donald, and Dorothy Twohig, eds. *The Diaries of George Washington*. 6 vols. Charlottesville: University Press of Virginia, 1976–79.

Jackson, Melvin H. *Privateers in Charleston, 1793–1796: An Account of the French Palatinate in South Carolina*. Washington, DC: Smithsonian Institution Press, 1969.

Jameson, John Franklin. *Privateering and Piracy in the Colonial Period: Illustrative Documents*. New York: Macmillan, 1923.

Jarvis, Michael J. *In the Eye of All Trade: Bermuda, Bermudians, and the Maritime Atlantic World, 1680–1783*. Chapel Hill: University of North Carolina Press, 2010.
Jessup, Philip C., and Francis C. Deak. *Neutrality: Its History, Economics, and Laws*. 4 vols. New York: Columbia University Press, 1935–36.
Kaplan, Lawrence S., ed. *Colonies into Nation: American Diplomacy, 1763–1801*. New York: Macmillan, 1972.
Kert, Faye M. *Privateering: Patriots and Profits in the War of 1812*. Baltimore: Johns Hopkins University Press, 2015.
Ketcham, Ralph, ed. *Selected Writings of James Madison*. Indianapolis: Hackett, 2006.
Knott, Sarah. *Sensibility and the American Revolution*. Chapel Hill: University of North Carolina Press, 2009.
Koot, Christian. *Empire at the Periphery: British Colonists, Anglo-Dutch Trade, and the Development of the British Atlantic, 1621–1713*. New York: New York University Press, 2011.
Kramer, Lloyd. *Lafayette in Two Worlds: Public Cultures and Personal Identities in an Age of Revolution*. Chapel Hill: University of North Carolina Press, 1996.
Kulsrud, Carl J. "Armed Neutralities to 1780." *American Journal of International Law* 29 (July 1935): 423–447.
Kupperman, Karen Ordahl. "International at the Creation: Early Modern American History." In *Rethinking American History in a Global Age*, edited by Thomas Bender, 91–106. Berkeley: University of California Press, 2002.
Kurland, Philip B., and Ralph Lerner, eds. *The Founders' Constitution*. https://press-pubs.uchicago.edu/founders/.
Labaree, Leonard W., and Whitfield J. Bell Jr., eds. *The Papers of Benjamin Franklin*. 43 vols. New Haven, CT: Yale University Press, 1959–[2018].
Larson, Edward J. *The Return of George Washington, 1783–1789*. New York: HarperCollins, 2014.
Leibiger, Stuart. *Founding Friendship: George Washington, James Madison, and the Creation of the American Republic*. Charlottesville: University Press of Virginia, 1999.
Lemisch, Jesse. *Jack Tar vs. John Bull: The Role of New York's Seamen in Precipitating the American Revolution*. New York: Garland, 1997.
Lengel, Edward G. *General George Washington: A Military Life*. New York: Random House, 2005.
———. *Inventing George Washington: America's Founder, in Myth and Memory*. New York: Harper, 2011.
Maclay, Edgar Stanton. *A History of American Privateers*. New York: D. Appleton, 1899.
Madariaga, Isabel de. *Britain, Russia, and the Armed Neutrality of 1780*. New Haven, CT: Yale University Press, 1962.
———. *Catherine the Great: A Short History*. New Haven, CT: Yale University Press, 1990.

———. *Russia in the Age of Catherine the Great*. New Haven, CT: Yale University Press, 1981.

Manela, Erez. "The United States in the World." In *American History Now*, edited by Eric Foner and Lisa McGirr, 201–220. Philadelphia: Temple University Press, 2011.

Mansfield, Julia. "The Disease of Commerce: Yellow Fever in the Atlantic World, 1793–1805." PhD diss. Stanford University, 2018.

Marcus, Maeva, et al., eds. *The Documentary History of the Supreme Court of the United States, 1789–1800*. 8 vols. New York: Columbia University Press, 1985–[2007].

McCoy, Drew R. *The Elusive Republic: Political Economy in Jeffersonian America*. Chapel Hill: University of North Carolina Press, 1980.

McCullough, David. *John Adams*. New York: Simon and Schuster, 2001.

McMahon, Robert J., "Toward a Pluralist Vision: The Study of American Foreign Relations as International History and National History." In *Explaining the History of American Foreign Relations*, edited by Michael J. Hogan and Thomas G. Patterson, 35–50. 1991. 2nd ed., Cambridge: Cambridge University Press, 2004.

McManemin, John A. *Captains of the Privateers during the Revolutionary War*. Spring Lake, NJ, 1985.

Middlekauff, Robert. *The Glorious Cause: The American Revolution, 1763–1789*. New York: Oxford University Press, 1982.

Moats, Sandra. *Celebrating the Republic: Presidential Ceremony and Popular Sovereignty, from Washington to Monroe*. DeKalb: Northern Illinois University Press, 2010.

Montefiore, Sebag. *Prince of Princes: The Life of Potemkin*. New York: Thomas Dunne Books, 2000.

Moore, John Bassett, ed. *International Adjudications: Ancient and Modern*. 6 vols. New York: Oxford University Press, 1929–.

Morgan, William James. "American Privateering in America's War for Independence, 1775–1783." *American Neptune* 36 (April 1976): 79–87.

Morris, Richard B. *The Peacemakers: The Great Powers and American Independence*. New York: Harper and Row, 1965.

Myers, Jr., Minor. *Liberty without Anarchy: A History of the Society of Cincinnati*. Charlottesville: University Press of Virginia, 1983.

Nagel, Paul C. *John Quincy Adams: A Public Life, a Private Life*. New York: Alfred A. Knopf, 1997.

Nash, Gary. *The Urban Crucible: Social Change, Political Consciousness, and the Origins of the American Revolution*. Cambridge, MA: Harvard University Press, 1979.

Neff, Stephen C. *The Rights and Duties of Neutrals: A General History*. Manchester: Manchester University Press, 2000.

Newman, Simon P. *Parades and Politics of the Street: Festive Culture in the Early American Republic*. Philadelphia: University of Pennsylvania Press, 1997.

Novak, William J. "The Myth of the 'Weak' American State." *American Historical Review* 113 (June 2018): 752–772.

Orren, Michael B. *Power, Faith, and Fantasy: America in the Middle East, 1776 to the Present*. New York: W. W. Norton, 2007.

Painter, Thomas. *Autobiography of Thomas Painter, Relating His Experiences during the War of Revolution*. Privately published, 1910.

Palmer, R. R. *The Age of Democratic Revolution: A Political History of Europe and America, 1760–1800*. 2 vols. Princeton, NJ: Princeton University Press, 1959–64.

Palmer, William P., Henry W. Flournoy, Raleigh E. Colston, and Sherwin McRae, eds. *Calendar of Virginia State Papers and Other Manuscripts*. 11 vols. Richmond, 1875–93.

Patterson, David S. "The Department of State: The Formative Years, 1775–1800." *Prologue* 21 (Winter 1989): 315–328.

Perkins, Bradford. *The First Rapprochement: England and the United States, 1795–1805*. Berkeley: University of California Press, 1967.

Perl-Rosenthal, Nathan. *Citizen Sailors: Becoming American in the Age of Revolution*. Cambridge, MA: Harvard University Press, 2015.

———. "Private Letters and Public Diplomacy: The Adams Network and the Quasi-War, 1797–1798." *Journal of the Early Republic* 31 (Summer 2011): 283–311.

Peters, Ronald M., Jr. *The American Speakership: The Office in Historical Perspective*. Baltimore: Johns Hopkins University Press, 1990.

Peterson, Merrill D. *Thomas Jefferson and the New Nation: A Biography*. New York: Oxford University Press, 1970.

Petrie, Donald A. *The Prize Game: Lawful Looting on the High Seas in the Days of Fighting Sail*. Annapolis: Naval Institute Press, 1999.

Phelps, Glenn A. *George Washington and American Constitutionalism*. Lawrence: University Press of Kansas, 1993.

Piggott, Francis, and G. W. T. Omond. *Documentary History of the Armed Neutralities, 1780–1800*. London: University Press, 1919.

Pinkney, Helen R. *Christopher Gore: Federalist of Massachusetts*. Waltham, MA: Gore Place Society, 1969.

Pocock, J. G. A. *The Machiavellian Moment: Florentine Political Thought and the Atlantic Republican Tradition*. Princeton, NJ: Princeton University Press, 1975.

Poston, Brook. *James Monroe: A Republican Champion*. Gainesville: University Press of Florida, 2019.

Powell, John Harvey. *Bring out Your Dead: The Great Plague of Yellow Fever in Philadelphia in 1793*. New York: Arno, 1970.

Preble, George Henry, and Walter C. Green, eds. *Diary of Ezra Green, M.D., Surgeon on Board on the Continental Ship of War "Ranger."* Boston: Privately Published, 1875.

Prince, Carl E. *The Federalists and the Origins of the U.S. Civil Service*. New York: New York University Press, 1977.

Prince, Carl E., and Mollie Keller. *The U.S. Customs Service: A Bicentennial History*. Washington, DC: Department of Treasury, 1989.

Puls, Mark. *Henry Knox: Visionary General of the American Revolution*. New York: Palgrave Macmillan, 2008.
Purcell, Sarah. *Sealed with Blood: War, Sacrifice, and Memory in Revolutionary America*. Philadelphia: University of Pennsylvania Press, 2002.
Randolph, Edmund. *A Vindication of Mr. Randolph's Resignation*. Philadelphia, 1795.
Rao, Gautham. *National Duties: Custom Houses and the Making of the American State*. Chicago: University of Chicago Press, 2016.
——. "The New Historiography of the Early Federal Government." William and Mary Quarterly, 3rd ser., 77 (January 2020): 97–128.
Reardon, John J. *Edmund Randolph: A Biography*. New York: Macmillan, 1974.
Rediker, Marcus. *Between the Devil and the Deep Blue Sea: Merchant Seamen, Pirates, and the Anglo-American Maritime World, 1700–1750*. Cambridge, MA: Harvard University Press, 1987.
Ritcheson, Charles R. *Aftermath of Revolution: British Policy towards the United States, 1783–1795*. Dallas: Southern Methodist University Press, 1969.
Rosenfeld, Sophia. *Common Sense: A Political History*. Cambridge, MA: Harvard University Press, 2011.
Rouleau, Brian. *With Sails Whitening Every Sea: Mariners and the Making of an American Maritime Empire*. Ithaca, NY: Cornell University Press, 2014.
Royster, Charles S. *A Revolutionary People at War: The Continental Army and America Character, 1775–1783*. Chapel Hill: University of North Carolina Press, 1979.
Sadosky, Leonard J. *Revolutionary Negotiations: Indians, Empires, and Diplomats in the Founding of America*. Charlottesville: University of Virginia Press, 2009.
Scharf, J. Thomas. *History of the Confederate States Navy from Its Organization to the Surrender of the Last Vessel*. New York: Gramercy Books, 1996.
Scott, James Brown, ed. *The Armed Neutralities of 1780 and 1800: A Collection of Official Documents Preceded by the Views of Representative Publicists*. New York: Oxford University Press, 1918.
——. *Prize Cases decided in the United States Supreme Court, 1789–1918*. Oxford: Clarendon, 1923.
Sears, Louis Martin. *George Washington and the French Revolution*. Detroit: Wayne State University Press, 1960.
Shankman, Andrew. "Toward a Social History of Federalism: The State and Capitalism to and from the American Revolution." *Journal of the Early Republic* 37 (Winter 2017): 615–653.
Shapiro, Ian, ed. *The Federalist Papers*. New Haven, CT: Yale University Press, 2009.
Shields, David S. *Civil Tongues and Polite Letters in British America*. Chapel Hill: University of North Carolina Press, 1997.
Sleeper-Smith, Susan. *Indigenous Prosperity and American Conquest: Indian Women of the Ohio River Valley, 1690–1792*. Chapel Hill: University of North Carolina Press, 2018.

Stagg, J. C. A. *Mr. Madison's War: Politics, Diplomacy, and Warfare in the Early American Republic*. Princeton, NJ: Princeton University Press, 1983.
Stahr, Walter. *John Jay: Founding Father*. New York: Humbledon and London, 2005.
Stark, Francis R. "The Abolition of Privateering and the Declaration of Paris." PhD diss., Columbia University, 1897.
Starkey, David J. *British Privateering Enterprise in the Eighteenth Century*. Exeter, UK: University of Exeter Press, 1990.
Stinchcombe, William C. *The American Revolution and the French Alliance*. Syracuse, NY: Syracuse University Press, 1969.
———. "John Adams and the Model Treaty." In *The American Revolution and "A Candid World,"* edited by Lawrence S. Kaplan, 69–84. Kent, OH: Kent State University Press, 1977.
Stourzh, Gerald. *Benjamin Franklin and American Foreign Policy*. Chicago: University of Chicago Press, 1954.
Swanson, Carl E. *Predators and Prizes: American Privateering and Imperial Warfare, 1739–1748*. Columbia: University of South Carolina Press, 1991.
Syrett, Harold C., and Jacob E. Cooke, eds. *The Papers of Alexander Hamilton*. 27 vols. New York: Columbia University Press, 1961–87.
Taylor, Alan. *The Divided Ground: Indians, Settlers, and the Northern Borderlands of the American Revolution*. New York: Alfred A. Knopf, 2006.
Taylor, Robert J., Mary-Jo Kline, and Gregg L. Lint, eds. *The Papers of John Adams*. 19 vols. Cambridge, MA: Harvard University Press, 1977–2018.
Thomas, Charles Marion. *American Neutrality in 1793: A Study in Cabinet Government*. New York: Columbia University Press, 1931.
Truxes, Thomas M. *Defying Empire: Trading with the Enemy in Colonial New York*. New Haven, CT: Yale University Press, 2008.
Tuck, Richard. *The Rights of War and Peace: Political Thought and the International Order from Grotius to Kant*. New York: Oxford University Press, 1999.
Twohig, Dorothy, ed. *The Papers of George Washington, Presidential Series*. 20 vols. Charlottesville: University of Virginia Press, 1987–[2019].
Twohig, Dorothy, Philander D. Chase, Beverly H. Runge, and Frank E. Grizzard Jr., eds. *The Papers of George Washington, Retirement Series*. 4 vols. Charlottesville: University of Virginia Press, 1998–[99].
Ubbelohde, Carl. *The Vice-Admiralty Courts and the American Revolution*. Chapel Hill: University of North Carolina, 1960.
U.S. Senate. *Journal of the Executive Proceedings of the Senate of the United States of America*. Vol. 1. Washington, DC: U.S. Senate, 1828.
Van, Rachel Tamar. "Cents and Sensibilities: Fairness and Free Trade in the Early 19th Century." *Diplomatic History* 42 (2018): 72–89.
Varg, Paul A. *Foreign Policies of the Founding Fathers*. East Lansing: Michigan State University Press, 1963.

Vattel, Emer de. *The Law of Nations; or, Principles of the Law of Nature, Applied to the Conduct and Affairs of Nations and Sovereigns.* Edited by Joseph Chitty. Philadelphia: Johnson and Co., Booksellers, 1872.

Vattel, Emer de. *The Law of Nations; or, Principles of the Law of Nature, Applied to the Conduct and Affairs of Nations and Sovereigns, with Three Early Essays on the Origin and Nature of Natural Law and on Luxury.* Edited by Béla Kapossy and Richard Whatmore. Translated by Thomas Nugent. Indianapolis: Liberty Fund, 2008.

Vickers, Daniel. *Young Men and the Sea: Yankee Seafarers and the Age of Sail.* New Haven, CT: Yale University Press, 2005.

Volo, James M. *Blue Water Patriots: The American Revolution Afloat.* Westport, CT: Praeger, 2007.

Waldstreicher, David. *In the Midst of Perpetual Fetes: The Making of American Nationalism, 1776–1820.* Chapel Hill: University of North Carolina Press, 1997.

Welch, Richard E., Jr. *Theodore Sedgwick, Federalist: A Political Portrait.* Middletown, CT: Wesleyan University Press, 1965.

White, Ashli. *Encountering Revolution: Haiti and the Making of the Early Republic.* Baltimore: Johns Hopkins University Press, 2010.

White, Leonard D. *The Federalists: A Study in Administrative History, 1789–1801.* New York: Free Press, 1948.

———. *The Jeffersonians: A Study in Administrative History, 1801–1829.* New York: Free Press, 1951.

Whitridge, Arnold. *Rochambeau.* New York: Macmillan, 1965.

Williams, Frances Leigh. *A Founding Family: The Pinckneys of South Carolina.* New York: Harcourt Brace Jovanovich, 1978.

Wilmarth, Arthur E., Jr. "Elusive Foundation: John Marshall, James Wilson, and the Problem of Reconciling Popular Sovereignty and Natural Law Jurisprudence in the New Federal Republic." *George Washington Law Review* 72 (2003): 184–189.

Wilson, Rufus R., ed. *Heath's Memoir of the American War.* Freeport, NY: Books for Libraries, 1970.

Winslow, Richard E., III. *"Wealth and Honor": Portsmouth during the Golden Age of Privateering, 1775–1815.* Portsmouth, NH, 1988.

Wood, Gordon S. *The Americanization of Benjamin Franklin.* New York: Penguin, 2004.

———. *Empire of Liberty: A History of the Early Republic, 1789–1815.* New York: Oxford University Press, 2009.

———. *The Radicalism of the American Revolution.* New York: Vintage, 1992.

Young, Christopher J. "Connecting the President and the People: Washington's Neutrality, Genet's Challenge, and Hamilton's Fight for Public Support." *Journal of the Early Republic* 31 (Fall 2011): 435–466.

Ziesche, Philipp. *Cosmopolitan Patriots: Americans in Paris in the Age of Revolution.* Charlottesville: University of Virginia Press, 2010.

INDEX

Page numbers in italics refer to illustrations.

Adams, John, 4: as congressional delegate, 22, 23, 24, 27; as diplomat, 27, 28, 29, 30, 33, 34, 35, 36, 37, 38, 39, 41; as president, U.S., 135, 140; —, and Quasi-War, 140, 145; as president, U.S. Senate, 115; as vice president, U.S., 67, 115
Adams, John Quincy, 27, 36
admiralty authority, U.S., 92–93, 98, 106, 109, 121, 122, 125, 126, 144; and delegating to France, 92–93, 101, 106, 121; and *Glass v. Sloop* Betsey (1794), 120–22; *Jansen v. Vrow Christina Magdalena* (1794), 121
admiralty courts, American states, 19, 35, 92
admiralty courts, British, 12, 33, 116, 133; and vice-admiralty courts, colonial, 15, 16, 17, 134
Algeria, 127, 137, 138, 140; pirates of, 29, 137, 138, 146; vessels of, 138
Algiers, 130, 137, 144, 145; and James Leander Cathcart, 138; diplomacy, U.S., 138, 140; treaty with U.S. (1795), 138, 139; truce with Portugal, 130, 137, 138
alliances, American, 60: avoiding political, 3, 38, 144, 145, 159n90; with Europe, 27, 35, 38, 41, 44, 45, 49, 54, 58, 66, 131; and free trade, 2, 28, 40; wartime, 23, 24, 27, 34, 40. *See also* treaties, American Revolution; treaties, U.S.

allies, U.S.: Britain and France, 1, 5, 41, 61; neutral nations, 33–34
Americans abroad: as merchants, 7; as missionaries, 7; as scientists, 7. *See also* diplomats, U.S.
Anglo-French war (1793), 1, 5, 41, 57, 58, 59, 61, 62, 65, 70, 79, 82, 90, 127, 128, 133, 141, 144, 146; and Spain, 136
army, British, 40, 43, 45
army, Continental, 19, 20, 44, 46, 47, 50, 51, 123, 170n11
army, French, 44, 45; baron de Luckner, 56
artisans, maritime: blacksmiths, 15; caulkers, 15; coopers, 10; gunsmiths, 15; mastmakers, 15; riggers, 10; sailmakers, 10, 15; shipwrights, 10, 15
Atlantic Ocean, 2, 3, 5, 7, 9, 10, 12, 14, 16, 17, 19, 20, 22, 24, 25, 51, 61, 84, 86, 94, 107, 110, 114, 125, 127, 130, 133, 134, 139; and Straits of Gibraltar, 130, 137, 138, 184n65; and U.S. boundary, 108
attorney general, U.S., 5, 61, 62, 81, 124, 142; establishment of, 61
attorneys, U.S., 3, 6, 80, 170n17; and Christopher Gore, Massachusetts, 108–10, 134, 178n23; Richard Harison, New York, 91, 174n75; and indemnifications, 108; and privateering violations, 81, 86, 88, 144; William Rawle, Pennsylvania, 86, 90, 91, 93–94, 108, 172n47

199

Austria, 17, 32, 42, 56, 65, 70, 157n58, 159n90

Bank of the United States, 4. *See also* "Report on the Public Credit"
Barbary States, 39, 114, 115, 137, 140; and Barbary Coast, 6; Tripoli and Tunis, 137, 138. *See also* Algiers; Morocco
Boston, Massachusetts, 9, 10, 15, 16, 18, 20, 80, 81, 95, 108, 119, 135, 170n11; and public library, 27; Tea Party (1773), 18
Bourbon powers, 30, 32, 56, 57. *See also* France; Spain
Bradford, William: as attorney general, U.S., 124; Neutrality Proclamation (1794), 124
Britain, 1, 4, 6, 9, 12, 13, 14, 15, 16, 17, 19, 22, 24, 27, 28, 29, 30, 31, 32, 33, 34, 35, 36, 37, 39, 40, 41, 42, 43, 44, 49, 57, 59, 62, 64, 65, 69, 70, 73, 75, 79, 82, 84, 85, 90, 96, 100, 136, 138, 143; and assaults on American commerce, 60, 82, 103, 111, 113, 114, 115–16, 128, 129, 130, 131, 132, 133, 140, 144, 145; outstanding Revolutionary War issues, 8, 61, 131, 132, 133, 135, 140, 144; U.S. commercial treaty with, 131–32, 133, 134; U.S. diplomatic relationship with, 66, 73, 78, 118, 120, 123, 126, 134, 139. *See also* Hammond, George; treaties, U.S.: of Amity, Commerce, and Navigation, Britain/Jay's Treaty

cabinet, Washington's, 1, 4, 7, 57, 58, 59, 61, 71, 72, 73, 74, 78, 80–82, 84, 85, 95, 101, 185n3; bipartisan cast within, 62, 76, 77, 91, 141, 142, 143; compromises within, 5, 63, 64, 65, 68, 72–73, 74, 103, 104, 120, 141, 144, 146, 166n35; and Congress, U.S., 67–68, 98–99, 111, 112, 113, 120; enforcement of neutrality, 6, 16, 69, 78, 80–82, 84, 85–88, 89, 90, 91, 92, 99–102, 103, 109, 123, 124, 144; Federalist composition, 142, 143; ideological divide, 2, 4, 60, 61, 62, 66, 68, 71, 74, 76, 95, 96, 104, 105, 113, 120, 142; and *Little Sarah* crisis, 95–96, 102; members of, 62, 142; "Opinion on French privateers," 99–101, 102; recall of Genet, 101, 102, 104–7; "Rules on Neutrality," 99–101, 102; Supreme Court, questions to, 96, 97; and yellow fever, 112
Caribbean Sea, 7, 9, 12, 15, 16, 17, 20, 46, 111, 112, 117, 126, 127, 128, 129, 130, 132, 140, 145
Catherine II (empress of Russia; "Catherine the Great"), 30, *31*, 33, 36. *See also* League of Armed Neutrality
Charles IV (king of Spain), 135, 136
Charleston, South Carolina, 10, 15, 82, 83, 119; as hub of French privateering, 84, 85, 86, 90, 121, 173n73
Citizen Genet (privateer), 84, 86, 89–90, 120. *See also (prizes)* ships, American commercial: *Betsey*; ships, British commercial: *William*
citizens, U.S., 2, 4, 5, 7, 8, 9, 22, 51, 53, 62, 63, 64, 65, 71, 72, 75, 78, 79, 80, 81, 86, 87, 90, 94, 97, 101, 106, 110, 111, 114, 121, 123, 124, 125, 126, 127, 128, 130, 134, 135, 136, 138, 139, 140, 144, 145, 146
Clinton, George: as Genet's father-in-law, 122; and *Polly/Republican*, 91
colonies, North American, 9, 10, 14, 15, 18, 19, 24, 25, 26, 27, 28, 33, 34, 36, 37, 42, 43
commissions, French military, 87, 110–11, 124
commissions, privateering, 12, 19; for American colonists, 14; for Americans, 63, 83–84, 85, 87, 101, 106, 108, 109, 120, 125, 131; for nations at war (France, Britain), 86, 89, 91
Congress, Confederation, 38, 39, 40, 123, 131, 137

Index

Congress, Continental, 19, 22, 23, 24, 26, 27, 29, 30, 33, 34, 35, 36, 38, 43; Declaration of Independence, 16, 27, 106; "Secret Committee," 27
Congress, U.S., 3, 6, 39–40, 53, 61, 67–68, 76, 78, 80, 95, 98, 102, 105, 116, 118, 126, 130, 139, 144; and American commerce, protecting, 118, 125; annual presidential address to (1793), 7, 53, 112, 113–14, 115, 120, (1795) 138; convening of, 98–99, 112, 175n117; embargoes, U.S., 117, 118; enforcing neutrality, 103, 114, 138, 139, 140; Madison's resolutions, 115–16, 117, 118; power to declare war, 60, 69, 74; relocation of U.S. capitol, 112; Sedgwick's proposals, 116–17, 118
Consolato del mare, 13, 30, 151n27
Constitution, French, 48, 49, 50, 51, 52, 53, 54, 55, 56, 57
Constitution, U.S., 1, 4, 38, 39, 40, 49, 55, 60, 112, 121, 145; and competing interpretations of, 62, 73, 80; and Genet, 93, 105; separation of powers, 98, 105; and U.S. treaties, 93–94
consuls, American, 7, 116, 127–28, 131, 150n20, 182n4; Joel Barlow, Algiers, 138; exequaturs for, 128, 178n26; Fulwar Skipwith, 116, 127–30, 134
consuls, French, 13, 92, 93, 101, 107, 108, 109, 110, 120, 121, 150n20; Antoine Duplaine, 108–10; —, and seizure of *Greyhound*, 108; François Dupont, 93; exequaturs for, 109–10, 178n26
contraband, wartime, 14, 26, 28, 29, 32, 64, 131; and grains, 111, 130, 132; gunpowder, 13; weapons, 13
cotton: cotton gin, 5, 10; shipped to Liverpool and Manchester, England, 5
court cases, U.S.: *Glass v. Sloop* Betsey (1794), 120–22; *Jansen v. Vrow Christina Magdalena* (1794), 121; *Moodie v. Ship* Phoebe Anne (1796), 121; *Talbot v. Jansen* (1795), 121; *Williamson v.* Betsey (1795), 121
courts, U.S., 3, 16, 60, 89, 91, 92, 93, 96, 97, 98, 102, 103, 109, 110, 114, 120–22, 125, 126, 131, 145
Custis, John Parke, 22, 27, 153n91
customs houses, U.S., 4, 82. *See also* Treasury, Department of, U.S.
customs officers, British, 17, 18
customs officers, U.S., 3, 6, 80–82, 89, 100, 117, 170n11; William Ellery, Newport, Rhode Island, 81; and privateering violations, 80, 81, 88
Customs Service, U.S., 80. *See also* Treasury, Department of, U.S.

Dana, Francis, 36, 37, 38, 158n75. *See also* "militia diplomacy"; Russia
debt, revolutionary war, 3–4, 62, 83, 139. *See also* "Report on the Public Credit"
Declaration of Armed Neutrality, 31–32, 33, 35, 36, 156n45. *See also* Catherine II; Russia
Declaration of Independence, 16, 27, 106; and John Hancock, 16; Richard Henry Lee's resolution, 27, 155n21
Delaware Bay, 84, 85
Delaware River, 95, 96, 97; and Mud Island, fortification of, 95, 96, 175n106
Democratic-Republicans, 62, 68, 69, 74, 94, 104, 105, 115, 116, 133, 139, 141, 142, 143
Denmark, 2, 32, 34, 115, 132, 159n90
D'Estaing, Admiral, 44, 46, 47, 48, 51, 58; Continental army/navy, 44–45; death by guillotine, 57; Versailles National Guard, 49. *See also* Society of the Cincinnati
diplomacy: European, 28, 33, 34, 38, 40, 41, 43, 65; revolutionary, 24, 25, 26, 27, 33, 34, 36, 38, 40, 41; U.S., 3, 39, 40, 53, 60, 61, 78, 102, 113–14, 118, 125, 126, 137, 144, 145, 159n95; —, and costs of, 139

diplomats, European, 65, 79, 104, 110, 122, 142; marquis de Verac, 36
diplomats, U.S., 7, 24, 26, 27, 34, 35, 36, 38, 53, 54, 66, 79, 102, 104, 118, 120, 123, 126, 170n5, 181n116; Silas Deane, 30; Patrick Henry, 136; Arthur Lee, 30; Robert Livingston, 123. *See also* Jay, John; Pinckney, Thomas
district courts, U.S., 6, 91, 92, 109, 110, 121–22, 126, 170n17, 174n82; William Paca, judge, Maryland, 120; —, and *Glass v. Sloop* Betsey (1794), 120–21; Richard Peters, judge, Pennsylvania, 92; —, and *William* ruling, 92, 93

East India Companies: Dutch, 13; English, 13
Elizabeth I (queen of England), 14
embargoes, U.S., 116, 117, 118, 130, 144; end of, 117; extension of, 117; hardships, 117
Embuscade (French privateer), 84, 85, 89, 95; prizes: *Four Brothers*, 85; *Grange*, 84–86, 89, 95; *Little Sarah*, 89, 95–97, 102, 106; *Morning Star*, 85
"enemy goods make enemy ships," 13, 25, 114; and "Blue Water" wars, 12; and Rule of 1756, 16
Enlightenment ideas, 2, 8, 13, 23, 24, 25, 29, 30, 31, 66, 78, 102
Enlightenment philosophers, 2, 24, 25, 26, 27; and John Locke, 26; Montesquieu, 25, 26; Adam Smith, 25
envoys, U.S., 3, 6, 30, 118, 120, 127, 130, 131, 132, 135, 136, 140, 143, 144–45; in Algiers, 137; —, Thomas Barclay, 138; —, David Humphreys, 138; —, John Paul Jones, 138; —, John Lamb, 137; in Britain, and Samuel Bayard, 133, 183n32; and Caribbean shipping losses, 132, 133; in Spain, 134, 135; —, William Carmichael, 136; —, William Short, 136, 184n57

Europe, 9, 10, 12, 13, 16, 23, 24, 28, 32, 33, 34, 35, 36, 38, 39, 40, 49, 53, 54, 60, 61, 63, 64, 65, 66, 70, 76, 79, 98, 113, 114, 119, 127, 131
exports, colonial America, 9, 28; beef, 10; fish, 10; indigo, 10; pork, 10; rice, 10; wheat, 10

Fanny, 91, 93, 107. *See also* Hammond, George; *Sans Culotte*; ships, British commercial; *William*
Farewell Address, Washington's (1796), 5, 145
Fauchet, Jean Antoine, 122, 124, 142, 143. *See also* France: U.S. diplomatic relations with; Genet, Edmund Charles; ministers, European
Federalists, 49, 62, 68, 69, 71, 75, 104, 116, 123, 131, 142, 143
Florida, Spanish, 29, 83, 110, 113, 114, 125
foreign policy, U.S., 1, 7, 53, 60, 66, 68, 69, 71, 74, 75, 76, 77, 101, 102, 115, 120, 140, 141, 143, 144, 145, 146; executive branch dominance over, 3, 6, 60, 68, 69, 75, 77, 79, 102, 118, 139; partisan disagreements over, 65, 66–67, 68, 71, 75
France, 4, 6, 7, 8, 12, 13, 14, 16, 24, 27, 28, 29, 30, 31, 32, 33, 36, 39, 40, 42, 43, 46, 48, 49–55, 58, 79, 80, 84, 110, 135; American Revolution loans, 61, 83; assaults on U.S. commerce, 98, 111, 113, 114, 115, 116, 127, 140; assaults on U.S. sovereignty, 84, 87–88, 103, 110; French republic, 56, 66, 71, 105, 143; French revolutionary wars, 1, 49, 56, 57, 59, 61, 82, 87, 90, 101, 105, 130, 134, 136, 144; U.S. diplomatic relations with, 29, 45, 60, 62, 64, 65, 66–68, 69, 70, 77, 80, 81, 87, 101, 104–5, 106, 107, 113, 114, 122, 123, 128, 129, 131–32, 135, 140, 141, 142, 143, 144; U.S. trading partner, 29, 61, 111, 115; U.S. treaty obligations

to, 66–68, 69, 70, 87, 88–89, 94, 97, 122, 131–32, 133, 140, 141; —, and Convention of Mortefontaine (1800), 146. *See also* Genet, Edmund Charles; privateering: French; treaties, American Revolution

Franklin, Benjamin, 157n62: as diplomat, 26, 27, 28, 29, 30, 33, 34, 35, 36, 37, 38, 39, 41; and French Revolution, 53

"free ships make free goods," 13, 14, 16, 23, 24, 29, 30, 32, 34, 39, 98, 111, 113, 131, 132, 134, 151n29; neutral cargo, 13, 33; "neutrals," 17; Treaty of Utrecht (1713), 14

free trade, 1, 2, 9, 13, 14, 16, 22, 23, 24, 25, 26, 27, 28, 29, 30, 31, 32, 33, 34, 36, 38, 39, 40, 41, 65, 66, 97–98, 100, 132, 133, 137, 138

Genet, Edmund Charles: appeal to American public, 105; arrival of, 82, 85; "Citizen Genet," 3, 7, 82, *83*, 90, 94, 95, 101, 102, 103, 108, 120, 144, 171n29; and Cordelia Clinton, 122; death of, 122; and Democratic-Republicans, 105; and diplomatic improprieties, 83–84, 90, 106; and *Fanny*, 93; Franco-American treaties, interpretations of, 87, 88–89, 91, 92; and *Grange* case, 85; and Hamilton, 95; and *Henfield* case, 90, 94, 95; instructions from French government, 83; and Jefferson, 87, 88, 89, 90, 91, 92–93, 105, 110, 176–77n4, 177n15; and *Little Sarah/Petite Démocrate*, 95–97, 102, 106, 107; and *Polly/Republican*, 91, 92; privateering, U.S. policy, 99–101; privateering activities, 6, 83–85, 88, 89–90, 96, 99–100, 101, 104, 105, 106, 108, 110, 113, 114, 120; recall of, 7, 102, 103–5, 106, 107, 113, 122, 127, 144, 177n15; restitution, French prizes, 92; and Spanish Louisiana, 110–11, 136; and U.S. admiralty authority, 92–93, 94, 106; as U.S. citizen, 122; U.S. government, understandings of, 87, 90, 92, 93, 97, 105, 106, 176–77n4; and *William*, 91–93, 101, 107

Germantown, Pennsylvania: as temporary U.S. capitol, 112. *See also* Congress, U.S.: convening of; yellow fever

Glass v. Sloop Betsey (1794), 120–22, 134, 174n82. *See also* admiralty authority, U.S.

Gore, Christopher: commissioner, "seizure" commission, 134; district attorney, Massachusetts, 108–10, 178n23

government, British, 9, 14, 15, 16, 17; Lord Grenville, 132; order in council, June 8, 1793, 111, 113, 114, 130, 131, 132; order in council, November 6, 1793, 111, 113, 114, 117, 128, 130, 131, 132; Prohibitory Act (1775), 19; revenue acts, 27; taxes, colonial, 18; trade laws, 18, 22, 153n68. *See also* Hammond, George

government, French, 42, 45, 54, 55, 57, 82, 104, 122, 135; Committee on Public Safety, 143; Executive Council, 104; Girondins, 83, 122; Jacobins, 122; Legislative Assembly, 55, 56; National Assembly, 49, 50, 52, 53, 54, 55, 114; National Constituent Assembly, 52, 54, 55; National Convention, 57, 98, 143

government, republican, 4, 27, 47, 49, 50, 51, 57, 66, 144, 145

government, U.S., 2, 3, 6, 8, 49, 51, 60, 79, 80, 87, 90, 92, 93, 102, 106, 108, 126, 127, 140, 146; executive branch, 3, 60, 68, 69, 75, 77, 78, 90, 92, 99, 102, 103, 105, 108, 117, 118, 139; judicial branch, 3, 6, 26, 60, 90, 92, 93, 98–99, 114, 120, 121, 144

governors, colonial: as vice admirals, 15, 16

governors, state, 19, 78, 79, 80; George Clinton, New York, 91; as enforcers of neutrality, 6, 65, 86, 88, 91, 93, 100, 108, 110, 111, 117, 118, 123, 124, 144; governments, state, 19; and Pierre L'Enfant, 118; Thomas Mifflin, Pennsylvania, 92, 95, 96, 175n106; ship seizures, reporting of, 108

Grange (Scottish ship), 84, 85, 86, 89, 95; Genet's assistance, 85. See also *Embuscade*

Greyhound, 108–9. See also consuls, French; ships, American commercial: *Roland*

Grotius, Hugo: *De Jure Belli ac Pacis* ("The Law of War and Peace"), 66; *Mare Liberum* ("The Free Sea"), 25, 26; referenced in cabinet debate, 66

Hamilton, Alexander, 27, 159n96: and Congress, U.S., 98–99, 113; and defensive proposals, 116, 117, 118, 180n90; and embargoes, 117; *Federalist* 11, 39; and Genet, 95, 104, 105, 106; and *Henfield* verdict, 95; and Jay's Treaty, 131, 133; and *Little Sarah* crisis, 96; neutrality enforcement, 72, 80–81, 86, 87, 100; neutrality query, as author of, 62, 63, 64, 65, 165n23; —, and response to, 66–67, 68, 77; as "No Jacobin," 95; as "Pacificus," 59, 60, 68–71, 73, 74–75, 95; privateering, U.S. policy, 87, 88; "Report on the Public Credit," 3–4, 62, 73, 139; as secretary of the Treasury, 2, 3, 4, 5, 6, 7, 26, 59, 60, 61, 62, 63–67, 68, 71, 73, 75, 76, 80–82, 89, 100, 112, 142; and Supreme Court, U.S., 97

Hamilton: The Musical, 4

Hammond, George: as British minister to United States, 6, 79, 87, 142, 172n38; and *Fanny*, 91, 93, 107; and *Grange* case, 84, 85, 86, 89; Jefferson's letters to, 87–88, 96, 134; and *Little Sarah*, 96; memorials to Jefferson, 84–85, 90, 93; and privateering, U.S. policy, 87, 88, 99–101; and restoration, British prizes, 84, 85, 86, 88, 89, 91, 92, 99–101, 134; and *William* case, 89, 91, 92, 93

Helvidius essays, 60, 72–75, 77, 169n92; publication in *Gazette of the United States*, 73. See also Madison, James; Pacificus essays

Henfield, Gideon, 75, 89–90, 91, 93, 94, 95, 98, 121, 145, 173n64; acquittal of, 93; as "Citizen Henfield," 94; Democratic-Republican support, 94. See also privateers: American citizens as; Singleterry, John; *U.S. vs. Henfield*

Holland, 14, 34, 35, 61, 121, 156n45. See also Netherlands

House of Representatives, U.S., 69, 115, 116, 117, 118; and Jay's Treaty, 134; Frederick Muhlenberg, speaker of, 115, 179n65; Theodore Sedgwick, 116, 117, 118, 180n90. See also Congress, U.S.; Madison, James

Humphreys, David: as envoy to Algiers, 138; as minister to Portugal, 54, 57–58, 138, 163n57

impressment, American citizens, 39, 132, 140, 146; colonial, 11, 13, 17, 18, 19; and Knowles Riot (1747), 18

isolationism, in World Wars I and II, 2

Jay, John, 177n6; contributions to neutrality proclamation, 62, 63, 65, 121, 166n30; as diplomat, 38, 123, 131; as envoy to Britain, 118, 120, 123, 130–31, 132, 133, 134; Jay's Treaty/Treaty of Amity, Commerce and Navigation (1795), 133, 135, 137, 139, 141, 143; and Lord Grenville, 132; as U.S. Supreme Court Chief Justice, 94, 98, 113, 118, 120–21, 123, 131, 144, 183n22

Jefferson, Thomas, 127, 136, 143; author of Genet's recall, 105–7, 177n15; and Citizen Genet, 87, 88, 89, 90, 91–93, 95, 96, 97, 101, 104–7, 174n87, 176n4, 177n15; and Congress, U.S., 66–67, 98–99, 113; as Democratic-Republican, 2, 4, 59, 60, 68, 73, 76, 104, 105, 113, 123, 142, 143, 166n30; as diplomat, 39, 41; as governor, 27, 123; *Grange* case, 84–85; *Greyhound* case, 109–10; and "Helvidius," 59, 60, 68, 72, 73, 74, 75, 168n76, 169n88; *Henfield* case, 90, 95; and *Little Sarah* crisis, 95, 96, 97, 102; "mere English neutrality," 68; and Monticello, 112; neutrality enforcement, 79, 80, 81, 82, 85, 86, 87, 90, 91, 92, 93, 96, 97, 100, 106, 109–10, 111, 123, 134; neutrality proclamation, initial support for, 66–67, 77; —, distancing from, 71, 72–73, 74, 75; neutrality query, response to, 66–67, 77; opinion of Washington, 73, 74, 75, 76, 169n101; as president, U.S., 135, 139, 140, 145; privateering, U.S. policy, 87, 88, 89, 91, 99–101; "Report on Commerce," 115, 116, 117; resignation from cabinet, 115, 142; —, attempted, 73, 74, 76, 95, 105, 176n122; as secretary of state, U.S., 2, 4, 5, 6, 7, 26, 59, 60, 61, 62, 63, 64, 65, 68, 77, 79, 80–81, 82, 84–85, 86–88, 90, 91, 92, 93, 100, 105, 107, 108, 111, 113, 115, 123, 134, 138, 142; and Spanish Louisiana, 110–11; as supervisor of U.S. attorneys and marshals, 86, 90, 91, 108, 109–10; and Supreme Court, U.S., 97–98; on U.S. government, 90, 92, 93, 176n4

Jones, John Paul, 11, 138

judges, U.S., 3, 81, 90, 92, 94, 97, 173n59

Judiciary Act, U.S. of 1789, 92, 121, 170n17, 174n82; and admiralty authority, 92, 121

Kentucky, 61, 80; John Brown, U.S. senator, 123–24; and invasion of Louisiana, 101; recruitment activities in, 110, 124, 136; —, and in Georgia and South Carolina, 110; Isaac Shelby, governor, 110, 123

Knox, Henry, 26, 166n31; and Congress, U.S., 98, 113; as Hamilton's cabinet ally, 62, 71; and *Little Sarah* crisis, 96; and Navy, U.S., 118–20; neutrality enforcement, 86, 87, 91, 92, 93, 96, 99–100, 118; neutrality query, response to, 66–67, 77; as secretary of war, 5, 7, 16, 26, 62, 65, 96, 118, 142; and Spanish Louisiana, 110–11; and state governors, 86, 91, 92, 99–100, 111, 118; and state militias, 86, 92, 93; and Supreme Court, U.S., 97

Lafayette, marquis de, 47, 48, 52, 58, 101, 160n15, 161n23, 161n28; and Continental Army, 44–45; as "George Washington of France," 50, 162n45; in Olmutz prison, 57; in Paris National Guard, 50, 56; and republican government, 51, 54, 55–56; and Society of the Cincinnati, 46

La Rouerie, marquis de, 47, 48, 52, 58, 161n27; and Continental Army, 44, 160n15; death, 57; as delegate from Brittany, France, 50–51; and Society of the Cincinnati, 46, 161nn22–23

Law of Nations, The (Vattel), 25–26, 27; quoted in Pacificus essays, 3, 70; referenced in cabinet debate on neutrality, 66–67, 73

laws, U.S., 94, 96, 97, 99, 100, 103, 109, 110, 111, 112, 118, 120, 121, 125, 126, 144, 147n3

League of Armed Neutrality (1780), 2, 30, 31, 32, 33, 34, 35, 36, 38, 132, 159n93; member nations (Austria, Denmark, Holy Roman Empire, Netherlands,

League of Armed Neutrality (1780) (*continued*)
Norway, Portugal, Prussia, Russia, Sweden, Two Sicilies), 32; and United States, 132

League of Armed Neutrality (1794), 159n90

Lee, Henry "Lighthorse Harry": as governor, Virginia, 101; raising French regiment, 101; Washington's eulogy, 146

letters of marque, 151n33; colonial, 12, 15, 16; French, 13; revolutionary, 19, *21*; U.S., 40

letter writing, as political business: 7, 34, 79, 80, 90, 100, 108, 110, 114, 149n36, 161–62n34; of cabinet, 7, 62; of French officers, 41, 46–47, 48, 49, 50, 51, 52, 53, 54, 55, 56, 58, 60; of Catherine Macaulay Graham, 47; of William Heath, 76; of Edward Newenham, 47

Little Sarah/*Petite Democrate*, 89, 95–97; and cabinet debate about, 95–96; and Genet, 102, 106. See also *Embuscade*; ships, British commercial

Louis XVI (king of France), 50, 52, 55, 56; and American Revolution treaties, 29, 55; and execution of, 57, 62; and execution of Marie Antoinette, 122; as "Louis Capet," 67

Louisiana, Spanish: and French proposed invasion of, 5, 83, 101, 110–11, 123–24, 136; and Genet, 110–11, 113, 123, 124, 125; —, and Georgia, 110; —, and Kentucky, 110, 124, 136; —, and South Carolina, 110; U.S. purchase of, 139

Madison, James: congressional resolutions on trade, 115–16, 117, 118; as congressman, 72, 105, 112, 115–16, 117; as Democratic-Republican, 62, 115, 117, 123, 143; as "Helvidius," 59, 60, 72–73, 74, 75, 168n76; and Jefferson, 71, 72, 73, 74, 75, 76, 105, 115, 117; Montpelier home, 72, 73; opinion of Washington, 74–75, 76, 169n101; opposition to Anglo-French war, 75; as president, U.S., 139, 140, 145

maritime culture, U.S., 11, 16, 117; "able seamen," 11, 17, 18: "articles of a ship," 11; boarding houses, 10; coffee houses, 10; "sailor towns," 10; shipbuilding, 10, 15, 16, 81; taverns, 10, 15, 16

maritime risks, U.S., 11, 13, 17, 18, 20, 22. See also impressment

marshal, U.S., 81, 91, 108. See also state, secretary of, U.S.

Maryland, 10, 19, 84, 91, 120, 129, 134, 153n78; Baltimore, 119, 128, 129; and Chesapeake Bay, 10, 45, 91; William Vans Murray, U.S. congressman from, 84

Massachusetts, 18, 19, 20, 23, 108, 109, 116, 134, 153n78; coastal cities, 19; Harvard College, 27

Mediterranean Sea, 7, 13, 29, 114, 126, 127, 137, 138, 139, 140

mercantilism, 12, 24

merchants, U.S., 7, 9, 10, 11, 16, 84, 133; Thomas FitzSimons, 133, 135; Thomas Hancock, 16; Stephen Higginson, 81, 183n17

military force, use of, 96, 111, 119, 126, 139–40

"militia diplomacy," 34, 35, 36, 37, 157n58. See also Adams, John; Franklin, Benjamin

militias, state: as enforcers of neutrality, 3, 6, 86, 92, 93, 117, 118, 139, 144; in Pennsylvania, 93; and *William* case, 92, 93

ministers, European, 36, 64, 69, 79, 85, 87, 88, 100, 107, 108, 122; and ship seizures, 108

ministers, U.S., 6, 34, 38, 54, 57, 60, 79, 123, 161nn34–35; and Charles Cotesworth Pinckney, France, 143

Mississippi River, 5, 110, 113, 114, 124; and Pinckney's Treaty, 136, 137; Spanish control over, 61, 114
Model Treaty (1776), 22, 23, 24, 27, 28–29, 30, 33, 39, 67, 155n29. *See also* Adams, John
Monroe, James, 122n182; as Democratic-Republican, 121, 141; and French Revolution, 143; and Jay's Treaty, 143; as minister to France, 123, 129, 143; and Monroe Doctrine, 123; recall of, 123, 143, 144
Morocco, 39, 127, 137, 138, 140
Morris, Gouverneur, 45, 141, 163n59; on Lafayette, 162n45; recall of, 122, 143; as U.S. minister to France, 54, 60, 101, 104, 105, 106, 107, 110, 122, 143

Native American confederacies: Haudenosaunee, 42; Iroquois, 38
Native American nations: Delaware, 38; and neutrality, 37–38; Oneida, 37–38; Seneca, 42; Tuscarora, 38
Native Americans, 113; and American Revolution, 37–38; European alliances with, 61, 114, 131; and neutrality, 37–38; and warfare, 3, 14, 61
Navy, Continental, 9, 19; *Washington* (brigantine), 20; "Washington's Navy," 20
navy, French, 16, 20, 44, 45, 49, 84
Navy, Royal (British), 9, 11, 15, 17, 20, 30, 35, 44, 45, 84, 111, 115, 116, 129, 132, 144, 150n7
Navy, U.S., 3, 6, 89, 116, 117, 118, 126, 139–40; and Algiers, 138, 185n72; authorization of, 118; establishment of, 119–20, 138, 139; officers, 119; and Tripoli, 140; uniforms, 120; U.S.S. *Constellation*, 118, *119*
Netherlands, 2, 12, 14, 16, 32, 33, 36, 37, 65, 70, 79, 81, 90, 115, 116, 121, 159n93. *See also* Adams, John; Holland; "militia diplomacy"
neutrality, 1, 2, 3, 8, 14, 23, 24, 25–26, 30, 31, 32, 33, 34, 35, 36, 37–38, 39, 49, 58, 120, 126; Native American aspiration in American Revolution, 37–38
Neutrality Act (1794), 125–26, 144
neutrality policy, U.S., 3, 4, 5, 7, 8, 29, 38–39, 41, 49, 53, 54, 58, 60, 76, 77, 123, 131, 134, 139, 143
Neutrality Proclamation (1793), 1, 3, 5, 6, 7, 8, 24, 26, 75, 90, 101, 105, 106, 113, 125, 140, 144, 145–46; compromises, 64, 65, 72–73, 74, 77, 104, 142, 166n35; and Congress, U.S., 113–15; drafting of, 62, 63, 64, 66, 67; final statement, 65; formulation, 58, 59, 60, 62, 72–73, 77; issuance of, 64–65, 79; query, 63–64; —, and cabinet responses, 66–68; resolutions in support of, 106, 134
Neutrality Proclamation (1794), 5, 124–25, 126, 136, 144; and Spanish Louisiana, 110, 124–25, 136
Neutrality Proclamation, controversies (1793): constitutionality, 68–69, 72, 73, 74; consulting Congress, U.S., 67–68; opposition to, "Helvidius," 72, 73, 74; —, Jefferson, 71, 72, 73, 74, 75; —, Monroe, 123, 143; —, "Veritas," 68–69; support for, "Pacificus," 68–71, 95
Neutrality Proclamation, enforcement (1793): 6, 77, 78, 80, 82, 84–87, 88, 103, 127, 139, 141, 144; aiding U.S. citizens, 128–30, 133, 137–38, 140, 145; banning privateering in U.S. ports, 87, 99–102, 120, 144; and Congress, U.S., 113–15, 118, 120; *Henfield* verdict, 95; indemnification, 89, 100, 102, 108, 130, 132, 134, 144; internationally, 118, 122, 127, 131, 132, 133–40; jurisdiction, 81, 97–99, 100; lack of legal authority, 93, 94, 110, 125; prosecutions, 90, 91, 93–94; restoration of British prizes,

Neutrality Proclamation, enforcement (1793) (*continued*)
84, 85, 86, 88, 89, 91, 92, 100–102, 144; and Supreme Court, U.S., 97–98, 120–21; and U.S. policies, 99–101; and U.S. territorial boundaries, 107–8; weaknesses in, 88, 93, 94, 95–96, 110, 114

neutrality violations, 3, 5, 6, 26, 30, 31, 33, 60, 74, 75, 77, 78, 80, 81, 84, 85, 90, 91, 99, 100, 101, 102, 106, 108, 109, 110, 111, 113, 114, 115–16, 121, 122, 124, 125, 132, 144

New Orleans, Louisiana, 110, 136–37

Newport, Rhode Island, 15, 16, 44, 81

newspaper editors, U.S.: John Fenno, 69; Philip Freneau, 68

newspapers, U.S., 1, 59, 61, 66, 68, 75, 94, 110, 111; *American Daily Advertiser*, 145; *Gazette of the United States*, 69, 73; —, and John Fenno, 69; *General Advertiser*, 61, 124; *National Gazette*, 68, 94; —, and Philip Freneau, 68

New York City, 10, 15, 16, 18, 19, 44, 45, 95, 119

Norfolk, Virginia, 84, 106, 119

officers, American: George Rogers Clark, 124; Benjamin Logan, 124; John Montgomery, 124; Arthur St. Clair, 61, 124; John Sullivan, 44

officers, British: Edward Braddock, 43; Charles Cornwallis, 45

officers, French, 41, 44, 45, 46, 47, 48, 49, 50, 51, 52, 53, 54, 55, 56, 57, 58, 60, 161n23; and aristocratic liberalism, 47–48, 55, 161n24

Pacificus essays, 60, 68, 69–71, 72, 73, 74, 75, 77, 95, 164n2; Hamilton as author of, 68; publication in *Gazette of the United States*, 69; response to "Veritas," 68–69

Pacificus-Helvidius debate, 74–75

partisanship, 1, 60, 61, 75, 76, 77, 104, 105, 142, 143, 145, 146

Pennsylvania, 19, 42, 43, 86, 91, 92, 93, 95; and Ohio River, 42

Petite Democrate/Little Sarah, 89, 95–97, 102, 106

Philadelphia, Pennsylvania, 10, 15, 16, 19, 26, 73, 89, 90, 95, 118, 119, 124, 129, 130, 145; Library Company of, 27; as nation's capital, 1, 61, 68, 69, 72, 83, 84, 93, 94, 95, 97, 98, 105, 106, 107, 111, 112, 113, 122, 133, 135

Pickering, Timothy, 184n58; as secretary of state, U.S., 139, 143, 144; as secretary of war, U.S., 142

Pinckney, Thomas: as envoy, U.S. to Spain, 136, 137; as minister, U.S. to Britain, 130, 131

Pinckney's Treaty, Spain (1795), 2, 136–37, 139. *See also* treaties, U.S.

piracy, 12, 126; Algerian, 29, 137, 138; Corsairs (French), 13

Plan of Treaties. *See* Model Treaty

port cities, North America, 6, 9, 10, 11, 15, 16, 17, 18, 19, 22, 80, 106, 110, 135, 150n20; banning privateering in, 86–87, 144; fortification of, 118; and naval vessels, U.S., 119

Portugal, 14, 25, 32, 35, 54, 61, 79, 115; and Barbary States, 130, 137, 138

privateering, 1, 2, 6, 9, 12, 13, 14, 25, 152n45; British, 14, 15, 16, 20, 75; colonial, North American, 15, 16, 17, 18, 22, 24; —, in Connecticut, Maryland, Massachusetts, New Hampshire, New Jersey, New London, New York, Rhode Island, 19; —, in New London, Connecticut, 19; —, in Portsmouth, New Hampshire, 18; and Congress of Paris, 1856, 13; French, 60, 75, 78, 83, 84–87, 88, 89, 90, 92, 94, 96, 99, 101, 103, 104–5, 108–9, 122, 145;

revolutionary, American, 18, 19, 20, *21*, 22, 24, 28, 29, 33, 34; Spanish, 17, 36; and surety bonds, 12, 15; U.S., 22, 23
privateering, enforcement: banning in U.S. ports, 62, 87, 91, 95, 97, 99, 100, 102, 103, 113, 120, 125, 131, 144; banning U.S. citizens, 87, 94, 97, 99, 102, 145; departing U.S. ports, 87, 88, 96, 100, 125–26; indemnification of prizes, 88, 100–101, 133–35; prohibition on outfitting and recruitment, 64, 86, 87, 91, 95, 97, 99, 100, 125; prosecution of violators, 86, 90, 92, 93–95, 114, 121, 125; restoration of prizes, 84, 85, 86, 88, 89, 91, 92, 97, 99–100, 108, 121, 144; U.S. obligations, 86, 89–90, 97, 99–100, 108
privateers, 2, 3, 9, 12, 13, 15, 25, 99; American citizens as, 20, 60, 62, 75, 77, 83, 84, 85, 86, 90, 108, 121; British as, 14, 15, 17, 20, 86; colonial, North Americans as, 15, 16, 17, 21–22; French ships as, 93, 102, 106, 111, 116, and *Embuscade*, 84, 85, 89; prohibiting Americans as, 87, 94, 97, 99, 102, 144; revolutionary, U.S, 19, 20, 33; —, and *George Washington* (privateer), 20, 22; Spanish, 18; U.S. ships as: *Anti-George*, 84; *Citizen Genet*, 84, 86, 89; *Republican (Polly)*, 84, 91; *Roland*, 108; *Sans Culotte*, 84, 89. *See also specific privateers*
privateers, prizes, 12, 13, 15, 16, 17, 19, 20, 32, 64, 86, 87, 88, 89, 90, 92, 93, 95, 97, 99, 100, 101, 106, 108–9, 114, 120, 121
Prussia, 32, 39, 56, 57, 65, 70, 81, 90, 121

Randolph, Edmund, 26, 104, 166n31; as attorney general, U.S., 5, 7, 62, 68, 97, 112; as cabinet's swing vote, 65, 71, 74, 81, 86, 87, 96, 124; and Congress, U.S., 98–99; as Democratic-Republican, 141, 142, 143; and Genet's recall, 106, 122; and *Grange* case, 85; and Jay's Treaty, 131, 133, 135; Jefferson's dislike of, 71, 167n46; neutrality enforcement, 85, 86, 87, 91, 123–24, 130; Neutrality Proclamation (1793), author of, 65; neutrality query and response, 66–68, 77; and resignation, 141, 142, 143, 185n3; —, and controversy surrounding, 142, 143, 144, 186n7; as secretary of state, U.S., 111, 116, 118, 122, 123, 128, 130, 142; on U.S. sovereignty, 87, 90; *U.S. vs. Henfield* (1793), 90, 93–94; "Vexations and Spoliations on our Commerce," 116, 118, 128, 130, 131
"Report on the Public Credit," 3–4, 62, 73, 139. *See also* Alexander Hamilton
republican ideology, 47–48, 71, 95
Revolution, American, 2, 5, 8, 11, 18, 21, 23, 24, 30, 31, 34–35, 37, 38, 39, 40, 41, 44, 45, 46, 47, 48, 51, 52, 60, 61, 62, 83, 124, 128, 134, 138, 139; and French Revolution, 50, 51, 52, 105, 143, 162n35, 162n47; Sons of Liberty, 19; Sons of Neptune, 19; Yorktown, surrender at, 37, 45. *See also* officers, American; officers, French
Revolution, French, 49, 50, 51, 52, 54, 55, 56, 57, 58, 62, 143; Bastille, 50, 52; Chateaubriand, 52; "Declaration of Rights of Man and the Citizen," 50; Girondins, 83, 122; Jacobins, 122; Reign of Terror, 122, 143; Tennis Court Oath, 50, 52
revolutionary ideas, 24, 25, 27, 29, 55, 84
Rochambeau, comte de, 47, 48, 51, 56, 58; in American Revolution, 45–46; death of, 57; as marshal of France, 50
Russia, 2, 30, 31, 32, 33, 34, 35, 36, 37, 61, 132; Hermitage, 36; Hotel Paris, 36; Saint Petersburg, 36–37. *See also* Catherine II; Declaration of Armed Neutrality; League of Armed Neutrality

Sans Culotte (U.S. privateer), 84, 89, 91; and prizes: *Eunice* (British), 84; *Fanny* (British), 91

seamen, American, 7, 9, 10, 11, 15, 16, 17, 18, 19, 22, 115, 132, 135; and Algerian pirates, 137, 138; Nathaniel Fanning, 20; rescue of, 111, 117, 128, 130, 145; John Wachsmuth, 128

sea passports, U.S., 81–82; and embargoes, U.S., 117

"seizure" commission, 134–35; and indemnifications, 134–35; Jay Treaty and Article VII, 133–34; members, American (Christopher Gore, William Pinkney, and John Trumbull), 134; members, British (Nicholas Antsey and John Nicholl), 134; ships, American, *Betsey*, 134; —, *Sally*, 134–35

Senate, U.S., 67, 113, 114, 115, 116, 118, 125, 128; and constitutional powers, 60; and Jay's Treaty, 133; and Pinckney's Treaty, 136, 137

ship captains, American, 7, 9, 10, 11, 12, 15, 16, 17, 18, 84, 89; Joshua Barney, 128, *129*; William Culver, 107, 122; Gideon Henfield, 75, 89–90, 91, 93, 94, 95, 98, 121, 145, 173n64; Thomas Painter, 20; Christopher Prince, 20; John Singleterry, 75, 89–90, 91, 173n64; George Walker, 17

ships, American commercial, 82, 84, 117; and Algerian pirates, 137, 138, 184n65; *Betsey*, 134; *Betsey* (sloop), 120–21, 122; British attacks on, 111, 116, 130, 131, 132, 140, 144, 145; and compensation for, 131, 132, 133, 134–35, 140, 145; *Dauphin*, 137; *Delaware*, 116; *Hannah*, 107; *Maria*, 137; *Polly*, 91; and protection of, 134, 145; *Roland*, 108, 178n23; *Sally*, 133–35; *Sampson*, 128

ships, British commercial, 19, 20, 32, 84, 91, 100, 142; and Algerian pirates, 137;

and American privateering against, 108; compensation for, 134–35; French privateering against, 78, 84, 88, 89, 106; *Little Sarah*, 89, 95, 96, 97, 102, 106; as prizes: *Eunice*, 84; *Fanny*, 91, 93, 107; *Four Brothers*, 85; *Grange*, 84, 85, 86, 89, 95; *Greyhound*, 108–9; *Morning Star*, 85; *Neptune*, 17; *William*, 89, 91, 92, 93, 101, 107, 108

Singleterry, John, 75, 89–90, 91, 173n64. *See also* Henfield, Gideon; privateers: American citizens as

slavery, 3; and Africa, 10; and "Middle Passage," 10

Society of the Cincinnati, 48; American chapter, 46, 47; Diamond Ribbon Eagle, *47*; French chapter, 46, 47

sovereignty, U.S., 2, 6, 29, 39, 61, 69, 75, 83, 87, 90, 92, 93, 96, 102, 103, 104, 114, 123, 125, 126, 127, 132, 136, 137, 138, 139, 141, 144

Spain, 6, 13, 14, 15, 16, 17, 25, 30, 31, 32, 33, 37, 70, 79, 113, 114, 115, 116, 124, 126, 136, 184n54; King Charles IV, 135, 136; Pinckney's Treaty (1795), 136–37, 139, 140, 144

State, Department of, U.S., 6, 26, 76, 128, 171n19; establishment of, 60

state, secretary of, U.S., 2, 6, 27, 57, 59, 61, 62, 71, 72, 78, 79, 81, 82, 85, 86, 87, 88, 92, 96, 106, 107, 111, 115, 116, 128, 130, 131, 135, 138, 139, 142, 143, 170n14; establishment of, 60

Supreme Court, U.S., 6; and admiralty authority, 98, 144; cabinet's questions on neutrality, 96, 97–98; *Glass v. Sloop Betsey* (1794), 103, 120–21; John Jay, chief justice, 94, 98, 113, 118, 120–21, 123, 131, 144, 183n22; *Little Sarah* crisis, 94; and separation of powers, 98; James Wilson, justice, 94, 174n88

Sweden, 2, 30, 32, 34, 115, 120, 121, 132, 158–59n82

territorial boundaries, international, 85, 86
territorial boundaries, U.S., 5, 39, 85, 86, 87, 89, 91, 92, 93, 97, 100, 107–8, 126, 136, 144
trade: Caribbean, 15, 16, 128; Mississippi River, 114; transatlantic, 6, 9, 10, 11, 12, 18, 22, 27, 39, 53, 117
Treasury, Department of, U.S., 170n14; circulars, 80–81, 89, 100; commissioner of the revenue, U.S., 82; —, Tench Coxe, 82; customs houses, U.S., 4, 82; customs officers, U.S., 3, 6, 80–82, 89, 117, 144; customs service, U.S., 80; establishment of, 60, 165n8
Treasury, secretary of, U.S., 2, 59, 61, 62, 72, 75, 80, 81, 116, 142, 170n14
treaties, American Revolution: of Alliance, France (1778), 30, 39, 44, 55, 121; —, and American obligations under, 66–68, 69–70, 97; —, and Convention of Mortefontaine (1800), 146; —, and "guarantee clause," 64, 69–70, 166n27; of Amity and Commerce, France (1778), 30, 36, 44, 55, 61, 64, 133; —, and American obligations under, 66–68; —, and Articles, XVII and XXII, 87, 88–89, 156n37, 173n59; —, and bringing French prizes in U.S. ports, 64, 67, 81–82, 83, 86, 88–89, 92, 97; —, and Convention of Mortefontaine (1800), 146; —, and outfitting French privateers in U.S. ports, 86–87, 88, 89–90, 92, 97, 168n68; —, and *Moodie v. Ship* Phoebe Anne (1796), 121–22; of Amity and Commerce, Netherlands (1782), 36, 37, 81–82, 90, 121; of Amity and Commerce, Sweden (1782), 121, 158–59n82
treaties, U.S.: of Amity and Commerce, Morocco (1786), 39, 138; of Amity and Commerce, Prussia (1785), 39, 81, 90, 121; of Amity, Commerce, and Navigation, Britain/Jay's Treaty (1795), 2, 118, 130–31, 132, 133, 134, 139, 145; —, and commissions under, 133–35, 137, 139; —, and controversies surrounding, 133–34, 141, 143; —, and negotiations, 132–33, 135; —, and provisions of, 133–34; —, and resolutions against, 134; of Paris (1783), 38, 39, 131; of San Ildefonso/Treaty of San Lorenzo/Pinckney's Treaty, Spain (1795), 2, 136–37, 139

U.S. vs. Henfield, 95, 174n88; acquittal in, 93, 94, 98; defense team, 94; reversal of ruling, *Talbot v. Jansen* (1795), 121; U.S. government's case, 90, 93–94

Vattel, Emer de, 25–26, 27, 66–67, 70, 73. See also *Law of Nations*
Veritas essays, 68–69. See also newspapers, U.S.: *National Gazette*
Vermont, 61, 80
Virginia, 10, 19, 45, 48, 62, 71, 72, 84, 101, 123, 127, 146; colonial militia, 42–43; House of Burgess, 43

War, Department of, U.S., 117, 165n8; establishment of, 60
war, secretary of, U.S., 62
War of 1812, 123, 132, 140, 146
wars, colonial: of Austrian Succession (1740–48), 17, 42, 152n40; of Jenkin's Ear (1739–48), 15; and King George's War (1744–48), 17, 152n40; Nine Years' War (1688–97), 14, 152n38; Seven Years' War, 5, 14, 16, 18, 25, 42, 43; —, and India, 16; of Spanish Succession (1702–13), 14, 152n38
Washington, George, before and after presidency: and Martha Custis, 43, 112; death of, 186n19, 186n22; early years, 41–43; eulogy for, 146; and French officers, 41, 44, 45, 46, 47; as

Washington, George, before and after presidency (*continued*)
    military officer, 5, 7, 20, 33, 35, 40, 41, 42, 43, 44, 45, 46; and Mount Vernon, 43, 48, 112, 186n19; and political education, 7, 40, 41, 43–44, 58, 146; as privateer, 20, 22; and Society of the Cincinnati, 46, 48
Washington, George, presidency: as architect of neutrality policy, 1, 2, 5, 6, 7, 41, 53, 54, 55, 57–58, 59, 60, 62, 68, 73, 75, 77, 84, 90, 101, 113–14, 115, 120, 124, 125, 135, 139, 140, 141, 143, 144, 145, 146; avoiding European warfare, 1, 6, 22, 59, 61, 65, 75, 78, 85, 90, 95, 101, 118, 124, 125, 127, 131, 135, 139, 141, 144, 145, 146; and Congress, U.S., 67–68, 95, 98–99, 111, 112, 113, 114, 115, 116, 120, 125, 130, 136, 138, 140, 144; correspondence during, 41, 46, 47, 48, 49, 50, 51, 52–54, 55, 56, 58, 62, 76; and embargoes, 117, 118; enforcing neutrality, 78, 81, 82, 85, 86, 87, 88, 92, 99–102, 103, 110, 120, 124, 125, 126, 128; Farewell Address, 5, 145; and Genet, 89, 92, 95, 102, 103, 104, 105, 106, 107, 122; *Henfield* verdict, 95, 98; and Jay's Treaty, 133–34, 142; *Little Sarah* crisis, 95–97; as political negotiator, 4, 5, 7, 8, 59, 60, 62, 63, 64, 65, 68, 76, 78, 82, 85, 86, 87, 89, 96, 97, 99, 101, 103, 104, 106, 107, 113, 118, 120, 123, 141, 144, 146; presidential tours, 51, 123; "State of the Union" address (1790), 53; "State of the Union" address (1793), 113–14, 115, 140; "State of the Union" address (1795), 138; as statesman, 4, 6, 8, 73, 74, 75, 77, 114, 118, 120, 123, 126, 127, 128, 130, 131, 133, 134, 135, 136, 137, 138–39, 140, 141, 143, 144, 145, 146

Washington, Lawrence (Washington's half-brother), 41–42

Washington, Lund, 22

West Indies, 6, 10, 16, 17, 42, 44, 64, 66, 82, 84, 111, 131, 140; assaults on U.S. shipping, 116–17, 127, 128, 129, 130; —, and indemnifications, 134–35; and U.S. agents, and Nathaniel Cabot Higginson, 130, 133, 183n17

Whiskey Rebellion, 3, 142

William (Scottish ship): and Citizen Genet, 92–93, 101, 107; *Citizen Genet* (privateer), 89; district court ruling, 92, 93; and Hammond, 91, 92, 93; and Pennsylvania militia, 93; restitution for, 108

Wolcott, Oliver: secretary of Treasury, U.S., 142, 185n3

yellow fever, 111, 112–13

THE REVOLUTIONARY AGE

Embracing a broad chronology and geography, this series seeks to publish original scholarship on the revolutionary and counterrevolutionary upheavals that transformed the Atlantic world between 1750 and 1850.

Ireland and America: Empire, Revolution, and Sovereignty
Patrick Griffin and Francis D. Cogliano, editors

www.ingramcontent.com/pod-product-compliance
Lightning Source LLC
Chambersburg PA
CBHW021140230426
43667CB00005B/201